Embeddings in Natural Language Processing

Theory and Advances in
Vector Representations of Meaning

Synthesis Lectures on Human Language Technologies

Editor

Graeme Hirst, *University of Toronto*

Synthesis Lectures on Human Language Technologies is edited by Graeme Hirst of the University of Toronto. The series consists of 50- to 150-page monographs on topics relating to natural language processing, computational linguistics, information retrieval, and spoken language understanding. Emphasis is on important new techniques, on new applications, and on topics that combine two or more HLT subfields.

Embeddings in Natural Language Processing: Theory and Advances in Vector Representations of Meaning
Mohammad Taher Pilehvar and Jose Camacho-Collados
2020

Conversational AI: Dialogue Systems, Conversational Agents, and Chatbots
Michael McTear
2020

Natural Language Processing for Social Media, Third Edition
Anna Atefeh Farzindar and Diana Inkpen
2020

Statistical Significance Testing for Natural Language Processing
Rotem Dror, Lotem Peled, Segev Shlomov, and Roi Reichart
2020

Deep Learning Approaches to Text Production
Shashi Narayan and Claire Gardent
2020

Linguistic Fundamentals for Natural Language Processing II: 100 Essentials from Semantics and Pragmatics
Emily M. Bender and Alex Lascarides
2019

Grammatical Inference for Computational Linguistics
Jeffrey Heinz, Colin de la Higuera, and Menno van Zaanen
2015

Automatic Detection of Verbal Deception
Eileen Fitzpatrick, Joan Bachenko, and Tommaso Fornaciari
2015

Natural Language Processing for Social Media
Atefeh Farzindar and Diana Inkpen
2015

Semantic Similarity from Natural Language and Ontology Analysis
Sébastien Harispe, Sylvie Ranwez, Stefan Janaqi, and Jacky Montmain
2015

Learning to Rank for Information Retrieval and Natural Language Processing, Second Edition
Hang Li
2014

Ontology-Based Interpretation of Natural Language
Philipp Cimiano, Christina Unger, and John McCrae
2014

Automated Grammatical Error Detection for Language Learners, Second Edition
Claudia Leacock, Martin Chodorow, Michael Gamon, and Joel Tetreault
2014

Web Corpus Construction
Roland Schäfer and Felix Bildhauer
2013

Recognizing Textual Entailment: Models and Applications
Ido Dagan, Dan Roth, Mark Sammons, and Fabio Massimo Zanzotto
2013

Linguistic Fundamentals for Natural Language Processing: 100 Essentials from Morphology and Syntax
Emily M. Bender
2013

Semi-Supervised Learning and Domain Adaptation in Natural Language Processing
Anders Søgaard
2013

Embeddings in Natural Language Processing: Theory and Advances in Vector Representations of Meaning
Mohammad Taher Pilehvar and Jose Camacho-Collados

ISBN: 978-3-031-01049-1   paperback
ISBN: 978-3-031-02177-0   ebook
ISBN: 978-3-031-00188-8   hardcover

DOI 10.1007/978-3-031-02177-0

A Publication in the Springer series
SYNTHESIS LECTURES ON HUMAN LANGUAGE TECHNOLOGIES

Lecture #47
Series Editor: Graeme Hirst, *University of Toronto*
Series ISSN
Print 1947-4040   Electronic 1947-4059

Embeddings in Natural Language Processing

Theory and Advances in
Vector Representations of Meaning

Mohammad Taher Pilehvar
Tehran Institute for Advanced Studies

Jose Camacho-Collados
Cardiff University

SYNTHESIS LECTURES ON HUMAN LANGUAGE TECHNOLOGIES #47

ABSTRACT

Embeddings have undoubtedly been one of the most influential research areas in Natural Language Processing (NLP). Encoding information into a low-dimensional vector representation, which is easily integrable in modern machine learning models, has played a central role in the development of NLP. Embedding techniques initially focused on words, but the attention soon started to shift to other forms: from graph structures, such as knowledge bases, to other types of textual content, such as sentences and documents.

This book provides a high-level synthesis of the main embedding techniques in NLP, in the broad sense. The book starts by explaining conventional word vector space models and word embeddings (e.g., Word2Vec and GloVe) and then moves to other types of embeddings, such as word sense, sentence and document, and graph embeddings. The book also provides an overview of recent developments in contextualized representations (e.g., ELMo and BERT) and explains their potential in NLP.

Throughout the book, the reader can find both essential information for understanding a certain topic from scratch and a broad overview of the most successful techniques developed in the literature.

KEYWORDS

natural language processing, semantics, vector space model, word embeddings, contextualized embeddings, sense embeddings, graph embeddings, sentence embeddings

Contents

Preface

Semantic representation is one of the oldest areas of research in Natural Language Processing (NLP). This area lies at the core of language understanding and looks at ways to express meaning in a machine-interpretable form. Among different types of representation, vectors have always been a popular choice, owing to their simple geometrical intuition and versatility. In fact, vector representations (more recently, *embeddings*) have played a crucial role in improving the generalization ability of various NLP systems.

In the early 2010s, the field of semantic representation was dominated by word embeddings. One reason behind this success was that embeddings proved perfect complements for neural NLP models, which were getting increasing attention around those years. It did not take long for the research attention to be expanded to other areas of representation learning (e.g., graphs, sentences, senses), pushing the boundaries in those areas. More recently, a new branch has emerged, namely contextualized embeddings, in which representations and downstream NLP systems have become even more tied together. Contextualized models have proven effective not only in a wide range of NLP tasks but also in knowledge transfer across different languages.

This book presents an overview of the field of vector representation. As a significant extension and update of a survey article we had on the topic [Camacho-Collados and Pilehvar, 2018], this book reflects the subsequent development of the field, particularly for contextualized representations. Moreover, while the survey mainly focused on word-level embeddings, the book also discusses other types of embeddings that are commonly used in NLP, such as graph and sentence embeddings. Last but not least, this book was written with a different style and purpose, as our aim was to make it more accessible to a wider audience.

INTENDED READERSHIP

This book should be of interest to all AI researchers who work with natural language, especially those who are interested in semantics. Our goal is to introduce the topic of semantic representation to those who are new to the area and to provide those who are already familiar with the area with a broader perspective and a quick overview of recent developments and the state of the art in various branches. The book synthesizes the diverse literature on semantic representations and provides a high-level introduction to major semantic embedding models.

We note that in our overview of various techniques, we provide details only to the depth that is necessary to sketch the general shape of the field and provide a hint on how the research problem was approached. In these cases, we also provide relevant references to allow the reader to further investigate specific sub-areas. We hope this book can bring fresh researchers and practitioners up to speed on the recent developments in the field, while pointing out open problems and areas for further exploration.

COVERAGE AND OUTLINE

The book is split into nine chapters. The first two chapters provide basic concepts that can be helpful in understanding the remainder of the book. Chapters 3 to 7 are the core of this book, which discusses different types of embeddings. While there is some connection between these chapters, we tried to make them as self-contained and independent as possible. Chapter 8 discusses some of the implications of the common representation models, while Chapter 9 provides concluding remarks and future research prospects. In the following, we describe each individual chapter in more detail.

1. In Chapter 1, we start with a brief introduction on why **semantic representation** is an important topic in NLP and discuss its evolution path. We also explain the basics of **Vector Space Models**.

2. In Chapter 2, we provide some **background knowledge** on the fundamentals of NLP and machine learning applied to language problems. Then, we briefly describe some of the main knowledge resources that are commonly used in lexical semantics.

3. Chapter 3 discusses **word representations**, starting from a brief overview of conventional count-based models and continuing with the more recent predictive embeddings. We also describe some of the techniques for specializing embeddings, which serve to produce knowledge-enhanced and cross-lingual word embeddings, and common evaluation methods for word representations.

4. Chapter 4 covers various techniques for embedding structural knowledge resources, in particular semantic **graphs**. We will overview major recent methods for embedding graph nodes and edges and conclude with their applications and evaluation.

5. In Chapter 5, we focus on the representation of individual meanings of words, i.e., **word senses**. Two classes of sense representations (unsupervised and knowledge-based) are discussed, followed by evaluation techniques for each type of representation.

6. Chapter 6 is about the recent paradigm of **contextualized embeddings**. We first explain the need for such embeddings and then describe the most popular models and their connection to language models. The chapter also covers some of the efforts to explain and analyze the effectiveness of contextualized models.

7. Chapter 7 goes beyond the level of words, and describes how **sentences and documents** can be encoded into vectorial representations. We cover some of the widely used supervised

and unsupervised techniques and discuss the applications and evaluation methods for these representations. Given the book's main focus on word-level representation, this chapter provides partial coverage but also pointers for further reading.

8. Chapter 8 explains some of the **ethical issues and inherent biases** in vector representations (and, in particular, word embeddings), which recently have been a topic of concern. The chapter also covers proposals for debiasing word embeddings.

9. Finally, in Chapter 9 we present the **concluding remarks and open research challenges**.

We note that given its massive success, there has been a surge of interest in representation learning, resulting in rapid progress over the past few years, essentially making the state-of-the-art representation technique a moving target. Therefore, it is impossible to keep track of all the recent developments in the field; instead, we try to focus on some of the more established techniques and general concepts. In fact, during the writing of the book, the field of contextualized representation had changed so much that, upon the completion of the first draft, we had to go back to the corresponding chapter and significantly extend it with newer content. Nevertheless, as we mentioned, we tried to focus on the more general concepts and ideas that are relevant for understanding rather than individual systems that may change over time.

Finally, we would like to thank our editors, reviewers, colleagues, and all others who provided us with valuable feedback for improving the book. Also, we would like to thank our families for their patient support during the writing of this book.

Mohammad Taher Pilehvar and Jose Camacho-Collados
November 2020

CHAPTER 1

Introduction

Artificial Intelligence (AI) has been one of the most important topics of discussion over the past years. The goal in AI is to design algorithms that transform computers into "intelligent" agents. By intelligence here we do not necessarily mean an extraordinary level of smartness; it often involves basic problems that humans solve frequently in their day-to-day lives. This can be as simple as recognizing faces in an image, driving a car, playing a board game, or reading (and understanding) an article in a newspaper. The intelligent behavior exhibited by humans when "reading" is one of the main goals for a subfield of AI called Natural Language Processing (NLP). Natural language[1] is one of the most complex tools used by humans for a wide range of reasons, for instance to communicate with others, to express thoughts, feelings, and ideas, to ask questions, or to give instructions. Therefore, it is crucial for computers to possess the ability to use the same tool in order to effectively interact with humans.

From one view, NLP can be roughly divided into two broad subfields: Natural Language Understanding (**NLU**) and Natural Language Generation (**NLG**), with the two being tightly interwoven in many NLP applications. NLU deals with understanding the meaning of human language, usually expressed as a piece of text.[2] For instance, when a Question Answering (QA[3]) system is asked "do penguins fly?", the very first step is for it to understand the question, which in turn depends on the meaning of *penguin* and *fly*, and their composition. There are many challenges that make NLU an AI-hard problem.

- **Ambiguity.** One of the most important difficulties with human language lies in its ambiguous nature. Ambiguity can arise at different levels.

  - **Lexical ambiguity**. Words can simultaneously belong to multiple syntactic classes (parts of speech). For instance, *fly* can be a noun as well as a verb. This is called categorical ambiguity. A more subtle form of ambiguity arises when a word in a specific syntactic class can have multiple associated meanings (i.e., "senses"). This property of a word to denote multiple senses is referred to as *polysemy* words. For instance, the verb *fly* can describe different actions, including *traveling through the air* which is the intended meaning in the above example, or *operating an airplane*

---

[1]Human language is referred to as "natural", in contrast to programming or other artificial languages.

[2]The process of transcribing an utterance, i.e., converting speech to text, is the objective in Speech Processing, another subfield of AI.

[3]QA is one of the applications of NLP which deals with designing systems that automatically answer questions posed by humans in a natural language.

as in "the pilot flew to Cuba" or *move quickly or suddenly* as in "he flew about the place".[4] We will talk more about senses and how to model them in Chapter 5.

- **Syntactic ambiguity**. A sentence could be parsed syntactically in multiple ways. For instance, in the sentence "I saw a man on the hill with binoculars", we can attach *binoculars* to either *I* or to the *man*. As a result, different interpretations can be made depending on the choice of attachment. This is a well-known challenge in parsing, called prepositional phrase (PP) attachment. Syntactic ambiguity can also arise from conjunctions. For example, in "Avocado salad with cheese", is cheese a part of salad or separate from that?

- **Metonymic ambiguity**. Metonymy is the substitution of a concept, phrase or word being meant with a semantically related one. For instance, in "Cambridge voted to stay in the EU", it is definitely the people of Cambridge who voted and not the city itself.

- **Anaphoric ambiguity**. This type of ambiguity concerns the interpretation of pronouns. For instance, in "I have a laptop but recently bought a new one. I am going to give it away.", what does *it* refer to, the old one or the recently acquired one?

• **Common sense knowledge**. Addressing many of the ambiguities requires something that is not explicitly encoded in the context; it needs world knowledge or some reasoning. For instance, in the example for anaphoric ambiguity it is easy for a person with background knowledge to attach *it* to the old laptop. Referential ambiguities that need background knowledge for resolution are targeted by the Winograd Schema Challenge [Levesque et al., 2012] which is deemed to be alternative to the Turing Test for machine intelligence. Similarly, it would be easy for humans to identify the intended meaning of *mouse* in "I ordered a mouse from Amazon" given their background knowledge from the marketplace.

• **Figurative language.** Idioms such as "fingers crossed" and "all ears" and sarcasm are forms of figurative language that are extensively used by humans in both conversational and written form. Given that the interpretation of these expressions is not a direct function of the meanings of their constituent words, they pose a serious challenge for language understanding algorithms.

Many of the NLP applications require addressing one or more of the above challenges. For instance, Machine Translation (MT) often requires handling different types of ambiguity in order to transform meaning from a language to another, with both having their own implicit ambiguities. Similarly, Question Answering not only has to deal with ambiguities but also sometimes requires a grasp of background common sense knowledge for making inference about facts

---

[4]Definitions are extracted from WordNet (more about this lexical resource in Chapter 2). WordNet 3.0 lists 14 meanings (senses) for the verb *fly*.

and answering questions. Also, many tasks in NLP are designed to target specific research challenges. For instance, Word Sense Disambiguation deals with identifying the intended meaning of a word in a given context, coreference resolution is focused on resolving anaphoric ambiguity, and semantic similarity measurements assess the ability of models in representing the semantics of words or longer pieces of texts.

NLG can be viewed as the opposite of NLU: the goal is for a computer to generate text, or in other words to "talk" to humans through natural language, either to verbalize an idea or meaning, or to provide a response. NLG is difficult for several reasons.

- **Ambiguity.** In terms of ambiguity, there is a symmetry between NLU and NLG. Ambiguity in NLU is a one-to-many mapping from language to meaning (e.g., due to polysemy), whereas NLG typically involves a one-to-many mapping from meaning to language. For example, one concept can be expressed with many different words or phrases (synonymy). This challenge is amplified at the generation time as the computer often has to pick specific words from a massive vocabulary to verbalize a concept, while paying attention to the context, e.g., text domain, style, and being self-consistent.

- **Word order.** The property of natural languages to allow dynamic order of syntactic constituents can further complicate the generation process. This is especially the case for languages with relatively free word order, such as German, Russian, Farsi, and Turkic, in which the same sentence can be expressed with multiple grammatically plausible word orders.

- **Fluency.** Another major challenge during NLG is the need to accord with the grammatical rules of the language, while preserving an acceptable level of fluency. The generated text not only has to precisely express the concept, but it also needs to be fluent, which requires extensive semantic and syntactic linguistic knowledge.

As noted before, many applications in NLP involve both NLU and NLG. For instance, in Question Answering, first we need to understand the question to be able to generate an answer. Similarly, MT involves understanding of the source language text and then the generation of the target language text. Other similar scenarios include abstractive text summarization[5] and conversational AI.

Semantic representation, the topic of this book, deals with modeling semantics in a way that is interpretable for computers. Therefore, semantic representation lies in the core of most NLP models, from understanding to generation, and it is a crucial playmaker in the performance of downstream applications. In the following sections we will talk more about semantic representation. Most of the works discussed in this book deal with the English language. Therefore, some conclusions may or may not generalize to other types of language. While acknowledging

---

[5]In contrast to *extractive* text summarization in which the goal is to identify important sections of the text and to put these subsets together to generate a verbatim summary, in *abstractive* summarization the summary has to be reproduced from scratch, upon interpretation of the original text.

this limitation, we have also attempted to refer to other languages and their challenges in some chapters and sections, to help the reader assess the cross-lingual applicability of some of the concepts addressed in the book.

1.1   SEMANTIC REPRESENTATION

Imagine the word *desk*. When stored on a computer, this word is nothing but a sequence of four characters "d", "e", "s", and "k". But computers only understand zeros and ones. Hence, each character has to be stored as a pattern of bits. The number of bits depends on the encoding. For instance, the extended ASCII needs 8 bits for storing each character. Therefore, the word *desk* is *represented* as a sequence of 32 zeros and ones according to this encoding.[6] A five-character word, such as "table", will get a 40-bit long representation.[7] This approach is not adequate for representing the semantics of words, due to the following limitations.

1. The representation cannot incorporate semantic information of words. For example, the semantically similar words "table" and "desk" (or even synonymous words such as "noon" and "midday") will have totally different representations. We are ideally looking for a representation that can encode semantics of words.

2. The representation is character-wise. Therefore, the size of the representation depends on the length of the words (number of characters they have). The variable size is an unwanted property which further complicates the comparison of representations of different words. In fact, it is not straightforward to integrate these variable-sized representations into machine learning models, which generally "understand" feature-based representations.

Given these issues, the field of semantic representation has attempted at developing structures that can include the notion of *meaning* into the equation. In the following section we present vector space models, which represent one of the most successful attempts into semantic representation to date and the main topic covered in this book.

1.2   VECTOR SPACE MODELS

One of the solutions to address the variable-size issue of character-level representations to directly represent words rather than characters. This is the idea behind one-hot representation, which is the simplest form of word representation and established the basis of word vector space models.

One-hot representation.   Instead of mapping characters to 8-bit binary representations, one-hot representations can be viewed as an ASCII-like encoding that maps words to distinct fixed-sized patterns of zeros and ones. Assume we have 100 words in a vocabulary and

---

[6]ASCII encoding for "desk": 01100100 01100101 01110011 01101011.
[7]ASCII encoding for "table": 01110100 01100001 01100010 01101100 01100101.

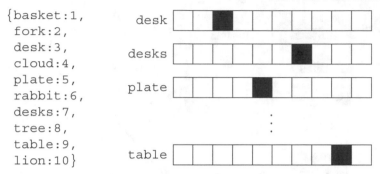

Figure 1.1: A toy vocabulary of ten words with their corresponding one-hot representations.

we would like to encode them as one-hot representations. First, we associate an index (between 1 to 100) to each word. Then, each word is represented as a 100-dimension array-like representation, in which all the dimensions are zero except for the one corresponding to its index, which is set to one (therefore the name "one-hot" encoding). Note that, one-hot encoding is different from our earlier ASCII-like representation in that it is highly sparse, i.e., it contains only a single 1 entry and the rest are set to zero. Figure 1.1 shows a toy example with a vocabulary of 10 words along with their indices (left) and one-hot representations (right). Despite its simplicity, one-hot encoding sets the foundations for more flexible Vector Space Models (to be elaborated in the next section).

One-hot representation addresses the second limitation discussed above. However, it still suffers from the first limitation: each word is assigned a different representation and there is no notion of "similarity" between them. Using this representation, it is not possible to encode the conceptual similarity between "noon" and "midday". Even worse, the two similar looking words such "desk" and "desks" (which would have similar string-based representations) are assigned completely different one-hot vectors.

Moreover, as one can guess from Figure 1.1, the dimensionality of one-hot representations grows with the number of words in the vocabulary. In a typical vocabulary, we should expect hundreds of thousands of words. Representing each word using one-hot representation is definitely too storage-intensive and would make the processing difficult (see dimensionality reduction in Chapter 3).

The Vector Space Model (VSM), first proposed by Salton et al. [1975], provides a more flexible solution to the limitations of one-hot representation. In this model, objects are represented as vectors in an imaginary multi-dimensional continuous space. In NLP, the space is usually referred to as the **semantic space** and the representation of the objects is called **distributed representation**. Objects can be words, documents, sentences, concepts, or entities, or any other semantic carrying item between which we can define a notion of similarity. In this chapter, we

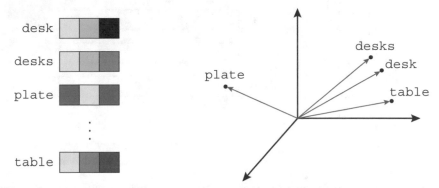

Figure 1.2: Representing the words in Figure 1.1 in 3-dimensional continuous vector space. Note the continuous embeddings in the vectors (compared to binary values in Figure 1.1) and the notion of spatial similarity between "desk", "desks", and "table".

mostly focus on words because many applications in NLP are based on VSM representation of words.[8]

Figure 1.2 shows a simple 3-dimensional semantic space that represents four words with their corresponding vectors. In fact, one-hot representation is a specific type of distributed representation in which each word is represented as a special type of vector which is only extended along one axis in the semantic space (the semantic space needs to have m dimensions where m is the number of words in the vocabulary). Moving from the *local* and discrete nature of one-hot representation to *distributed* and continuous vector spaces brings about multiple advantages. Most importantly, it introduces the notion of similarity: the similarity of two words (vectors) can be measured by their distance in the space. Moreover, many more words can fit into a low dimensional space; hence, it can potentially address the size issue of one-hot encoding: a large vocabulary of size m can fit in an n-dimensional vector space, where $n \ll m$. Dimensionality of representations is particularly important for recent machine learning models in which it can have a direct impact on the number of parameters of the model.

Figure 1.3 provides a more realistic example with many more words in a 2-dimensional space. Usually, semantic spaces have many more dimensions that can be illustrated. Therefore, we usually leverage dimensionality reduction techniques (cf. Chapter 3) to reduce the size of the semantic space to two or three for visualization purposes. In Chapter 2, we will describe the process of learning different types of distributed word representations.

VSM has been one of the most successful ideas in NLP; it is undoubtedly the prevalent solution for representing semantics for reasons such as being mathematically well defined and for the availability of a large set of algebraic tools. The geomteric metaphor of meaning is also supported by research in conceptual spaces for cognitive knowledge representation [Gärdenfors,

---

[8]Throughout this book, unless explicitly specified, by representation we often refer to word representations.

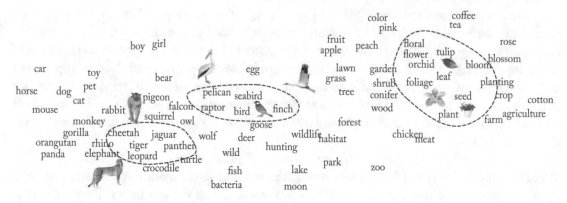

Figure 1.3: A sample word vector space reduced to two dimensions using t-SNE [Maaten and Hinton, 2008]. In a semantic space, words with similar meanings tend to appear in the proximity of each other, as highlighted by these word clusters (delimited by the red dashed lines) associated with *big cats*, *birds*, and *plants*.

2004, Landauer and Dumais, 1997]. Cognitive representations assume humans characterize objects with respect to the features they possess (features such as weight, color, taste, or temperature). Brain models similarities between entities according to the similarities between their features.

Distributed representations have established their effectiveness in NLP tasks such as information extraction [Laender et al., 2002], semantic role labeling [Erk, 2007], word similarity [Radinsky et al., 2011], word sense disambiguation [Navigli, 2009], or spelling correction [Jones and Martin, 1997], *inter alia*. The process of constructing distributed representations has undergone a long history of development in the past few decades but their constitutional property has remained unchanged: distance in the vector space denotes a notion of semantic similarity. It is important to note that distributed representation is not only limited to words; it can be applied to any other type of concepts or textual forms, such as word senses, entities, sentences, or documents (all to be covered in this book). Turney and Pantel [2010] provide a comprehensive survey of conventional VSM techniques in NLP.

1.3   THE EVOLUTION PATH OF REPRESENTATIONS

The Vector Space Model [Salton et al., 1975] was initially centered around modeling documents in information retrieval systems. The initial success persuaded other researchers, such as Schütze [1993], Lund et al. [1995], and Landauer and Dumais [1997], to extend the model from documents to other forms, particularly words. The compatibility of vector-based representations with conventional and modern machine learning and deep learning methods has significantly helped the model to prevail as the dominant representation approach for the past few decades.

The *distributional hypothesis* [Firth, 1957, Harris, 1954] which stipulates that words occurring in the same contexts tend to have similar meanings, has been the foundation for automatically constructing word VSM. However, different interpretations of the hypothesis and ways of collecting "similarity" cues and constructing the space have been proposed. Earlier approaches were based on collecting word statistics from large text corpora, usually in terms of occurrence and co-occurrence frequency. Hence, they are usually referred to as *count*-based techniques (Section 3.1). These representations are often large and need some sort of dimensionality reduction (Section 3.1.2).

The deep learning tsunami hit the shores of NLP around 2011 [Manning, 2015]. Word2vec [Mikolov et al., 2013c] was one of the massive waves from this tsunami and once again accelerated the research in semantic representation. Despite not being "deep", the proposed model was a very efficient way for constructing compact vector representations, by leveraging (shallow) neural networks. Since then, the term "embedding" almost replaced "representation" and dominated the field of lexical semantics. The fresh blood in the veins of lexical semantics resulted in dozens of specialized embedding techniques, such as sense embedding (Chapter 5), retrofitted embeddings (Section 3.4), and cross-lingual embeddings (Section 3.5), many of which are based on Word2vec and capture different kind of knowledge. This also accelerated research in other areas of representation, such as embeddings of nodes and relations in structured knowledge resources, such as semantic networks.

Word embeddings proved to be very efficient at capturing semantics, with their integration in various NLP systems resulting in considerable performance improvements [Baroni et al., 2014]. However, they still suffered from a major limitation: they fall short of modeling the dynamic nature of words. Words can exhibit different syntactic and semantic properties depending on the context in which they appear. For instance, the term *mouse* can refer to unrelated meanings (rodent and computer device). Word embeddings are, however, static in nature. By static here we mean that the same embedding is used for the word *mouse* independently from the context in which it appears. In other words, different meanings of the word are conflated into a single vectorial representation.[9]

The latest wave is the so-called contextualized representations. The approach is aimed at addressing the static nature of word embeddings by allowing the embedding for a word to be dynamically adapted to the context in which the word appears. Differently from conventional word embeddings, the input to these models is not words in isolation, but words along with their contexts. Contextualized representations are currently dominating almost all standard NLP benchmarks. Chapter 6 talks about this new type of representations.

---

[9]Yaghoobzadeh et al. [2019] showed that static word embeddings can provide a good representation of the frequent meanings of a word, despite conflating them into a single vector. However, they fall short when representing less frequent meanings.

CHAPTER 2

Background

2.1 NATURAL LANGUAGE PROCESSING FUNDAMENTALS

NLP lies at the intersection of linguistics and computer science. In this section, we cover some fundamental notions of linguistics and NLP which will be recurrent in most of the chapters. While the coverage of these topics will be quite shallow, this will give the reader a basic understanding which should be enough to follow the rest of the book.

2.1.1 LINGUISTIC FUNDAMENTALS

Linguistics, as an area of study, comprises many subfields, among which we find phonetics, phonology, pragmatics, lexicography, psycholinguistics, discourse, and others such as syntax, morphology, and semantics. While in this book we will not cover these topics in-depth, we recommend Bender [2013] and Bender and Lascarides [2019], which cover the most important aspects of linguistics directly related to NLP. In the following, we provide a brief overview of three major fields of study in linguistics that are related to the topic of this book.

Syntax. Syntax deals with the structure of sentences. It defines the rules and principles that specify the order in which words are put together in a sentence in a given language. For instance, syntax of the English language denotes that sentences in this language should have the subject–verb–object (SVO) order (where the subject comes first, followed by the verb, and then the object) whereas syntax for Farsi or Korean languages generally follows the SOV order. Grammar is a more general concept which involves syntax but also other rules governing a language, such as morphology.

Morphology. Morphology deals with the structure of words and studies their constituent parts (roots, stems, prefixes, and suffixes). It shows how words are formed and how they are related to each other in a language. A language like Farsi is morphologically rich given that, for instance, a verb in this language can take many inflected forms, whereas languages such as English are less morphologically diverse.

Semantics. Semantics is the area of linguistics that studies meaning. This is clearly the area which is the central focus of this book. In fact, what we generally expect from an embedding is a machine-readable representation that encodes the semantics (or meaning) of a word, a sentence, etc. While there are different branches of semantics, this book mainly deals with lexical semantics, which is the branch that studies word meaning. Then there are also a few chapters (especially Chapter 7) where compositional semantics, i.e., how to combine smaller pieces into larger units such as sentences or documents, comes into play.

2.1.2   LANGUAGE MODELS

Language Models (LM) are intended to distinguish grammatical from ungrammatical sequences in a specified language [Chomsky, 1957]. In other words, given a phrase or a sentence in a language, a LM has to identify if it is fluent or plausible according to the grammar of that language or not. For instance, a language model is expected to identify "high air pollution" as a fluent sequence in English that accords with its grammar, whereas "high pollution air" as unfluent or ungrammatical.

The statistical approach to language modeling usually makes an n-th order Markov assumption and estimates the probability of a given sequence based on the statistics of n-gram[1] frequencies in a large text corpus, usually followed by a smoothing operation. Statistical LM is one of the major components of Statistical Machine Translation (SMT), which was the prominent MT paradigm before the introduction of Neural Machine Translation (NMT).[2] The LM component of SMT systems is responsible for generating fluent translations in the target language. Roughly speaking, among a set of candidate translations, the LM unit picks the one that has the highest probability of it being said by a native speaker.

Statistical LM suffers from data sparsity given that the number of possible n-grams in a language grows exponentially with respect to the vocabulary size and sequence length, a phenonemon also known as the curse of dimensionality. Neural language models (NLMs) address the sparsity issue of count-based LMs by moving from the local one-hot representation of words to a continuous distributed one (see Section 3.2). To this end, during sequence modeling each word is represented as a continuous vector, incorporating the notion of vector space similarity. The continuous representation of words pushes the language model to learn grammatical and semantic *patterns* instead of exact sequences of words. This in turn results in a smooth modeling that allows the NLM to assign high probabilities to unobserved sequences based on similar patterns (semantic and functional similarity) that were observed during training.

In this manner, language modeling has largely benefited from distributed representations. Interestingly, the benefit has recently turned out to be mutual. The application of LM has vastly expanded from MT and generation-oriented tasks to representation learning. In fact, most of the recent successful word representation techniques are closely tied to language modeling.

It is shown by different researchers that to achieve the simple objective of predicting the next word (or a set of missing words), language models encode complex syntactic and semantic information [Goldberg, 2019, Jawahar et al., 2019]. Owing to this, the recent NLMs that are usually trained on massive amounts of text have been the dominating approach for semantic

---

[1]An n-gram is defined as any sequence of n items from a text corpus. For example, "air pollution" is a 2-gram or a *bigram*.
[2]For an in-depth overview of SMT, the reader can refer to Koehn [2009].

representation. In Chapter 6 we will discuss contextualized representations and explain their close ties with language models. In the following section, we provide more details on neural networks applied to NLP, for language modeling and other tasks.

2.2   DEEP LEARNING FOR NLP

In the early 1990's, a revolution in the field of NLP gradually led to a shift from hand-coded knowledge and rules, expert systems, hand-tooled grammars, lexicons, and morphological analyzers, and from Chomskyan linguistic theories to corpus-based Machine Learning [Charniak, 1995]. Since then, Machine Learning (ML) has empowered many applications in NLP. For almost two decades, statistical ML techniques were the favorite paradigm for many NLP tasks and dominated most of the benchmarks. The general approach was to train shallow models on usually high dimensional and sparse hand-crafted features. Classification-based NLP tasks, such as sentiment analysis, topic categorization, and word sense disambiguation, were conventionally approached using classifiers such as Support Vector Machines (SVM) and Maximum Entropy (MaxEnt), whereas Conditional Random Field (CRF) was the predominant solution for structured prediction tasks, e.g., Named Entity Recognition (NER) and chunking.

In the past decade, a new revolution has taken place. After a highly successful introduction in Machine Vision, deep learning soon expanded its dominance to NLP. A seminal work in this branch is that of Collobert et al. [2011] who showed that a simple neural network, with no explicit intervention during training, can outperform feature-based techniques across several tasks, such as NER and Part-of-Speech tagging. Word2vec [Mikolov et al., 2013a] is another major contribution in this direction. Again, a simple neural network was shown to be highly efficient and effective in capturing the semantics of words compared to computationally expensive statistical techniques, which in the main also required an extra step of dimensionality reduction. In Chapter 3 we will elaborate further on Word2vec.

Another impactful deep learning technique that revolutionized many of the NLP systems is the Long Short-Term Memory (LSTM) network (Section 2.2.2). For several years, LSTMs were the optimal solution for encoding sequences into dense continuous representations, with several desirable properties that were lacking in previous models, such as their ability to capture word order and long-distance dependencies. Prior to LSTMs, sentence-level representation techniques were either limited to simplistic models, such as bag of words (BoW), or had to resort to local word orderings, such as n-grams. Convolutional neural networks grew in parallel with LSTMs and proved to be powerful in tasks such as sentiment analysis and topic categorization. However, they did not attain the popularity of LSTMs since they cannot capture word order on their own. For a comprehensive overview of neural networks and their application to NLP, the reader might refer to the book of Goldberg [2017].

Bag of Words (BoW). A *bag* or a *multiset* is a modified *set* that allows repetitions. BoW is a simple model in which a word sequence (such as a sentence or a document) is represented as its bag of words, disregarding grammar and word order but keeping word repetitions. For instance, the BoW representation for the sentence "A binary star is a star system consisting of two stars orbiting around their common barycenter." would be the following:
"a:2, binary:1, star:2, is:1, system:1, consisting:1, of:1, two:1, stars:1, orbiting:1, around:1, their:1, common:1, bycenter:1".

Depending on the application, instances such as function words are often disregarded in the BoW representation (these words discarded in the preprocessing step are often known as *stopwords*). BoW is one of the oldest ways of representation in the context of linguistics [Harris, 1954]. Despite its simplicity, BoW constitutes an efficient baseline for tasks such as text classification.

2.2.1   SEQUENCE ENCODING

Unlike words, it is not feasible to pre-train embeddings for all word sequences (phrases, sentences, etc.) in a natural language, given that the number of possible sequences can be infinite. Therefore, the representation for a text sequence is often computed as a combination of its words' representations. Chapter 7 talks about the representation of longer pieces of texts, such as sentences and documents.

The most trivial *combination* strategy is to average the representations of unique words in the sequence. In other words, the sequence is represented as the *centroid* point of its content words' vectors in the space. An important issue with this representation is that all words play equal role in the final representation of the sequence, with only frequency being taken into account. However, it is natural to expect that some words in the sequence might be more central to its meaning. Another important issue with this BoW model stems from the fact that it disregards the order of words. We know that word order can play a crucial role in terms of semantics. For instance, the semantically different sequences "the dog chases the cat" and "the cat chases the dog" (and many other ungrammatical sequences constructed using these words) will have identical BoW representations. Recurrent Neural Networks (RNNs) have successfully addressed the above issues in NLP.

2.2.2   RECURRENT NEURAL NETWORKS (RNNS)

RNNs are a special type of neural architecture characterized by recurrence: unlike feedforward networks (such as fully connected and CNNs), RNNs have feedback loops allowing the network to exhibit temporal dynamic behavior, and can thus "remember the past". By *remember the past*, we mean that RNNs have a memory that enables them to recall previous states, trying to mimic the human process of reading text in which a sequence is interpreted word by word, while keeping a memory of previously seen words. Feedforward networks often receive the input at once;

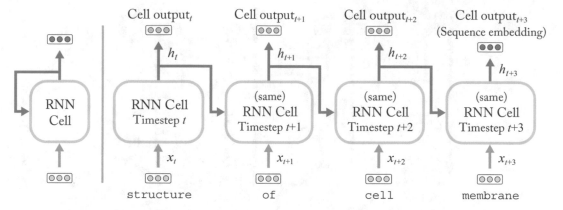

Figure 2.1: Left: RNNs have a loop that allows the network to remember the past words in the sequence. The loop is unrolled on the right side, illustrating how the RNN functions. Note that the same RNN cell is applied in different time steps to the words in the sequence.

hence, unless some additional measure is taken, they have no means of capturing the order in sequential data.[3]

Figure 2.1 shows a high-level illustration of a simple recurrent neural network. The same RNN cell receives the input word embeddings in a sequence of timesteps. The output for each timestep is computed by combining the current input and the output from the previous timestep. This output (vector) will be passed as an additional input to the next timestep and this recurrence repeats until the end of the sequence is reached. The simplest form of combination can be to multiply each of these vectors with their corresponding weight matrices, and then add them to construct the output for the current timestep. In this way, RNNs can recall the past which can be crucial for accurate encoding of semantics. At timestep t, the output embedding h_t from the RNN cell is computed using the following formula:

$$h_t = f(Wx_t + Uh_{t-1} + b_o). \tag{2.1}$$

In Equation 2.1, $f()$ represents an activation function of choice (e.g., sigmoid), x_t is the input embedding at time t (for the tth word) and h_{t-1} is the output (embedding) from the previous timestep $(t-1)$. The parameter b is the bias term and W and U are the weight matrices to be learned during the training. The final h embedding (for the last timestep, or after reading the last word in the sequence) can be taken as the embedding for the sequence.

---

[3]We will see in Section 6.2 how a feedforward network, called the Transformer, can be also effectively used for sequence encoding.

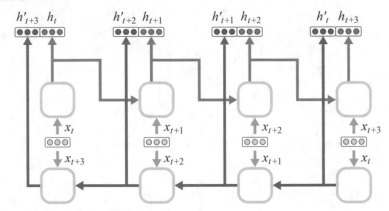

Figure 2.2: Bidirectional RNN. The text sequence is fed to the network in both directions to allow each timestep to have access to future inputs.

RNN Variants

Since their adoption, RNNs have been prominent in NLP for numerous tasks. In the following, we provide details on different variants and models.

Bidirectional RNN   A widely used extension of RNN is the Bidirectional RNN (BiRNN). In this case, the input sequence is fed from beginning to end and also from end to the beginning. This would allow a cell state to have access to future timesteps, i.e., the next words in the input sequence. Figure 2.2 illustrates the architecture of BiRNN. The resulting h vector for BiRNNs is formed by combining (e.g., concatenating) the output vectors h and h' from the two directions. It is not difficult to think of cases in which having *future* context might help. For instance, in the sentence "cell is the biological unit of all living organisms", unless we have seen words that are to the right of the ambiguous word *cell*, it is impossible to have a clear understanding of the intended meaning of this word. BiRNNs are shown to be beneficial to many NLP tasks, such as MT [Cho et al., 2014b].

Stacked RNNs   It is also possible to stack multiple layers of RNN, on top of each other, a setting which has been shown to help in some tasks. For instance, Google Translate makes use of a stack of eight LSTM layers to encode and another eight layers to decode the sequence in source and target languages [Wu et al., 2016]. In the case of stacked RNNs, instead of taking the final h_t as the output of the intermediate layers, all h_t values from different timesteps are passed in the same order as input to the subsequent RNN cell (next layer).

Vanishing gradient problem.   Backpropagation is the most widely used algorithm for training neural networks. To minimize the loss function, backpropagation computes the *gradient* of the loss function with respect to the weights. In order to avoid redundant cal-

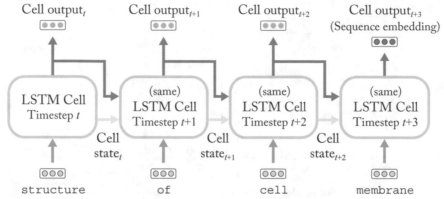

Figure 2.3: Long Short-Term Memory (LSTM) features a *carry track* that transfers the cell state across timesteps, allowing long-term dependencies to be captured.

culations, the gradients are calculated using the chain rule from the last layer where the loss is computed, iterating backward. Therefore, the gradient value can vanish[a] quickly as we move backward toward the *front* layers. This difficulty is usually referred to as vanishing gradient problem and can make it impossible to train deep neural networks. The impact of vanishing gradient in recurrent networks (which are deep with respect to timesteps) is that it impedes an effective capturing of long-term dependencies [Bengio et al., 1994]. In other words, this problem limits the memory of simple RNNs, as discussed above, and their capability to effectively remember the past.

[a]Or explode, depending on the activation function.

RNN-Based Models

In this section we provide more details on specific models based on RNNs, in particular LSTMs and GRU.

LSTM LSTM is a variation of RNN that tries to address the vanishing gradient problem. Figure 2.3 shows a high-level view of an LSTM network. In this illustration, the main difference with simple RNNs (Figure 2.1) lies in the *carry* track which transfers cell states across timesteps. The carry track works as the memory of this network. An internal mechanism, called *gate*, allows the memory in LSTMs to last longer.

Figure 2.4 shows the internal architecture of an LSTM cell. Given an input word (embedding) x_t and a cell state c_t that contains the memory from the previous timesteps, the output of the current timestep h_t in the LSTM cell is computed using the following set of equations:

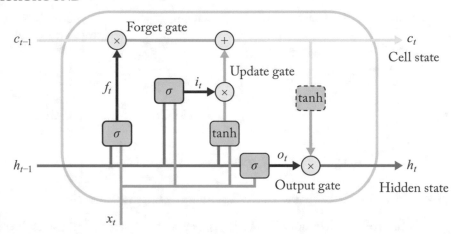

Figure 2.4: The internal structure of an LSTM cell. At timestep t, the cell *reads* an input x_t and updates the values of cell state c_t and hidden state h_t (the output of the current timestep) using three gates that control the extent to which signals can flow.

$$f_t = \sigma(W_f x_t + U_f h_{t-1} + b_f)$$
$$i_t = \sigma(W_i x_t + U_i h_{t-1} + b_i)$$
$$o_t = \sigma(W_o x_t + U_o h_{t-1} + b_o) \tag{2.2}$$
$$c_t = f_t \circ c_{t-1} + i_t \circ \tanh(W_c x_t + U_c h_{t-1} + b_c)$$
$$h_t = o_t \circ \tanh(c_t),$$

where $\circ$ is the element-wise product, σ is the sigmoid function, and f_t, i_t, and o_t are the respective activation vectors for the forget, input (update), and output gates. There are three main gates in the LSTM cell that regulate the flow of information.

- The **forget** gate decides what needs to be removed from the memory. This extent, characterized by the vector f_t, is computed based on the previous state h_{t-1} and the current input x_t (line 1 in Equation 2.2). Having f_t as a vector of 1's allows all the memory to be kept, while having all 0's does the opposite. Obviously, other values of f_t allow partial retention/forgetting of the memory.

- The **input** (update) gate controls the extent to which a new value should be placed in the memory. The activation vector for this gate is i_t which, similarly to f_t, is computed based on the previous state h_{t-1}, and the current input x_t, but with different weight matrices, W_i and U_i (line 2 in Equation 2.2). The activation is multiplied by a transformed version of x_t and h_{t-1} and the resulting vector is added to the carry track c_{t-1} to form the updated cell state c_t (line 4 in Equation 2.2).

- The **output** gate controls the extent to which the *state* should be changed to compute the output of the current timestep. The output activation o_t is computed in a similar manner, by combining signals from h_{t-1} and x_t (line 3 in Equation 2.2).

The current cell state c_t is transformed through tanh and multiplied by o_t to form the output of this timestep, i.e., h_t (last line in Equation 2.2). Similarly to other RNNs, the final cell state h_t, upon reading the last token in the sequence, can be taken as the encoded representation of the sequence. Note that the forget gate on the carry track does not involve any activation; therefore, it is theoretically possible to flow all the information through this gate and avoid the vanishing gradient problem.

GRU   There are several variants of LSTM. For instance, Gers et al. [2003] augmented LSTMs with *peephole* connections: the activation values f_t, i_t, and o_t are computed not only based on x_t and h_{t-1}, but also based on the cell state (c_t for the latter activation and c_{t-1} for the other two activations). Greff et al. [2017] provide a comprehensive survey of different LSTM variants.

A famous variant is the Gated Recurrent Unit (GRU). Proposed by Cho et al. [2014b], GRU combines forget and input (update) gates into a single *update* gate, and merges cell and hidden states. GRU makes use of the following equations to compute the ouput h_t:

$$
\begin{aligned}
z_t &= \sigma(W_z x_t + U_z h_{t-1} + b_z) \\
r_t &= \sigma(W_r x_t + U_r h_{t-1} + b_r) \\
\tilde{h}_t &= \tanh(W_h x_t + U_h(r_t \circ h_{t-1}) + b_h) \\
h_t &= (1 - z_t) \circ h_{t-1} + z_t \circ \tilde{h}_t,
\end{aligned}
\tag{2.3}
$$

where z_t and r_t are the respective activation vectors for the update and reset gates. Figure 2.5 shows the internal structure of a GRU cell. As can be seen from the above equations and from the figure, GRU is simpler than LSTM (it has fewer parameters). Therefore, it is less computationally expensive and faster to run.

Sequence Transduction

The RNN architectures discussed so far encode a text sequence into a fixed size representation. These models are mainly suitable for cases in which a fixed-size representation for the whole input sentence is required; for instance, in sentence-level classification tasks, such as sentiment analysis. However, such RNN architectures are not suitable for tasks in which the output can vary in size. MT is a prototypical example. In this task, the translation of an input sentence can change in size, depending on the input and other factors, and this size is usually not known a-priori.

A branch of models called sequence transduction or sequence to sequence (Seq2Seq) models [Sutskever et al., 2014] are suitable candidates for tasks such as MT which require input sequences to be transformed or *transduced* to the corresponding output sequences (of variable

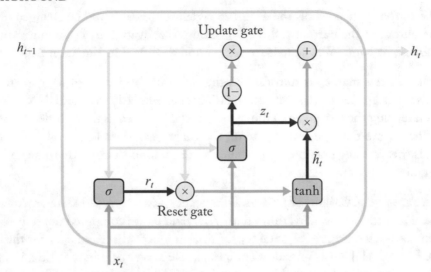

Figure 2.5: Gated Recurrent Unit (GRU) simplifies the architecture of LSTM by a few modifications, such as combining forget and input (update) gates into a single *update* gate, and merging cell and hidden states.

size). In other words, a Seq2Seq model converts sequences from one form to another form, e.g., questions to answers in Question Answering, or large pieces of texts to short texts in text summarization.

Figure 2.6 shows the high-level architecture of a typical Seq2Seq model. The model is based on the encoder-decoder structure [Sutskever et al., 2014] which is a widely used choice for Seq2Seq models. Here, two RNN networks (usually LSTM or GRU) function as the encoder and decoder modules of this structure. The encoder transduces an input sequence $(x_1, ..., x_n)$ to a sequence of continuous representations $\mathbf{r} = (r_1, ..., r_n)$. The task of the decoder is to decode the sequence $\mathbf{r}$ into an output sequence $(y_1, ..., y_m)$. The decoder is initialized with the final cell output and state of the encoder. Having a special start-of-sentence token (such as "<Start>"), the decoder generates the first output token. The output token is the most probable word according to the softmax layer which spans over the vocabulary.

The model is *auto-regressive*. In order to generate the second output token, it consumes the previously generated symbols as additional input. In other words, at any timestep the RNN receives as its input the generated token from the previous timestep. The decoder keeps generating tokens until another special token that denotes the end-of-sequence (such as "<End>") is generated.

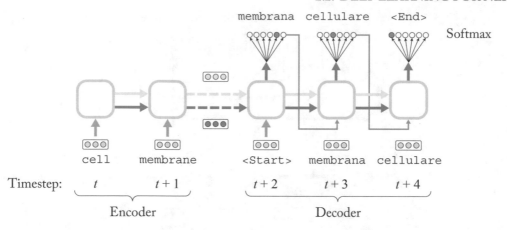

Figure 2.6: Sequence transduction based on an encoder-decoder architecture (used for translation from source to target language).

Attention Mechanism

One issue with the encoder-decoder transduction model is that all the necessary information of the source sentence needs to be compressed into a fixed-length vector. This is especially problematic for longer sentences [Cho et al., 2014a].

Attention mechanism [Bahdanau et al., 2015] is an alignment technique to circumvent this problem. While generating output and at each timestep, the decoder performs a soft search in order to find the set of words that are most important for generating the current output token. This allows the decoder to focus on those parts of the input sequence where relevant information is concentrated. In other words, the encoder is not forced to squash all the information of the source sentence in a single fixed-size vector. Instead, it encodes the input sentence into a sequence of vectors which are later used by the decoder to generate the output sequence.

Figure 2.7 provides an illustration of the attention mechanism in an encoder-decoder sequence transduction model. While generating *cellulare*, it is natural to expect the model to look at the source word *cell*, rather than *membrane*. This is handled by the alignment vector a', which is usually computed by combining decoder's current output $\bar{h}_{t'+1}$ and all cell outputs (sequence h) as follows:

$$a(t) = \frac{e^{score(h,\bar{h})}}{\sum_t e^{score(h,\bar{h}_t)}}, \tag{2.4}$$

where $score(h, \bar{h})$ can be as simple as the dot product $h^T \bar{h}$ or other parametrized forms such as $h^T W \bar{h}$. The alignment vector denotes those positions to which more attention needs to be paid. For the case of our example, $a_{t'+1}$ assigns more weight to *cell* than to *membrane*. The context vector c is then computed as the weighted average of h values (weighted by a).

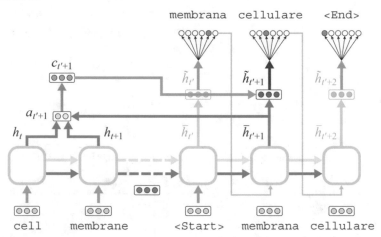

Figure 2.7: Global attention mechanism in encoder-decoder sequence transduction. During decoding, at each timestep ($t' + 1$ in the figure), the model computes an *alignment* weight vector $a_{t'+1}$ according to the current cell output $\overline{h}_{t'+1}$ and all source outputs (sequence h). The global context vector $c_{t'+1}$ is then computed as the weighted average of source outputs (weighted by $a_{t'+1}$). The attentional output $\tilde{h}_{t'+1}$ is finally computed based on $c_{t'+1}$ and $\overline{h}_{t'+1}$.

$$c_{t'} = \sum_t a_{t'} h_t \tag{2.5}$$

The context vector carries information about those source tokens which are most useful to the decoder for generating the next output token. The attentional output is finally computed using the following general formula:

$$\tilde{h}_{t'} = f(W_c[c_{t'}; \overline{h}_t]), \tag{2.6}$$

where f is the activation function of choice (e.g., tanh). The above procedure (and the architecture in Figure 2.7) is in fact the *global context* attention mechanism proposed by Luong et al. [2015], which resembles that of Bahdanau et al. [2015] with some simplifications.

Luong et al. [2015] also proposed a *local context* attention mechanism which aims at reducing the computational cost by constraining the context. As opposed to the global mechanism which computes the context vector based on all input words, the local mechanism focuses on a small set of input words and computes the context vector based on this set only. To this end, while generating an output token, the model first identifies a single source token to which most attention has to be paid. Then, the context vector is computed as the weighted average of words in a window centered around the chosen source token. Luong et al. [2015] showed that the local attention mechanism not only speeds up the computation, but it also results in performance improvements in the context of NMT.

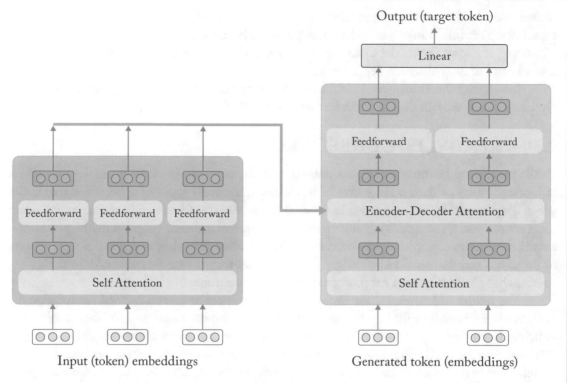

Figure 2.8: High-level architecture of the Transformer model. The sequence transduction model, which in the case of this figure translates from English to Italian, consists of stacks of encoders and decoders (more details in Chapter 6).

2.2.3   TRANSFORMERS

Until mid-2017, RNNs were the optimal choice for encoding text sequences into fixed-size representations. However, the introduction of a model called Transformer [Vaswani et al., 2017] revolutionized the field of MT, introducing a new, substantially more powerful, alternative for RNNs.

Before Transformers, the general belief was that it is not possible to capture long-range dependencies without resorting to some sort of recurrence. What makes the Transformer interesting is that the architecture is a feedforward model with no recurrence—its only memory is based on the attention mechanism. Despite this, Transformer-based models have significantly outperformed RNNs, dominating most benchmarks for a wide range of NLP tasks that require encoding text sequences.

Figure 2.8 provides a high-level illustration of the Transformer model. Similarly to RNN-based sequence transduction models, the Transformer has an encoder-decoder architecture. However, unlike RNNs that receive input tokens sequentially, one token at a time, the Transformer model takes all the tokens in the sequence at once and in parallel. This parallel functionality makes the Transformer substantially more efficient than RNN for parallel processing. Moreover, it allows the model to *attend* to far contexts while *reading* a specific word, enabling it to capture of long-distance dependencies.

Given that the Transformer architecture is tightly related with the language model-based representations, we will discuss them further in Chapter 6.

2.3   KNOWLEDGE RESOURCES

While most deep learning techniques presented in the previous section are usually trained on (annotated) texts as their main source of input, there are many types of approaches that make use of linguistic knowledge encoded in external resources. These knowledge resources can serve different purposes, from deriving more structured representations to simply providing extra linguistic information. Knowledge resources exist in many flavors as they describe different aspects of linguistic and real-world knowledge. In this section we give an overview of knowledge resources that are usually used for concept representation learning.

The nature of knowledge resources varies with respect to several factors. Knowledge resources can be broadly split into two general categories: expert-made and collaboratively constructed. Each type has its own advantages and limitations. Expert-made resources (e.g., WordNet) feature accurate lexicographic information such as textual definitions, examples and semantic relations between concepts. On the other hand, collaboratively constructed resources (e.g., Wikipedia or Wiktionary) provide features such as encyclopedic information, wider coverage, multilinguality, and up-to-dateness.[4]

In the following, we describe some of the most important resources in lexical semantics that are used for representation learning, namely WordNet (Section 2.3.1), Wikipedia, and related efforts (Section 2.3.2), and mergers of different resources such as BabelNet and ConceptNet (Section 2.3.3).

2.3.1   WORDNET

A prominent example of an expert-made resource is **WordNet** [Miller, 1995], which is one of the most widely used resources in NLP and semantic representation learning. The basic constituents of WordNet are *synsets*. A synset represents a unique concept which may be expressed through nouns, verbs, adjectives, or adverbs and is composed of one or more lexicalizations (i.e., synonyms that are used to express the concept). For example, the synset of the concept defined as "the series of vertebrae forming the axis of the skeleton and protecting the spinal cord" comprises six lexicalizations: *spinal column, vertebral column, spine, backbone, back*, and *rachis*. A word can belong to multiple synsets, denoting different meanings. Hence, WordNet can also be viewed

---

[4]In addition to these two types of resource, another recent branch is investigating the automatic construction of knowledge resources (particularly WordNet-like) from scratch [Khodak et al., 2017, Ustalov et al., 2017]. However, these output resources are not yet used in practice, and they have been shown to generally lack recall [Neale, 2018].

as a sense inventory. The sense definitions in this inventory are widely used in the literature for sense representation learning.[5]

WordNet can alternatively be viewed as a semantic network in which nodes are synsets and edges are lexical or semantic relations (such as hypernymy or meronymy) that connect different synsets. The most recent version of WordNet version (3.1, released in 2012) covers 155,327 words and 117,979 synsets. In its way to becoming a multilingual resource, WordNet has also been extended to languages other than English through the Open Multilingual Word-Net project [Bond and Foster, 2013] and related efforts.

2.3.2   WIKIPEDIA, FREEBASE, WIKIDATA, DBPEDIA, AND WIKTIONARY

Collaboratively constructed knowledge resources have had a substantial contribution in a wide range of fields, including NLP. **Wikipedia** is one of the most prominent examples of such resources. Wikipedia is the largest multilingual encyclopedia of world knowledge, with individual pages for millions of concepts and entities in over 250 languages. Its coverage is steadily growing, thanks to continuous updates by collaborators. For instance, the English Wikipedia alone receives approximately 750 new articles per day. Each Wikipedia article represents an unambiguous concept (e.g., *Spring (device)*) or entity (e.g., *Washington (state)*), containing a great deal of information in the form of textual information, tables, infoboxes, and various relations such as redirections, disambiguations, and categories. A similar collaborative effort was **Freebase** [Bollacker et al., 2008]. Partly powered by Wikipedia, Freebase was a large collection of structured data, in the form of a knowledge base. As of January 2014, Freebase contained around over 40 million entities and 2 billion relations. Freebase was finally shut down in May 2016 but its information was partially transferred to Wikidata and served in the construction of Google's Knowledge Graph. **Wikidata** [Vrandečić, 2012] is a project operated directly by the Wikimedia Foundation with the goal of turning Wikipedia into a fully structured resource, thereby providing a common source of data that can be used by other Wikimedia projects. It is designed as a document-oriented semantic database based on *items*, each representing a topic and carrying a unique identifier. Knowledge is encoded with *statements* in the form of property-value pairs, among which definitions (descriptions) are also included. **DBpedia** [Bizer et al., 2009] is a similar effort toward structuring the content of Wikipedia. In particular, DBpedia exploits Wikipedia infoboxes, which constitute its main source of information.

Finally, Wiktionary is another Wikimedia project that, unlike Wikipedia, focuses on linguistic knowledge. In this case, it includes a vast amount of information for words, including definitions, descriptions, etymologies, pronunciations, and a thesaurus.

---

[5]It is also worth mentioning that not all linguists share the notion of *sense* as defined in WordNet. For example, Kilgarriff [1997] offers an alternative view on this topic.

2.3.3   BABELNET AND CONCEPTNET

The types of knowledge available in the expert-made and collaboratively constructed resources make them often complementary. This has motivated researchers to combine various lexical resources across the two categories [McCrae et al., 2012, Niemann and Gurevych, 2011, Pilehvar and Navigli, 2014]. A prominent example is **BabelNet** [Navigli and Ponzetto, 2012], which merges WordNet with a number of collaboratively constructed resources, including Wikipedia. The structure of BabelNet is similar to that of WordNet. Synsets are the main linguistic units and are connected to other semantically related synsets, whose lexicalizations are multilingual in this case. The relations between synsets come from WordNet plus new semantic relations coming from other resources such as Wikipedia hyperlinks and Wikidata. The combination of these resources makes BabelNet a large multilingual semantic network, containing 15,780,364 synsets and 277,036,611 lexico-semantic relations for 284 languages in its 4.0 release version.

ConceptNet [Speer et al., 2017] is a similar resource that combines semantic information from heterogeneous sources. In particular, ConceptNet includes relations from resources like WordNet, Wiktionary, and DBpedia, as well as common-sense knowledge acquired through crowdsourcing and games with a purpose. The main difference between ConceptNet and BabelNet lies in their main semantic units: ConceptNet models words whereas BabelNet uses WordNet-style synsets.

2.3.4   PPDB: THE PARAPHRASE DATABASE

A different kind of resource is the ParaPhrase Database [Ganitkevitch et al., 2013, Pavlick et al., 2015, PPDB]. PPDB is a lexical resource containing over 150 million paraphrases at different linguistic levels: lexical (single word), phrasal (multiword), and syntactic. In addition to gathering paraphrases, PPDB also has a graph structure where words are viewed as nodes and the edges represent mutual paraphrase connections.

CHAPTER 3

Word Embeddings

Section 1.2 briefly discussed the Vector Space Model (VSM). We saw in that section how objects can be represented using continuous vectors in a multidimensional space and how distances in this space can denote the similarities between objects. However, we did not discuss how these spaces are constructed. In other words, the following question remained unanswered: how can we place hundreds of thousands of words in a space such that their positioning corresponds to their semantic properties? In this chapter, we will talk about the foundations behind constructing semantic spaces, particularly for words.

The quick answer to the above question is that semantic spaces are constructed automatically by analyzing word co-occurrences in large text corpora. But, how can word co-occurrences denote semantic similarity? The principal idea here is the **distributional hypothesis** [Firth, 1957], according to which "a word is characterized by the company it keeps." More simply put, words that appear in similar contexts tend to have similar meanings. For instance, *Jupiter* and *Venus* tend to have similar semantics since they usually appear in similar contexts, e.g., with words such as *solar system*, *star*, *planet*, and *astronomy*. Therefore, one can collect statistics of word co-occurrences and infer semantic relationships.

Word representation learning is usually framed as an unsupervised or self-supervised procedure, in that it does not require any manual annotation of the training data. Raw texts, which are usually available at scale, can be reliably used for computing word co-occurrence statistics. Therefore, word representation techniques can automatically learn semantic spaces without the need to resort to external supervision or manual intervention. In fact, one of the winning points of VSMs, when compared to other knowledge representation approaches, is that they can be directly computed from unlabeled corpora. This is a very desirable property that has allowed VSMs to be highly flexible and extendable, and therefore to dominate the field of semantic representation for many years.

However, there are several obstacles to inferring word semantics from co-occurrence statistics. We will talk about a few of these issues in this book. For instance, in addition to the celestial body meaning, *star* can refer to a well-known celebrity. Having *star* in the context of *actress* and *Jupiter* should not lead to establishing a semantic relationship between these two words. We will talk more about the ambiguity issue in Chapter 5.

In this chapter, we will specifically talk about word embeddings. Word embeddings are in fact a special type of distributed word representation that are constructed by leveraging neural networks, mainly popularised after 2013, with the introduction of Word2vec. Word embeddings are usually classified as **predictive models** because they are computed through language modeling objectives, such as predicting the next or a missing word. Before talking about predictive models in Section 3.2, we need to briefly describe the conventional **count-based** (Section 3.1) representations as they lay the foundation for word embeddings. We will then see the different variants and specialisation techniques for improving word embeddings, such as character embeddings (Section 3.3) and knowledge-enhanced embeddings (Section 3.4), and briefly discuss cross-lingual semantic spaces (Section 3.5). This chapter concludes by common evaluation benchmarks for word embeddings (Section 3.6).

3.1   COUNT-BASED MODELS

The classical approach for constructing VSMs mainly relies on word frequencies; therefore, the approach is usually referred to as *count-based*. Broadly speaking, the general idea in count-based models is to construct a matrix based on word frequencies. Turney and Pantel [2010] categorize count-based models based on their matrices into three general classes.

- **Term-document.** In this matrix, rows correspond to words and columns to documents. Each cell denotes the frequency of a specific word in a given document. Salton et al. [1975] first used this matrix for representing documents in order to measure the semantic similarity of pairs of documents. Two documents with similar patterns of numbers (similar columns) are deemed to be having similar topics. The term-document model is document centric; therefore, it is usually used for document retrieval, classification, or similar document-based purposes.

- **Word-context.** Unlike the term-document matrix which focuses on document representation, word-context matrix aims at representing words. Landauer and Dumais [1997] proposed using this type of matrix for measuring word similarity, following the work of Deerwester et al. [1990]. Thanks to an extension of the notion of context, this type of modeling enabled a more flexible definition which allowed a wide spectrum of possibilities, spanning from neighboring words to windows of words, grammatical dependencies, selectional preferences, or whole documents. The word-context matrix became a standard form of modeling, enabling different applications and tasks, such as word similarity measurement, word sense disambiguation, semantic role labeling, and query expansion.

- **Pair-pattern.** In this matrix, rows correspond to pairs of words and columns are the patterns in which the two have occurred. Lin and Pantel [2001] used this to find similarity of patterns, e.g., "X is the author of Y" and "Y is written by X". The matrix is suitable for measuring relational similarity: the similarity of semantic relations between pairs of words, e.g., *linux:grep* and *windows:findstr*. Lin and Pantel [2001] first proposed the *extended distributional hypothesis*: patterns that co-occur with similar pairs (contexts) tend to have similar meanings. This approach is also similar to the *distributional memory* framework proposed by Baroni and Lenci [2010]. In this framework the co-occurrence matrix is replaced by a third order tensor where explicit links between words are included.

The earliest VSM applied to NLP considered a document as a vector whose dimensions were the whole vocabulary [Salton et al., 1975]. Weights of individual dimensions were initially computed based on word frequencies within the document. Different weight computation metrics have been explored, but mainly based on frequencies or normalized frequencies [Harman, 2005, Jones, 1972, Salton and McGill, 1983]. This methodology has been successfully refined and applied to various NLP applications such as information retrieval [Lee et al., 1997], text classification [Soucy and Mineau, 2005], and sentiment analysis [Turney and Littman, 2003], to name a few. In this book we will focus on newer forms of representation (i.e., embeddings). We would recommend the extensive survey of Turney and Pantel [2010] which provides a comprehensive overview of earlier VSMs and their applications, for more detailed information.

The document-based VSM has been also extended to other lexical items like words. In this case a word is generally represented as a point in a vector space. A word-based vector has been traditionally constructed based on the normalized frequencies of the co-occurring words in a corpus [Lund and Burgess, 1996], by following the initial theories of Harris [1954]. The main idea behind word VSM is that words that share similar contexts should be close in the vector space (therefore, have similar semantics). Figure 1.3 shows an example of a word VSM where this underlying proximity axiom is clearly highlighted.

3.1.1   POINTWISE MUTUAL INFORMATION

Raw frequencies do not provide a reliable measure of association. A "stop word" such as *the* can frequently co-occur with a given word, but this co-occurrence does not necessarily reflect a semantic relationship since it is not discriminative. It is more desirable to have a measure that can incorporate the informativeness of a co-occurring words. Positive Pointwise Mutual Information (PPMI, or PMI in general) is such a measure [Church and Hanks, 1990]. PMI normalizes the probability of the co-occurrence of two words by their individual occurrence probabilities:

$$PMI(w_1, w_2) = \log_2 \frac{P(w_1, w_2)}{P(w_1)P(w_2)}. \tag{3.1}$$

Equation 3.1 shows how PMI is calculated from probabilities, where $P(x)$ is an estimate of the probability of word x, which can be directly computed based on its frequency in a given corpus, and $P(w_1, w_2)$ is the estimated probability that w_1 and w_2 co-occur in a corpus. In short, PMI checks if w_1 and w_2 co-occur more than they occur independently. A stop word has a high P value, resulting in a reduced overall PMI value. PMI values can range from $-$ inf to $+$ inf. Negative values indicate a co-occurrence which is less likely to happen than by chance. Given that these associations are computed based on highly sparse data and that they are not easily interpretable (it is hard to define what it means for two words to be very "unrelated"), we usually ignore negative values and replace them with 0, hence Positive PMI (PPMI).

3.1.2   DIMENSIONALITY REDUCTION

The word-context modeling is the most widespread way to compute count-based word representations. Usually, words that co-occur with the target word are taken as its *context*. Therefore, the number of columns[1] in this matrix is equal to the number of words in the vocabulary (i.e., unique words in a corpus). This number can easily reach hundreds of thousands or even millions, depending on the underlying corpus. This can potentially be a limiting factor, given that large vectors are less favorable due to storage space and computational reasons. To circumvent this limitation, a dimensionality reduction procedure is usually applied to VSM representations.

Dimensionality reduction is performed by simply dropping those *contexts* (i.e., columns) which are less informative or important (for instance, frequent function words). This can be done using feature selection techniques. Another way to reduce dimension is by merging or combining multiple columns into fewer new columns. The latter case is the basis for Singular Value Decomposition (SVD), which is a common approach for dimensionality reduction of VSMs.

SVD consists of factorizing a given $m \times n$ matrix into three component matrices $U \Sigma V^*$, where Σ is $m \times n$ diagonal matrix whose diagonal entries are called "singular values". One can reconstruct the original matrix based on these three. But, interestingly, it is also possible to reconstruct an approximation of the original matrix (with smaller dimensionality). To this end, one can pick only the set of k largest singular values (discarding the rest) and use that to reconstruct an $m \times k$ approximation of the original matrix. With SVD, word representations are now reduced in size from n dimensions to k (where $k \ll n$). Reducing dimensionality can bring additional advantages, such as eliminating noise. Note that the new k columns of the new SVD matrix generally do not have any natural interpretation, unlike the n columns of the original matrix, before SVD is applied.

3.1.3   RANDOM INDEXING

Dimension reduction techniques, such as SVD, tend to be highly compute-intensive, both in terms of memory requirement and execution time. In addition, the whole SVD computations need to be done from scratch every time new data is encountered, making SVD a one-time procedure. One of the key features of neural networks is their ability to efficiently learn dense representations, without the need for collecting huge co-occurrence matrices. In Section 3.2, we

---

[1]The number of columns and rows in the word-context matrix would be equal if we are interested in representing all words. Nonetheless, this is a simplified assumption and there are some settings where this may not hold in practice. For example, in some settings we may want to distinguish whether a word appears in the left or right context (e.g., the words occurring prior to *drives* (*person* or *driver*) would be different from the words occurring immediately after (*cars* or *trucks*). Alternatively, words may also be marked with part-of-speech or parser tags.

will see some techniques that leverage neural networks to directly learn low-dimensional word representations.

However, before delving into predictive models, it is worth mentioning Random Indexing (RI) [Sahlgren, 2005], an older technique that incrementally computes low-dimension word spaces without relying on co-occurrence matrices. RI first generates unique and random low-dimensional[2] representations for words, called *index* vectors. Then, in an incremental process while scanning through the text corpus, each time a word c is observed in the context of a target word w, the index vector for w is updated by adding to it the index vector of c. The resulting representations are an approximation of the co-occurrence matrix, but with a significantly lower dimensionality, and without the need for costly SVD computations. Moreover, RI representations can be update after the initial training, and once new data is at disposal.

3.2 PREDICTIVE MODELS

Learning low-dimensional vectors from text corpora can alternatively be achieved by leveraging neural networks. The representations that are generated using neural networks are commonly referred to as *embedding*, particularly due to their property of being dense and low dimensional. Neural networks were suitable candidates for this purpose due to their efficiency and speed in processing large amounts of texts and for their ability in learning dense representations [Bengio et al., 2003, Collobert and Weston, 2008, Collobert et al., 2011, Turian et al., 2010]. However, their success was limited due to hardware and software limitations of deep learning. In the last decade, together with the growth of deep learning, neural network-based representations (embeddings) have almost fully replaced the conventional count-based models and dominated the field. Given that neural word embeddings are usually trained with some sort of language modeling objective, such as predict a missing word in a context, they are also referred to as predictive models. Word embeddings were popularized by Word2vec [Mikolov et al., 2013a].

Word2vec. Word2vec [Mikolov et al., 2013d] is based on a simple but efficient feedforward neural architecture which is trained with language modeling objective. Two different but related Word2vec models were proposed: Continuous Bag-Of-Words (CBOW) and Skip-gram. The CBOW model aims at predicting the current word using its surrounding context, minimizing the following loss function:

$$E = -\log(p(\vec{w_t}|\vec{W_t})), \tag{3.2}$$

where w_t is the target word and $W_t = w_{t-n}, ..., w_t, ..., w_{t+n}$ represents the sequence of words in context. The Skip-gram model is similar to the CBOW model but in this case the goal is to predict the words in the surrounding context given the target word, rather than predicting the target word itself.

---

[2]Usually, index vectors are sparse and their dimensionality is in the order of thousands.

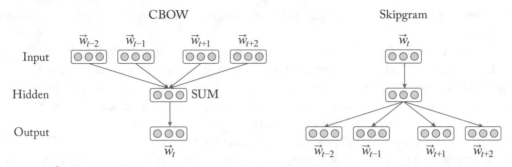

Figure 3.1: Learning architecture of the CBOW and Skip-gram models of Word2vec [Mikolov et al., 2013a].

Figure 3.1 shows a simplification of the general architecture of the CBOW and Skip-gram models of Word2vec. The architecture consists of input, hidden and output layers. The input layer has the size of the word vocabulary and encodes the context as a combination of one-hot vector representations of surrounding words of a given target word. The output layer has the same size as the input layer and contains a one-hot vector of the target word during the training phase. Interestingly, Levy and Goldberg [2014b] proved that Skip-gram can be in fact viewed as an implicit factorization of a Pointwise Mutual Information (PMI) co-occurrence matrix (Section 3.1.1).

Another prominent word embedding architecture is GloVe [Pennington et al., 2014], which tries to perform the meaning embedding procedure of Word2vec in an explicit manner. The main idea behind GloVe is that the ratio of co-occurrence probabilities of two words, w_i and w_j, with a third probe word w_k, i.e., $P_{(w_i,w_k)}/P_{(w_j,w_k)}$, is more indicative of their semantic association than a direct co-occurrence probability, i.e., $P(w_i, w_j)$. To achieve this, they propose an optimization problem which aims at fulfilling the following objective:

$$w_i^T w_k + b_i + b_k = \log(X_{ik}), \qquad (3.3)$$

where b_i and b_k are bias terms for word w_i and probe word w_k and X_{ik} is the number of times w_i co-occurs with w_k. Fulfilling this objective minimizes the difference between the dot product of w_i and w_k and the logarithm of their number of co-occurrences. In other words, the optimization results in the construction of vectors w_i and w_k whose dot product gives a good estimate of their transformed co-occurrence counts.

Note that GloVe does not make use of neural networks. However, Levy et al. [2015] consider it as a predictive model, mainly since GloVe was proposed with the new wave of neural word embeddings and was different from conventional count-based models in that it uses

Stochastic Gradient Descent to optimize a non-convex objective, whereas SVD guarantees an optimal decomposition (according to its objective).

In recent years, more complex approaches that attempt to improve the quality of word embeddings have been proposed, including models exploiting dependency parse-trees [Levy and Goldberg, 2014a] or symmetric patterns [Schwartz et al., 2015], leveraging subword units [Bojanowski et al., 2017, Wieting et al., 2016], representing words as probability distributions [Athiwaratkun and Wilson, 2017, Athiwaratkun et al., 2018, Vilnis and McCallum, 2015], learning word embeddings in multilingual vector spaces [Artetxe et al., 2018b, Conneau et al., 2018b], or exploiting knowledge resources (more details about this type in Section 3.4).

3.3   CHARACTER EMBEDDINGS

Even when the vocabulary of a word embedding space is large, we can encounter situations in certain applications where a word is out of vocabulary (OOV) as it was not covered in the training corpus (or was not included in the final vocabulary of the word embedding space for other reasons such as space or memory limitations). The default solution for such cases is to assign a random embedding to the OOV word. This is indeed not a good solution, especially if it is a word that plays a central role in our understanding of the context and in decision making.

There is a literature on modeling words that are unseen in the training data. Given that many of the OOV words can be morphological variations of existing words in the vocabulary, a large body of work has focused on this type of unseen word representation [Botha and Blunsom, 2014, Lazaridou et al., 2013, Soricut and Och, 2015]. To this end, usually a morphological segmenter is used to break inflected words into their components and to compute representations by extending the semantics of an unseen word's morphological variations. For instance, an unseen word like *memoryless* can be broken into *memory* and *less*. An embedding can be induced for the unseen word based on the embeddings of its individual components *memory* and *less* which are more frequent and probably seen during training.

Alternatively, the word can be broken into constituent subwords, i.e., group of characters that are not necessarily semantically meaningful. Character-based word representations date back to 1993, with the pioneering work of Schütze [1993] that used letter fourgrams (instead of word forms) mainly in order to reduce the size of the co-occurrence matrix for computational purposes. FastText [Bojanowski et al., 2017] is a recent prominent example in this direction which uses subword units as a way of tackling the OOV problem. In addition to words appearing in the training corpus, the model learns embeddings for n-grams of these words. Then, in the case of an unseen word, the corresponding embedding is induced by averaging the vector representations of its constituent character n-grams. This provides a quick solution for OOV embedding, but not an optimal one given that two words can have similar n-gram constituents but be dissimilar in terms of semantics. Similar to this approach, Byte Pair Encoding (BPE) [Sennrich et al., 2016, Witten et al., 1994] and WordPiece [Schuster and Nakajima, 2012] offer a solution to build a dictionary of subwords of a pre-given size. These methods are based on probabilities based on the likelihood of seen subword units in the training corpus and constitute a common solution for building a reduced vocabulary for contextualized embedding models, which will be covered in Chapter 6.

Another approach for unseen word representation is to exploit knowledge from external lexical resources, such as WordNet, in order to induce an embedding for the unseen word (with the assumption that the word is covered in WordNet). For instance, Pilehvar and Collier [2017] extract from WordNet a set of semantically similar words to the OOV word and combine their embeddings to form an embedding for the OOV word. Bahdanau et al. [2017] take a similar approach and leverage the definition of the missing word (again taken from WordNet) to induce its representation. However, as explained above, these techniques make the assumption that the OOV word is covered in the underlying lexical resource, which might not be necessarily true.

Finally, it is also possible to change the architecture of the NLP system so that it receives sequences of characters as its input, instead of the usual sequence of word tokens. Such character-based models are usually coupled with LSTM networks, with the hope to capture character order and also sequential patterns. Such character-based models have been successfully tested in different NLP tasks, including language modeling [Graves, 2013, Kim et al., 2016, Sutskever et al., 2011], part-of-speech tagging [Dos Santos and Zadrozny, 2014, Ling et al., 2015], syntactic parsing [Ballesteros et al., 2015], and MT [Kalchbrenner et al., 2016, Lee et al., 2017].

3.4   KNOWLEDGE-ENHANCED WORD EMBEDDINGS

As explained throughout this chapter, word vector representations (e.g., word embeddings) are mainly constructed by exploiting information from text corpora only. However, there is also a line of research which tries to combine the information available in text corpora with the knowledge encoded in lexical resources. This knowledge can be leveraged to include additional information not available in text corpora in order to improve the semantic coherence or coverage of existing word vector representations. Moreover, knowledge-enhanced word representation techniques are closely related to knowledge-based sense representation learning (see Section 5.2), as various models make use of similar techniques interchangeably.

The earlier attempts to improve word embeddings using lexical resources modified the objective function of a NLM for learning word embeddings (e.g., Skip-gram of Word2vec) in order to integrate relations from lexical resources into the learning process [Xu et al., 2014, Yu and Dredze, 2014]. A more recent class of techniques, usually referred to as *retrofitting* [Faruqui et al., 2015], aims at improving pre-trained word embeddings with a post-processing step. Given any pre-trained word embedding space, the main idea of retrofitting is to move closer words which are connected by a specific relationship in a given semantic network.[3] The main objective function to minimize in the retrofitting model is the following:

---

[3]FrameNet [Baker et al., 1998], WordNet, and the Paraphrase Database [Ganitkevitch et al., 2013, PPDB] are used in their experiments.

$$\sum_{i=1}^{|V|}\Big(\alpha_i\|\vec{w}_i - \vec{\hat{w}}_i\| + \sum_{(w_i,w_j)\in N} \beta_{i,j}\|\vec{w}_i - \vec{w}_j\|\Big),\qquad(3.4)$$

where $\vec{w}_i$ represents the output retrofitted vector, $\vec{\hat{w}}_i$ represents the original word embedding in the pre-trained model, $|V|$ represents the size of the vocabulary, N is the input semantic network represented as a set of word pairs, and α_i and $\beta_{i,j}$ are adjustable control values.

Building upon retrofitting, Speer and Lowry-Duda [2017] exploited the multilingual relational information in ConceptNet for constructing embeddings in a multilingual space, and Lengerich et al. [2018] generalized retrofitting methods by explicitly modeling pairwise relations. Other similar approaches are those by Pilehvar and Collier [2017] and Goikoetxea et al. [2015], which analyze the structure of semantic networks via Personalized Page Rank [Haveliwala, 2002] for extending the coverage and quality of pre-trained word embeddings, respectively. Finally, Bollegala et al. [2016] modified the loss function of a given word embedding model to learn vector representations by simultaneously exploiting cues from co-occurrences and semantic networks.

Recently, a new branch that focuses on specializing word embeddings for specific applications has emerged. For instance, Kiela et al. [2015] investigated two variants of retrofitting to specialize word embeddings for similarity or relatedness, and Mrksic et al. [2017] specialized word embeddings for semantic similarity and dialogue state tracking by exploiting a number of monolingual and cross-lingual linguistic constraints (e.g., synonymy and antonymy) from resources such as PPDB and BabelNet.

In fact, as shown in this last work, knowledge resources also play an important role in the construction of multilingual vector spaces. The use of external resources circumvents the need for compiling large parallel corpora, which have traditionally been the main source for learning cross-lingual word embeddings in the literature [Ruder et al., 2017, Upadhyay et al., 2016]. These alternative models for learning cross-lingual embeddings exploit knowledge from lexical resources such as WordNet or BabelNet [Goikoetxea et al., 2018, Mrksic et al., 2017], bilingual dictionaries [Ammar et al., 2016, Artetxe et al., 2016, Doval et al., 2018, Mikolov et al., 2013b] or comparable corpora extracted from Wikipedia [Vulić and Moens, 2015]. In the following section, we provide more details on these approaches and cross-lingual word embedding learning in general.

3.5   CROSS-LINGUAL WORD EMBEDDINGS

Cross-lingual word embeddings are an extended notion of word embeddings where words from two or more languages are represented in the same shared low-dimensional vector space. Intuitively, these spaces preserve similar semantic properties to those found in standard monolingual word embeddings.

For a more comprehensive overview of cross-lingual word embeddings, we recommend the book of Søgaard et al. [2019]. In the following, we split the different types of word embeddings according to their source of supervision: sentence-level (Section 3.5.1), document-level (Section 3.5.2), word-level (Section 3.5.3), and unsupervised (Section 3.5.4).

3.5.1   SENTENCE-LEVEL SUPERVISION

Sentence-level supervision models generally rely on parallel corpora,[4] of the same type used for MT, e.g., Europarl [Koehn, 2005]. This is extensive for many high-resource language pairs, but sometimes hard to obtain, at least publicly, for other less-resources languages. Given their similarity to MT, methods used to learn cross-lingual embeddings with this type of supervision are often interchangeable to processes embedded in the MT pipeline. Examples of cross-lingual embeddings learned from sentence alignments can be found in the works of Hermann and Blunsom [2014] and Lauly et al. [2014], who use compositional functions and autoencoders, respectively.

3.5.2   DOCUMENT-LEVEL SUPERVISION

Document-level supervision involves full comparable documents (not necessarily translations) which verse about the same topic. The most prominent example of this kind of supervision is Wikipedia, where documents in different languages explain the same concept or domain. Moreover, fully translated documents can also be used for supervision. Therefore, this supervision is generally easier to obtain than sentence translations. For instance, Vulić and Moens [2016] make use of Wikipedia pages of the same concept or entity in different languages. These different Wikipedia pages are not exact translations of each other but rather deal with the same topic.

3.5.3   WORD-LEVEL SUPERVISION

To learn cross-lingual embeddings with word-level supervision, only a bilingual dictionary is necessary. This strategy has been quite attractive for some time due to this cheap supervision, as bilingual dictionaries are easily available for hundreds of language pairs.

These methods are in the main based on linear alignments that map words from the input languages to their translations in the target language. A prominent example of such method is the proposal of Mikolov et al. [2013b]. Specifically, they proposed to learn a matrix $\mathbf{W}$ which minimizes the following objective:

$$\sum_{i=1}^{n} \|\vec{x}_i \mathbf{W} - \vec{z}_i\|^2, \tag{3.5}$$

---

[4]A parallel corpus is a collection of text documents in one language, each of which is translated into a different language.

where $\vec{x}_i$ is the vector representation of some word x_i in the source language and $\vec{z}_i$ is the vector representation of the translation z_i of w_i in the target language. This optimization problem corresponds to a standard least-squares regression problem, whose exact solution can be efficiently computed. Note that this approach relies on a bilingual dictionary containing the training pairs $(x_1, z_1), ..., (x_n, z_n)$. However, once the matrix $\mathbf{W}$ has been learned, for any word w in the source language, we can use $\vec{x}\mathbf{W}$ as a prediction of the vector representation of the translation of w. In particular, to predict which word in the target language is the most likely translation of the word w from the source language, we can then simply take the word z whose vector $\vec{z}$ is closest to the prediction $\vec{x}\mathbf{W}$.

The restriction to linear mappings might intuitively seem overly strict. However, it was found that higher-quality alignments can be found by being even more restrictive. In particular, Xing et al. [2015] suggested to normalize the word vectors in the monolingual spaces, and restrict the matrix $\mathbf{W}$ to an orthogonal matrix (i.e., imposing the constraint that $\mathbf{WW}^T = 1$). Under this restriction, the optimization problem (3.5) is known as the orthogonal Procrustes problem, whose exact solution can still be computed efficiently. Another approach was taken by Faruqui and Dyer [2014], who proposed to learn linear transformations $\mathbf{W}_s$ and $\mathbf{W}_t$, which, respectively, map vectors from the source and target language word embeddings onto a shared vector space. They used Canonical Correlation Analysis to find the transformations $\mathbf{W}_s$ and $\mathbf{W}_t$ which minimize the dimension-wise covariance between $\mathbf{XW}_s$ and $\mathbf{ZW}_t$, where $\mathbf{X}$ is a matrix whose rows are $\vec{x}_1, ..., \vec{x}_n$ and similarly $\mathbf{Z}$ is a matrix whose rows are $\vec{z}_1, ..., \vec{z}_n$. Note that while the aim of Xing et al. [2015] is to avoid making changes to the cosine similarities between word vectors from the same language, Faruqui and Dyer [2014] specifically want to take into account information from the other language with the aim of improving the monolingual embeddings themselves. On top of this, Artetxe et al. [2018a] proposed a multi-step framework in which they experiment with several pre-processing and post-processing strategies. These include whitening (which involves applying a linear transformation to the word vectors such that their covariance matrix is the identity matrix), re-weighting each coordinate according to its cross-correlation (which means that the relative importance of those coordinates with the strongest agreement between both languages is increased), de-whitening (i.e., inverting the whitening step to restore the original covariances), and dimensionality reduction step, which is seen as an extreme form of re-weighting (i.e., those coordinates with the least agreement across both languages are simply dropped). They also consider the possibility of using orthogonal mappings of both embedding spaces into a shared space, rather than mapping one embedding space onto the other, where the objective is based on maximizing cross-covariance. Other approaches that have been proposed for aligning monolingual word embedding spaces include models which replace Equation (3.5) with a max-margin objective [Lazaridou et al., 2015] and models which rely on neural networks to learn nonlinear transformations [Lu et al., 2015].

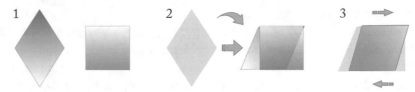

Figure 3.2: Two-stage procedure for mapping two monolingual word embedding spaces together [Doval et al., 2018].

Postprocessing. By restricting transformations to orthogonal linear mappings, these methods rely on the assumption that the monolingual embeddings spaces are approximately isomorphic [Barone, 2016, Doval et al., 2020]. However, it has been argued that this assumption is overly restrictive, as the isomorphism assumption is not always satisfied [Søgaard et al., 2018]. For this reason, it has been proposed to go beyond orthogonal transformations by modifying the internal structure of the monolingual spaces, either by giving more weight to highly correlated embedding components, as is the case for unsupervised variants [Artetxe et al., 2018a], or by complementing the orthogonal transformation with other forms of post-processing. As an example of this latter strategy, Doval et al. [2018] fine-tune the initial alignment by learning an unconstrained linear transformation which aims to map each word vector onto the average of that vector and the corresponding word vector from the other language.

Figure 3.2 shows a common pipeline including an orthogonal transformation and a final post-processing to further approach the resulting embedding spaces.

3.5.4 UNSUPERVISED

This branch of cross-lingual embeddings deals with those approaches that do not need for any kind of external supervision. Generally, unsupervised models learn language-specific embeddings from monolingual corpora and then learn a bilingual dictionary based on the distribution of these embeddings. This bilingual dictionary can also be learned using distant supervision techniques, such as constructing dictionaries from identical tokens [Smith et al., 2017] or numerals [Artetxe et al., 2017] or exploiting structural similarities of the monolingual vector spaces.

From this branch techniques to learn a bilingual dictionary automatically from the monolingual embeddings can be split into two main categories: adversarial and distributional. A prominent work in the former category is that of Conneau et al. [2018b]. This approach relies on adversarial training [Goodfellow et al., 2014], similar as in earlier models [Barone, 2016, Zhang et al., 2017b] but using a simpler formulation, based on the model in (3.5) with the orthogonality constraint on $\mathbf{W}$. The main intuition is to choose $\mathbf{W}$ such that it is difficult for a classifier to distinguish between word vectors $\mathbf{z}$ sampled from the target word embedding and vectors $\mathbf{xW}$, with $\mathbf{x}$ sampled from the source word embedding (where $\mathbf{x}$ and $\mathbf{z}$ are expected to be translations or near translations). There have been other approaches to create this initial bilingual dictionary without supervision via adversarial training [Hoshen and Wolf, 2018, Xu et al., 2018, Zhang et al., 2017a] or stochastic processes [Alvarez-Melis and Jaakkola, 2018]. These approaches have attempted to improve the robustness of the initial adversarial alignment, which have been shown not robust in different settings and especially on far languages [Søgaard et al., 2018]. As for non-adversarial techniques, Artetxe et al. [2018b] obtain the initial seed dictionary automatically by leveraging the similarity histogram distribution of words in the source and target languages. The underlying idea is that word translation in different languages will have similar distributions with respect to their distance to the other words in the vocabulary.

Finally, once this bilingual dictionary is constructed, cross-lingual embeddings are learned by making use of the word-level techniques presented in Section 3.5.3.

3.6   EVALUATION

In this section, we present the most common evaluation benchmarks for assessing the quality of word representations. Depending on their nature, evaluation procedures are generally divided into intrinsic (Section 3.6.1) and extrinsic (Section 3.6.2).

3.6.1   INTRINSIC EVALUATION

Intrinsic evaluation refers to a class of benchmarks that provide a generic evaluation of the quality and coherence of a vector space, independently from their performance in downstream applications. Different properties can be intrinsically tested, with semantic similarity being traditionally viewed as the most straightforward property for evaluating meaning representations. In particular, the semantic similarity of small lexical units such as words, where compositionality is not involved, has received the most attention. Word similarity datasets exist in many flavors.

It is also worth distinguishing the notions of similarity and relatedness. Two words are deemed to be semantically *similar* if they share many properties (e.g., *bike* and *motorcycle*, *lime* and *lemon*) whereas they are semantically *related* as long as they have any semantic relationship, such as meronymy (e.g., *wheel* and *bike*), antonymy (*sunset* and *sunrise*), or they are topically related (e.g., *tiger* and *zoo*). While words that are semantically similar can often be substituted with each other in a context, related words might just co-occur in the same context (e.g., *movie* and *popcorn*), without being substitutable.

The original WordSim-353 dataset [Finkelstein et al., 2002] conflates these two notions. Agirre et al. [2009] divided the word pairs in the dataset into two subsets with the aim of distinguishing similarity and relatedness. Genuine similarity datasets include RG-65 [Rubenstein and Goodenough, 1965] and MC-30 [Miller and Charles, 1991], which only contain 65 and 30 word pairs, respectively, or SimLex-999 [Hill et al., 2015], consisting of 999 word pairs. For a more comprehensive survey on semantic relatedness evaluation procedures, the reader could refer to Taieb et al. [2019].[5]

As far as intrinsic evaluation benchmarks are concerned for languages other than English, very few word similarity datasets exist. Equivalents of the original English RG-65 and WordSim-353 datasets have been constructed by translating these datasets either by experts [Granada et al., 2014, Gurevych, 2005, Joubarne and Inkpen, 2011], or by means of crowdsourcing [Leviant and Reichart, 2015]. Similarly, for the cross-lingual representations, most intrinsic evaluation benchmarks are constructed based on standard English word similarity datasets [Camacho-Collados et al., 2015, Hassan and Mihalcea, 2011, Miller and Charles, 1991]. The procedure consists in aligning word pairs across different versions of the same dataset in different languages. However, these datasets are either too small to allow for a reliable comparison of models and for drawing concrete conclusions, or they inherit the conflated similarity scale of the WordSim-353 dataset. SemEval-2017 [Camacho-Collados et al., 2017] and Multi-SimLex [Vulić et al., 2020] were aimed at addressing these issues by introducing several relatively large multilingual and cross-lingual datasets annotated by experts according to refined scales.

In addition to word similarity, measuring relational similarity between words has been used as a means for evaluating word representations, especially word embeddings. One of the popular evaluation benchmarks for this purpose, referred to as *word analogies*, was constructed by Mikolov et al. [2013c]. Given a pair (e.g., *brother* and *sister*) and a third word (e.g., *grandson*) the goal of the task is to find the pairing word for the third word that matches the semantic relationship between the words in the first pair (e.g., *granddaughter*). The original analogy dataset of Mikolov et al. [2013c] was then refined and extended by Gladkova et al. [2016]. Other intrinsic evaluation procedures include synonymy selection [Jarmasz and Szpakowicz, 2003, Landauer and Dumais, 1997, Reisinger and Mooney, 2010, Turney, 2001], outlier detection[6] [Blair et al., 2016, Camacho-Collados and Navigli, 2016, Stanovsky and Hopkins, 2018], and selectional preferences and concept categorization [Baroni et al., 2014]. For more information, Bakarov [2018] provides a more comprehensive overview of intrinsic evaluation benchmarks.

Problems with Intrinsic Evaluations

Several problems have been pointed out by various researchers regarding intrinsic evaluation procedures such as word similarity [Faruqui et al., 2016] and word analogies [Linzen, 2016, Schluter, 2018]. An important limitation is that word similarity benchmarks often consider only the *attributional* similarity of words, i.e., the extent of correspondence between the properties of two words (their attributes). However, different tasks in NLP address different notions of similarity, which might not match attributional similarity. For instance, word embeddings to be used for a POS tagging model do not need to encode fine-grained semantic distinctions, e.g., having identical representations for *cat* and *tiger* might not be an issue, as they both belong to

---

[5] A suitable online resource is ACL Wiki: https://aclweb.org/aclwiki/Similarity_(State_of_the_art).

[6] The task of outlier detection is also known as word intrusion detection [Murphy et al., 2012] or outlier odd-man-out [Stanovsky and Hopkins, 2018].

the same grammatical category (i.e., noun). However, for a Question Answering system, fine-grained distinctions such as the one *south* and *north* might be critical: there is a huge difference between answering "around sunset" and "around sunrise" when asked "when is best to visit the museum?". The SimLex-999 dataset [Hill et al., 2015] is explicitly designed with the intention to highlight this notion of similarity: for instance, the score assigned to the pair *sunset:sunrise* is lower than that for *bed:bedroom* and *paper:wood*.

Given the different conceptions of the notion of similarity, one might expect different types of word embeddings may be more suited than others for certain NLP tasks. In fact, it has been shown in several studies that intrinsic evaluation protocols do not always correlate with downstream performance. Tsvetkov et al. [2015] showed that performance on standard word similarity benchmarks has a low correlation with results on tasks such as sentiment analysis, metaphor detection, and text classification, whereas Chiu et al. [2016] found that, strikingly, there is a negative correlation between word similarity performance and results in Named Entity Recognition.

Tsvetkov et al. [2015] proposed an alternative intrinsic evaluation, called QVEC, which is based on aligning a word embedding matrix to the matrix of features extracted from manually crafted lexical resources. Specifically, they use SemCor [Miller et al., 1993], a large sense-annotated corpus, to construct a custom word-context matrix where rows are words and columns are WordNet supersenses (which are 41 in total). The columns in this matrix are aligned with the columns in the corresponding word representation matrix (which is to be evaluated) by maximizing correlation. The central assumptions is that dimensions in the latter matrix correspond to linguistic properties in the former matrix. The degree of "semantic content" is then computed as the total correlation among these two matrices. It was shown that QVEC can produce better estimates of downstream performance when compared to standard word similarity evaluations.

Another important problem with intrinsic evaluation is due to hubness. A hub in the semantic space is a word that has high cosine similarity with a large number of other words [Lazaridou et al., 2015]. Pairs of words with similar frequency tend to be closer in the semantic space, thus showing higher word similarity than they should [Schnabel et al., 2015].

Ignoring the polysemous nature of words is another issue with most existing intrinsic evaluation benchmarks. Most word similarity benchmarks do not check for the ability of embedding models to capture different meanings of a word. For an embedding model to succeed on these benchmarks, it is often enough to encode the most frequent meaning of a word. In Chapter 5, we will talk in detail about a different type of embedding that is aimed at capturing various meanings (or *senses*) of the same word.

3.6.2   EXTRINSIC EVALUATION

Extrinsic evaluation procedures aim at assessing the quality of vector representations when used as input features to a machine learning model in a downstream NLP task. In addition to intrinsic evaluation procedures, extrinsic evaluation is necessary to understand the effectiveness of word representation techniques in real-world applications. This is especially relevant given the problems of currently practiced intrinsic evaluations listed above. Indeed, one of the most important advantages of word embeddings lies in their ability to improve generalization power of machine learning models [Goldberg, 2017].

In this regard, any NLP application that deals with lexical semantics can be used for testing the quality of word representations. In their seminal work on the use of neural networks for NLP, Collobert et al. [2011] used a wide range of tasks including part of speech tagging, chunking, named entity recognition, and semantic role labeling. Although the goal in this work was not the explicit evaluation of word embeddings, one can use the framework for comparing various word embeddings by introducing them to the model as input features while fixing the network configuration. Text classification tasks such as sentiment analysis, metaphor detection, and topic categorization have also been used in the context of word embedding evaluation [Schnabel et al., 2015, Tsvetkov et al., 2015].

Extrinsic evaluations reflect the performance of a word embedding in a downstream scenario, but, similarly to intrinsic evaluations, they are prone to limitations which make them insufficient as a sole basis for evaluating word embeddings. The first limitation is shared to some extent between intrinsic and extrinsic evaluations, and comes from the fact that different NLP tasks might highly differ in their nature. In fact, word embedding performance does not necessarily correlate across tasks [Schnabel et al., 2015]. This makes it impossible to prescribe a single best-performing solution for all NLP tasks. For instance, word embeddings suitable for part of speech tagging might perform no better than random embeddings on sentiment analysis. Conclusions drawn from such evaluations should be limited to the specific task or the group of similar tasks, as the same conclusions will probably not generalize to other tasks of different nature.

The second limitation arises from the fact that it is difficult to control all the factors that come into play in extrinsic evaluation frameworks. In a typical NLP system, there are many parameters that impact final performance; sometimes even small changes in the configuration might drastically change the results. This makes it more difficult to draw general reliable conclusions from extrinsic evaluations. An embedding model performing well in a specific system configuration, for instance in sentiment analysis, might not necessarily perform well in other sentiment analysis systems or even in different configurations of the same model. Therefore, one should be very careful with the use of evaluation benchmarks, and more importantly, with the conclusions they make. It is always recommended to employ a mixture of intrinsic and extrinsic evaluations, and to test a diverse range of datasets and tasks.

CHAPTER 4

Graph Embeddings

Graphs are ubiquitous data structures. They are often the preferred choice for representing various type of data, including social networks, word co-occurrence and semantic networks, citation networks, telecommunication networks, molecular graph structures, and biological networks. Therefore, analyzing them can play a central role in various real-world scenarios, such as drug design, friendship recommendation in social networks, semantic modeling in language, and communication pattern extraction.

For instance, consider Zachary's famous Karate Club social network [Zachary, 1977] in Figure 4.1 (left). The network has 34 members which are shown as nodes in the graph. Edges in this graph denote if any pair of members had interactions outside of the club. Representing this social network as a graph facilitates its interpretation and analysis. With the first look, one can quickly have an idea on the rough number of friends each member of this network has in average, identify communities in the network, or find those members (nodes) who have so many friends and that they are central in a community or bridge different communities.

The primary challenge in graph embedding is to find a way to represent the data stored in a graph in a machine-interpretable or mathematical format which would allow the application of machine learning models. In other words, the high-dimensional, non-Euclidean graph structure needs to be encoded into a numerical or feature-based form.

We view the task of graph embedding from two different perspectives.

1. **Node embedding,** where the aim is to embed the nodes of a graph into a continuous semantic space with the objective of preserving relative "distances" (to be discussed in the following section).

2. **Relation embedding,** where the graph edges, i.e., the relationships between nodes, are the target of attention for embedding. We further categorize relation embedding techniques into **knowledge-based** (Section 4.2) and **unsupervised** models (Section 4.3).

4.1 NODE EMBEDDING

Going back to Zachary's Karate graph in Figure 4.1 (left), a standard clustering algorithm would detect four communities in the graph, which are highlighted by different colors in the figure. On the right side, a 2D embedding space is shown which represents nodes in the same graph, calculated using a node embedding technique, namely Graph Convolutional Networks (GCN;

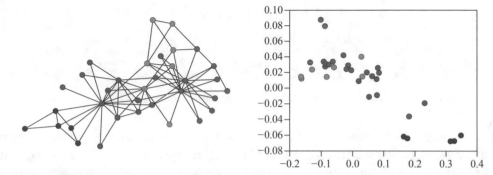

Figure 4.1: Zachary Karate Club graph (left) and the corresponding embedding space computed by Graph Convolutional Networks (GCN). Communities, as detected by modularity-based clustering [Brandes et al., 2008], are illustrated by different colors. Graph embedding tries to encode properties of graph nodes (such as neighborhood) in a continuous multidimensional space (in this case 2D). Figure from Kipf and Welling [2017].

cf. Section 4.1.4). Clearly, the embedding has done a good job in preserving the neighborhood properties of the graph.

Representing graph nodes as numerical vectors[1] in continuous spaces can have many advantages, such as facilitating the visualization and analysis of the global position of a node and that of its neighbors. For instance, one can easily compute the similarity between two nodes or obtain a clustering of the nodes (similar to the one shown in the figure) by using a simple clustering technique based on distances in the space.

Traditional node representation techniques focused on features such as graph statistics (e.g., node degree), motifs [Milo et al., 2002], graph kernels [Vishwanathan et al., 2010], or carefully designed features to model sub-structures [Liben-Nowell and Kleinberg, 2003]. Like other feature-engineered models, this approach suffers from unreliable adaptability; features might not be applicable to a new domain and thinking of new features is an arduous process.

Recent years have seen a surge of techniques that try to bypass the need for feature engineering. In fact, the trend in graph representation is analogous to that for words: directly embed units as low-dimensional vectors into a continuous imaginary space without any pre-processing or feature extraction. In graph embedding, units are nodes (in contrast to words) and the objective is to preserve structural properties of the graph, such as node neighborhood, rather than semantic or syntactic properties.

Graph embedding techniques can be broadly divided into three main categories:

1. matrix factorization-based methods,

2. random-walk based algorithms, and

---

[1]For instance, the nodes in the Karate's graph example are represented by a vector of two numbers.

3. graph neural networks.

4.1.1   MATRIX FACTORIZATION METHODS

Similarly to word representations, conventional techniques to node representation rely on extracting a set of pairwise similarity statistics for nodes coupled with dimensionality reduction. For the case of words, co-occurrence counts serve as a proxy for estimating the similarity of words. Given that co-occurrence matrices are generally large, dimensionality reduction needs to be applied to compress word vectors into fewer dimensions (cf. Chapter 2). Similar statistical measures can be used for estimating node similarity in graphs. For instance, the existence of an edge between two nodes reflects their similarity. Therefore, the adjacency matrix of a graph (which expresses the edges in the graph) can serve as a measure to estimate the pairwise similarities among the graph's nodes.

This class of techniques are referred to as Matrix Factorization (**MF**) because they represent graph properties (e.g., pairwise node similarity) as a matrix and compute embeddings for individual nodes by factorizing the matrix. The final goal in this case is to compute embeddings for nodes such that the similarity between these embeddings (often computed as their product) is highly correlated with the estimates given by graph-based node similarity measures. MF methods are generally inspired by dimensionality reduction techniques such as Laplacian Eigenmaps [Belkin and Niyogi, 2003], Locality Preserving Projections [He and Niyogi, 2004], and Principal Component Analysis [Pearson, 1901].

The main distinguishing factor between different MF methods lies in their way of estimating the similarity between nodes. Various statistical measures have been proposed. Earlier ones usually model only first-order relationships between nodes, such as edges denoted by the adjacency matrix used by the Graph Factorization algorithm [Ahmed et al., 2013], whereas more recent works try to capture higher-order relationships in terms of some power of the adjacency matrix (GraRep; [Cao et al., 2015]), or Jaccard neighborhood overlaps (HOPE; [Ou et al., 2016a]).

4.1.2   RANDOM WALK METHODS

The measure of node similarity used by MF techniques is *deterministic* in that it relies on a set of fixed statistical features. MF is generally not scalable especially for very large networks for which gigantic matrices need to be constructed. Random Walk (**RW**) based methods are different in that they leverage a *stochastic* way for determining the similarity.

The core idea behind the RW method is to perform a series of truncated random walks on the graph, sampling nodes seen during each walk in order to transform the graph's structure into a collection of paths (node sequences). These paths can be viewed as artificial sentences. Similarly to natural language where semantically similar words tend to co-occur frequently, artificial sentences carry information about similar (topologically related) vertices in the graph.

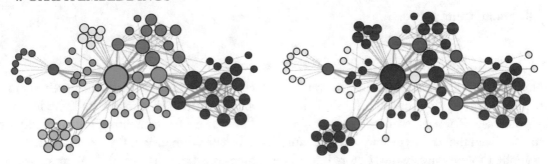

Figure 4.2: Representations learned for different configurations of Node2vec: left $q = 2$, right $q = 1$ ($p = 1$ for both settings). Graph nodes correspond to characters in the novel "Les Misérables" and edges connect coappearing characters. Representations are clustered using k-means; clusters are shown by colors. Using controlled random walks in Node2vec, one can adjust the notion of similarity: macro or structural similarity in the left sub-figure, micro or homophily (local) in the right sub-figure. Figure from Grover and Leskovec [2016].

Earlier methods [Hughes and Ramage, 2007, Pilehvar et al., 2013] take the direct normalized visit probabilities as vectors. These RW-based node representations significantly outperformed conventional deterministic graph analysis approaches (such as normalized graph distance [Wu and Palmer, 1994]) when used for encoding semantic networks in a wide range of lexical semantic applications [Pilehvar and Navigli, 2015]. This was especially noticeable when the obtained representations were compared using a rank-based distance measure, instead of the widely-used Cosine distance [Pilehvar et al., 2013]. However, conventional RW-based measures suffer from a major limitation: high dimensionality.

Newer RW-based techniques employ neural networks to address the dimensionality issue. **DeepWalk** [Perozzi et al., 2014] and **Node2vec** [Grover and Leskovec, 2016] are two prominent techniques in this category. The core idea here is to benefit from the efficiency of the Word2vec algorithms (cf. Section 3.2) for node representation. Word2vec receives sentences as its input and computes embeddings for its individual words. The gist of DeepWalk is to transform the structure of a graph to a series of sequences, or artificial sentences whose "words" are nodes. Random walks fit very effectively in this framework. These sentences are then used as input to the Skip-gram model and embeddings for individual words (i.e., graph nodes) are computed.

Node2vec [Grover and Leskovec, 2016] is an extension of DeepWalk which provides a more flexible random walk that can control for the notion of node similarity: homophily vs. structural. Figure 4.2 shows representations computed using the two configurations of Node2vec. Specifically, Node2vec introduces two *bias* parameters which control the behavior of random walks: p and q. The parameters control the tendency of the walk to stay in the neighborhood (homophily or local similarity), or to leave in exploration of other parts of the graph (macro or structural similarity).

Imagine a walk moving from node u to v. The random choice of the next node to visit from v is biased by an unnormalized transition probability α. With $\alpha = 1$, the walk visits a node which is at distance 1 from the starting node u. With probability $\alpha = 1/q$, the walk moves deeper in the network; setting q to a small value would bias the walk toward *outward* nodes, i.e., nodes that have distance 2 from starting node u. Parameter p performs a complementary role. The walk revisits the previous node, i.e., u, immediately with probability $1/p$. This keeps the walk close to the starting point; therefore, samples mostly comprise of nodes within a small locality. This gives a local view of the graph, capturing communities or homophily.

The two walk strategies resemble DFS (depth-first search) and BFS (breadth-first search). Setting p and q to model microscopic view of the neighborhood is similar in merit to BFS. In contrast, DFS tends to move further away from the source, modeling the macroscopic view of the neighborhood.

Structural roles.   Most node embedding approaches that are covered in this book have the underlying assumption that nearby nodes in the graph should be associated with similar embeddings, placed in close proximity of each other in the semantic space. We can think of tasks where the *role* played by a node in a graph is at the center of attention rather than relative position. Node2vec provides a solution to this using the *bias* terms (see Figure 4.2). For instance, for a target task it might be important to model similarities between nodes that act as bridges between different communities, which might not necessarily be close to each other in the graph. Embedding "structural roles" of nodes has been an active field of research with several proposals, such as Struc2vec [Ribeiro et al., 2017], GraphWave [Donnat et al., 2018], DRNE [Tu et al., 2018], and xNetMF [Heimann et al., 2018].

It is also worthwhile to mention another technique, called **LINE** [Tang et al., 2015], which is not strictly RW-based, but closely related. LINE combines two different objectives to learn node embeddings: first-order and second-order. The first-order objective is analogous to the BFS search in Node2vec. The second-order objective forces nodes with similar neighborhoods to have similar embeddings. The latter objective assumes that nodes with many common neighbors are probably similar to each other. In other words, if we take the neighours of a node as its context, nodes with similar distributions over contexts are deemed to be similar.

4.1.3   INCORPORATING NODE ATTRIBUTES

It is common for graph nodes to be associated with some attributes. Graphs in NLP are no exception. For instance, nodes (synsets) in WordNet are associated with various forms of textual data: synonymous words or phrases, glosses (definition), and example sentences. The above techniques all make use of graph structure only, ignoring all this information.

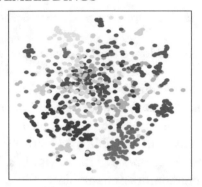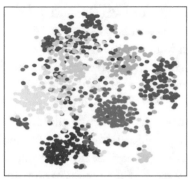

Figure 4.3: Embedded Cora citation network [McCallum et al., 2000] before (left) and after (right) enriching the graph with additional edges. The Cora dataset contains 2,708 machine learning papers linked by citation relationships into a graph. Documents belong to seven different categories, shown by different colors. Graph embedding carried out using DeepWalk and dimensionality reduction using t-SNE. Reprint from Kartsaklis et al. [2018].

Graph attributes, such as node content, can be used as a complementary source of information to the usually non-optimal structure of the networks. For instance, consider the synsets containing the frequently used meanings of *computer_monitor* and *TV*. The two synsets are separated by 10 nodes in WordNet 3.0 which is a large distance given that the maximum depth of a nominal leaf node in WordNet is no more than 20. However, these are similar concepts that are also defined in WordNet with similar glosses.[2] A node embedding technique that merely takes into account the structure of WordNet would place these two semantically similar concepts at distant regions in the space. However, leveraging glosses would force these representations to look more similar, i.e., it pulls together the corresponding points in the space.

The non-optimality of graph structures has been highlighted in the literature. For instance, Kartsaklis et al. [2018] showed for two different graphs that embedding the nodes based on structure only might not lead to desirable results. They proposed a technique for using node attributes in order to enrich networks with additional edges. They showed that an enriched graph can significantly improve the performance of DeepWalk in different NLP tasks. Figure 4.3 shows this improvement on one of the graphs, i.e., the Cora citation network.

There are several variants of RW-based models that try to augment the structural data with other attributes, such as node content and label information. TriDNR [Pan et al., 2016], DDRW [Li et al., 2016], and DANE [Gao and Huang, 2018] are instances of such models. TriDNR is one of the most prominent techniques in this paradigm. The model follows RW-based methods and captures structural node relationships using random walks. However, it additionally exploits the content of nodes as well as edge labels for improving representations. The

---

[2]TV: "an electronic device that receives television signals and displays them on a screen", and computer_monitor: "a device that displays signals on a computer screen".

authors of TriDNR experimented with the document classification task in two citation networks in which papers are nodes and their titles are the content of the nodes. They showed that significant improvements can be obtained by incorporating additional attributes that are ignored by structure techniques such as DeepWalk and Node2vec.

Moreover, many of the graphs in NLP are actually hierarchies (directed rooted trees) that are transformed into graphs (undirected trees). WordNet is an example of a hierarchical tree structure with additional lexical-semantic links. Synsets (nodes) at higher levels refer to more abstract concepts whereas they tend to be more specific and fine-grained when moving deeper in the tree. Representing such structures as graphs (especially with non-directed edges) would discard all this semantic information. As a solution to this problem, Nickel and Kiela [2017] propose representing nodes as Poincaré balls[3] which take into account both similarity and the hierarchical structure of the taxonomy given as input.[4]

One might be interested in learning coarse node representations, i.e., representing nodes at larger scales of relationships and their membership in hierarchies of communities. Walklets [Perozzi et al., 2017] is an approach for multi-scale representation that facilitates this goal. The approach is similar to DeepWalk with the only difference that certain nodes are skipped from paths, in order to learn higher-scale relationships or coarse representations as if the focus area in the graph is larger.

4.1.4   GRAPH NEURAL NETWORK METHODS

Given the dominance of deep learning, node embedding techniques that are based on neural networks have also been proposed. In fact, despite the short age, there is an extensive branch of techniques that either directly make use of deep learning models, such as autoencoders, for node representation or are inspired by ideas borrowed from deep learning, such as convolution operations.

This section provides a brief overview of the literature in neural network-based graph embedding. We can broadly classify NN-based models into two main categories: **autoencoder-based techniques** and **graph convolutional networks**.

Autoencoder-Based Models

Autoencoders are usually the first choice among neural network architectures for dimensionality reduction. The network learns, in an unsupervised manner, to encode a given representation into a dense embedding from which it can reconstruct the same input. This property of autoencoders makes them a suitable candidate for substituting matrix factorization techniques.

Figure 4.4 illustrates the general procedure behind a simple autoencoder-based node embedding model. Generally, these models comprise two stages in the pipeline. First, they analyze the structure of the network in order to extract a *context* vector for each node, which can char-

---

[3]A Poincaré ball is a hyperbolic space in which all points are inside the unit disk.
[4]WordNet is used as the reference taxonomy in the original work.

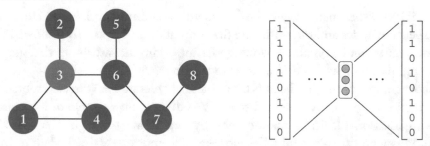

Figure 4.4: A toy graph with 8 nodes ($|V| = 8$) on the left and the general overview of an autoencoder-based node embedding technique on the right. For a target node ("3" in the figure) a context vector is extracted (simple adjacency statistics in this case). Autoencoder compresses the context vector into a much smaller embedding (with dimensionality $d \ll |V|$) for the corresponding node (shown at the middle). Autoencoder-based models mainly differ in the context vector used or in the architecture of the autoencoder.

acterize its local (or higher order) neighborhood. Then, an autoencoder is used to compress the context vector into a dense low-dimensional embedding.

SDNE [Wang et al., 2016] and DNGR [Cao et al., 2016] are two of the most prominent models in this class. SDNE constructs the context vector simply based on the adjacency matrix (similar to what is shown in Figure 4.4). DNGR leverages random walks for computing the context vector. Similarly to DeepWalk and Node2vec, DNGR carries out a series of truncated random walks to estimate pointwise mutual information between a target node and all other nodes in the graph. This is taken as a node's context vector and is fed for compression to the autoencoder network. DNGR is similar to ADW [Pilehvar et al., 2013] in the construction of the context vector.[5] However, ADW simply takes the context vector, without any compression, as the final representation whereas DNGR compresses these into smaller embeddings.

One big limitation of autoenoder-based models lies in their global context vector, which is essentially equal in size to the number of nodes in the graph. This can make the procedure very expensive for large graphs. For instance, it might be manageable for relatively smaller graphs, such as WordNet with around 120K nodes, to be embedded using autoencoder-based models. However, for larger networks, such as BabelNet's semantic network [Navigli and Ponzetto, 2010] that has millions of nodes, an autoencoder-based method will certainly suffer from lack of **scalability** (very high number of parameters in the network).

Moreover, most of the node embedding techniques that are discussed so far are by design transductive [Hamilton et al., 2017a], i.e., it is not straightforward to generate embeddings for nodes not seen during training, unless additional training is carried out. This can be limiting for evolving graphs, e.g., BabelNet (Live version) which is constantly updated with new concepts

---

[5]ADW takes the Personalized PageRank vector for each node as its corresponding representation.

that are created by Wikipedians. A transductive model would fail at keeping up with the updates as the training has to be carried out from scratch for a new node embedding to be computed.

Convolution-Based Models

Driven by ideas from computer vision, convolutional methods try to address the scalability and generalizability issues of previous techniques by resorting to local neighborhood rather than global information. The main reason behind naming this branch as *convolutional* lies in the process of combining neighboring nodes' embeddings to construct a target embedding, which is analogous to the convolution operation in computer vision (CNNs, [Hamilton et al., 2017a]). GCNs [Kipf and Welling, 2017] and **GraphSAGE** [Hamilton et al., 2017b] are two of the most prominent models in this category.

The basic idea is simple: to compute the embedding for a target node, look at the embeddings of neighboring nodes. The neighboring nodes are in turn embedded using their neighbors. This process is usually carried out in an iterative manner (the number of iterations is often referred to as *depth*).

More specifically, for a target node t, in each iteration *aggregate* the embeddings of neighboring nodes. The aggregation can be a simple element-wise mean, such as in the case of GCNs. The resulting aggregated embedding is then *combined* with the previous estimate of t's embedding (from the previous iteration). GCNs use a weighted sum for this stage. Models differ in how they define aggregation and combination. For instance, GraphSAGE uses concatenation for its aggregation and tests max-pooling networks and LSTMs as combination functions.

Thanks to the local nature of the context lookup in convolutional models (as opposed to autoencoder-based models that require the global associations for each node with respect to all the other nodes in the graph) they can address both generalizability and scalability issues. An embedding for a new node can be easily computed based on the learned aggregation and combination functions, and by looking up the existing embeddings for neighboring nodes.

4.2   KNOWLEDGE-BASED RELATION EMBEDDINGS

This section provides an overview of representation techniques targeting concepts and named entities from knowledge bases only. A large body of research in this area takes knowledge graphs (or semantic networks) as signals to construct representations of entities (and relations), specifically targeted to the knowledge base completion task.[6] A pioneering work in this area is TransE [Bordes et al., 2013], a method for embedding both entities and relations. In this model, relations are viewed as translations which operate in the same vector space as entities. Given a knowledge base represented as a set of triples $\{(e_1, r, e_2)\}$), where e_1 and e_2 are entities and r is the relation between them, the main goal is to approach the entities in a way that $\vec{e_1} + \vec{r} \approx \vec{e_2}$ for all triples in the space (i.e., $\forall (e_1, r, e_2) \in N$). Figure 4.5 illustrates the main idea behind the model.

---

[6]Given an incomplete knowledge base as input, the knowledge base completion task consists in predicting relations that are missing from the original resource.

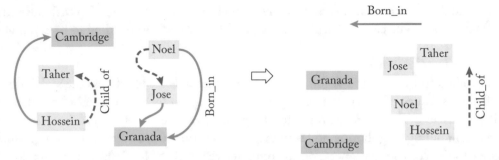

Figure 4.5: From a knowledge graph to entity and relation embeddings. Illustration idea is based on the slides of Weston and Bordes [2014].

This objective may be achieved by exploiting different learning architectures and constraints. In the original work of Bordes et al. [2013], the optimization is carried out by stochastic gradient descent with an L_2 normalization of embeddings as an additional constraint. Following this underlying idea, various approaches have proposed improvements for different parts of the learning architecture.

- TransP [Wang et al., 2014b] is a similar model that improved the relational mapping part by dealing with specific properties present in the knowledge graph.

- Lin et al. [2015] proposed to learn embeddings of entities and relations in separate spaces (TransR).

- Ji et al. [2015] introduced a dynamic mapping for each entity-relation pair in separate spaces (TransD).

- Luo et al. [2015] put forward a two-stage architecture using pre-trained word embeddings for initialization.

- A unified learning framework that generalizes TransE and NTN [Socher et al., 2013a] was presented by Yang et al. [2015].

- Finally, Ebisu and Ichise [2018] discussed regularization issues from TransE and proposed TorusE, which benefits from a new regularization method solving TransE's regularization problems.

These have been some of the most relevant works on knowledge base embeddings in recent years, but given the multitude of papers on this topic, this review was by no means exhaustive. A broader overview of knowledge graph embeddings, including more in-depth explanations, is presented by Cai et al. [2018] or Nguyen [2017], the latter focusing on the knowledge base completion task.

4.3   UNSUPERVISED RELATION EMBEDDINGS

Modeling the interaction of a pair of concepts has been widely investigated since at least Turney [2005]. For instance, intuitively for a human the relation between *mason* and *stone*, and *carpenter* and *wood* are similar, as they can both be integrated in a larger set of *work-with* relations. There have been attempts to store these relations in knowledge resources, as we showed in Section 2.3. However, the discrete nature of these relations has motivated a new field of study, which investigates their representation as parts of continuous vector spaces. While there are approaches that attempt to add continuity to discrete knowledge sources (see Section 4.2), it seems that the complex nature of relations in the real world requires us to use fully continuous models of relations, instead of grafting continuity onto fundamentally discrete models of relations.

Another way to model these relationships between concepts is by leveraging a text corpus, as in the case of word embeddings (see Chapter 3). In fact, a common way to model these relations is precisely via standard word embeddings [Mikolov et al., 2013d], through the word analogy task.

> **Word analogy.**   Word analogy has become a popular task in NLP since Mikolov et al. [2013d] who showed that Word2vec word embeddings are able to capture linguistic relationships going beyond purely semantic similarity by exploiting word vector differences. For instance, $\overrightarrow{king} - \overrightarrow{man} + \overrightarrow{woman}$ would result in a vector that is close to $\overrightarrow{queen}$.
>
> Lately there have been some works aiming at understanding where these analogies come from. In general, it has been shown that word embeddings are not actually recovering general relations, but rather some specific ones for which similarity or proximity in the vector space plays an important role [Levy et al., 2014, Linzen, 2016, Nissim et al., 2020, Rogers et al., 2017]. For instance, Bouraoui et al. [2018] shows how word embeddings can capture relations such us superlative or capital but then other relations cannot be retrieved by simple arithmetic operations from word embeddings. For a more detailed overview of the properties of word analogies, we would recommend the work of Allen and Hospedales [2019] or Allen et al. [2019].

In the following we discuss the two main of paradigm to learn relation embeddings, namely co-occurrence and predictive models. While there is extensive literature for modeling specific types of semantic relations, such as taxonomic [Cocos et al., 2018, Espinosa-Anke et al., 2016, Hearst, 1992, Shwartz et al., 2016], we focus on those approaches that aim at modeling any type of relation.

Co-occurrence based models.   In one of the earlier works, Turney [2005] proposed a singular value decomposition (SVD) model. This model encoded different linguistic patterns of words and how they are connected. A similar more recent work is that of Riedel et al. [2013] who represent word pairs as vectors, in this case combining co-occurrence statistics with information encoded in a knowledge graph. More recently, Jameel et al. [2018] proposed an unsupervised

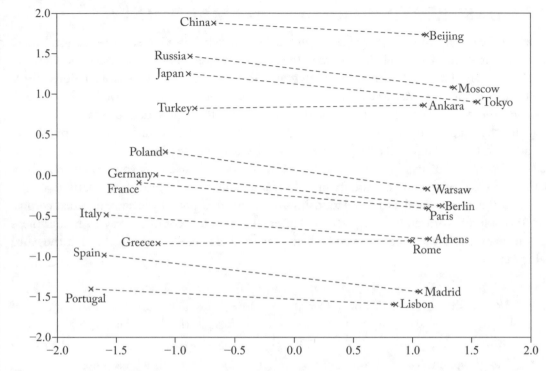

Figure 4.6: Word analogies in Word2vec. Image borrowed from Mikolov et al. [2013c].

method for learning relation vectors which is inspired by the GloVe word embedding model. Their training objective is to learn vector representations $\mathbf{r_{ab}}$ of word pairs and vector representations $\tilde{\mathbf{w}}_\mathbf{c}$ of context words, such that the dot product $\mathbf{r_{ab}} \cdot \tilde{\mathbf{w}}_\mathbf{c}$ predicts the strength of association between occurrences of the context word c and the word pair (a, b) in a sentence. For this purpose, they considered a number of generalizations of PMI to three arguments. A simpler and more efficient alternative was proposed by Espinosa-Anke and Schockaert [2018], where relation vectors were learned by averaging the word vectors of the context words appearing in sentences that contain the word pair (a, b) and then using a conditional autoencoder. These averaging methods have been further refined by exploiting latent variable models that assign probabilities to words based on their association to the given word pair [Camacho-Collados et al., 2019].

Predictive models. The aforementioned methods have the disadvantage that they can only learn relation vectors for pairs of words that co-occur in the same sentence sufficiently often. To address this, a number of methods have been proposed which learn word vectors that are aimed at modeling relational properties [Joshi et al., 2019, Washio and Kato, 2018a,b]. Specifically, these works train a neural network that maps the concatenation of two word vectors $\mathbf{w_a} \oplus \mathbf{w_b}$

to a vector $\mathbf{r}_{ab}$ which represents the relation between the words *a* and *b*. This network is trained such that $\mathbf{r}_{ab}$ captures the contexts in which the words appear, where contexts correspond to learned vector encodings of dependency paths [Washio and Kato, 2018b] or LSTM-based neural encodings of surface patterns [Joshi et al., 2019, Washio and Kato, 2018a].

4.4   APPLICATIONS AND EVALUATION

This section provides a brief overview of the most common evaluation setups for graph embedding techniques. The discussion is divided based on the embedding type into node embedding and relation embedding. We also briefly discuss some of the applications of these embeddings.

4.4.1   NODE EMBEDDING

Node embedding evaluation is usually centered around the notion of similarity between node embeddings. We briefly discuss some of the existing evaluation setups below.

- **Node classification.** One of the major applications of node embeddings is node classification, i.e., assigning labels to nodes based on rules learned from the labeled subset nodes. This procedure can be viewed as label propagation in the graph. Given its supervised nature and ease of evaluation, node classification is one of the first choices for evaluating node embeddings. For instance, one can view WordNet as a graph and compute embeddings for its nodes (synsets). Having domain labels (such as *zoology* or *transport*) for a set of synsets, the task would be to assign labels to unlabeled synsets.

- **Node clustering.** This is similar to node classification with the difference that labels are not pre-defined. Node clustering often involves computing similarities between nodes and grouping them based on these similarities. One application of node clustering would be to reduce the sense granularity of WordNet by grouping together senses of a word that are similar.

- **Node ranking.** Given a target node, the task of node ranking consists in recommending the top K nodes according to certain criteria, e.g., similarity. For instance, what are the three most semantically similar synsets to a given synset in WordNet. Node ranking has a wide range of applications, such as friend recommendation in social networks, question answering, and personalized advertisement, just to name a few.

- **Graph visualization.** The goal is to visualize a given graph in a low-dimensional space, usually 2D, to get a high-level overview of the properties of the graph. Nodes belonging to different categories can be shown with different colors. Figure 4.1 is an example of visualization. Given that node embeddings are usually of high dimensions (> 3), which is not directly visualizable, it is necessary to apply dimensionality reduction techniques, such as Principal Component Analysis (PCA) [Jolliffe, 1986] and t-distributed

Stochastic Neighbor Embedding (t-SNE) [Maaten and Hinton, 2008] on the node embeddings, prior to visualization. Visualization can serve as a qualitative testbed for evaluating node embeddings. Moreover, it can have applications in other fields, such as software engineering and biology, social network analysis, and bioinformatics [Herman et al., 2000].

- **Network compression.** *Reconstruction error* is a common way to quantify the ability of node embedding techniques to encode structural information of a graph. According to this procedure, given the node embeddings computed for a graph, the graph is reconstructed. Reconstruction error is then computed as the difference between the original and the reconstructed graphs. For instance, reconstruction can be viewed as predicting the edges of the original graph, and the error in this case can be directly computed as the accuracy of this prediction task. It is shown by different researchers [Ou et al., 2016b, Wang et al., 2016] that typical graphs can be reconstructed to a good accuracy from their node embeddings. This way, node embeddings can be considered as compressed forms of the topological information encoded in the structure of graphs and can be effectively used to store it.

4.4.2   RELATION EMBEDDING

The main application of relation embeddings is link prediction. It is often the case that the richness of relations in an underlying semantic network has a direct impact on the performance of a model using that resource [Agirre and Soroa, 2009, Pilehvar et al., 2013]. Relations in networks are often constructed according to observed interactions between nodes. For instance, WordNet's graph is usually enriched with relations extracted from manually disambiguated glosses. Therefore, given that glosses cannot contain all possible semantic relationships, the resulting semantic network can still be incomplete.

The task in link prediction consists in predicting missing edges in a graph. This can be extended to the task of verifying existing edges in the graph, if the graph is expected to have spurious edges due to its construction procedure. Other applications of link prediction include friend suggestion in social friendship networks or biological network analysis [Goyal and Ferrara, 2018].

As far as unsupervised relation embeddings are concerned (cf. Section 4.3), their main application has been to model relationships between pairs of words. In downstream applications, they have been integrated into pipelines for language understanding tasks such as reading comprehension [Joshi et al., 2019], text classification [Camacho-Collados et al., 2019, Espinosa-Anke and Schockaert, 2018], or relation extraction [Baldini Soares et al., 2019].

CHAPTER 5

Sense Embeddings

In this chapter, we introduce a type representation aimed at modeling unambiguous lexical items.[1] These representations emerged in order to address one of the main limitations of word-level representation techniques, meaning conflation.

Meaning Conflation Deficiency. The prevailing objective of representing each word type as a single point in the semantic space has a major limitation: It ignores the fact that words can have multiple meanings and conflates all these meanings into a single representation. The work of Schütze [1998] is one of the earliest to identify the meaning conflation deficiency of word vectors. Having different (possibly unrelated) meanings merged into a single representation can hamper the semantic understanding capabilities of an NLP system. In fact, word embeddings have been shown to be unable to effectively capture the different meanings of a word, especially infrequent ones, even when these meanings occur in the underlying training corpus [Yaghoobzadeh and Schütze, 2016]. The meaning conflation can have additional negative influence on accurate semantic modeling, e.g., semantically unrelated words that are similar to different senses of a word are pulled toward each other in the semantic space [Neelakantan et al., 2014, Pilehvar and Collier, 2016]. For example, the two semantically unrelated words *rat* and *screen* are pulled toward each other in the semantic space due to their similarity to two different senses of *mouse*, i.e., rodent and computer input device. See Figure 5.1 for an illustration. Moreover, the conflation deficiency violates the triangle inequality of Euclidean spaces, which can reduce the effectiveness of word space models [Tversky and Gati, 1982].

In order to alleviate this deficiency, a new direction of research tried to directly model individual word senses. In this chapter, we focus on this line of research, which has some similarities with respect to word representation learning and its own peculiarities. There are two main branches to sense modeling, unsupervised (Section 5.1) and knowledge-based (Section 5.2).[2] In Section 5.3, we additionally present common evaluation procedures and applications of such representations.

---

[1]This chapter is largely inspired by our previous survey [Camacho-Collados and Pilehvar, 2018]—Sections 3 and 4.
[2]While there exist methods for learning sense embeddings based on language models and contextualized embeddings (Chapter 6), this chapter covers only those methods prior to their introduction.

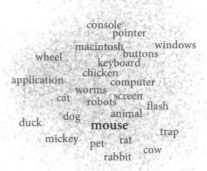

Figure 5.1: An illustration of the meaning conflation deficiency in a 2D semantic space around the ambiguous word *mouse* (dimensionality was reduced using PCA; visualized with the embedding projector of Tensorflow). Having the word with its different meanings represented as a single point (vector) results in pulling together semantically unrelated words, such as *computer* and *rabbit*.

5.1 UNSUPERVISED SENSE EMBEDDINGS

Unsupervised sense representations are constructed on the basis of information extracted from text corpora only. Word sense induction, i.e., the automatic identification of possible meanings of words, lies at the core of these techniques. An unsupervised model induces different senses of a word by analyzing its contextual semantics in a text corpus, and represents each sense based on the statistical knowledge derived from the corpus. Depending on the type of text corpus used by the model, we can split unsupervised sense representations into two broad categories according to their training corpus: (1) techniques that make use of monolingual corpora only (Section 5.1.1) and (2) techniques that leverage multilingual corpora (Section 5.1.2).

5.1.1 SENSE REPRESENTATIONS EXPLOITING MONOLINGUAL CORPORA

This section reviews sense representation models that use unlabeled monolingual corpora as their main source of information. These approaches can be divided into two main groups.

1. **Clustering-based** (or **two-stage**) models [Erk and Padó, 2008, Liu et al., 2015a, Van de Cruys et al., 2011], which first induce senses and then learn representations for these (Section 5.1.1),

2. **Joint training** [Li and Jurafsky, 2015, Qiu et al., 2016], which perform the induction and representation learning together (Section 5.1.1).

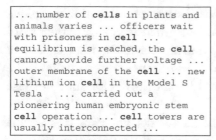 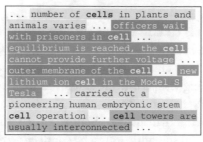 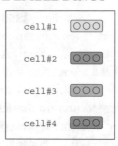

(1) Get occurrences of a word   (2) Analyze contexts and   (3) Compute sense
     from text corpora   induce senses of the word   representation

Figure 5.2: Unsupervised sense representation techniques first induce different senses of a given word (usually by means of clustering occurrences of that word in a text corpus) and then compute representations for each induced sense.

Two-Stage Models

The *context-group discrimination* of Schütze [1998] is one of the pioneering works in sense representation. This approach, based on *automatic* word sense disambiguation, was an attempt to address the knowledge-acquisition bottleneck for sense annotated data [Gale et al., 1992] and circumvent the need for reliance on external resources. The basic idea of context-group discrimination is to automatically induce senses from contextual similarity. Senses for an ambiguous word are computed by **clustering** the contexts in which it occurs. Specifically, each context C of an ambiguous word w is represented as a context vector $\vec{v}_C$, computed as the centroid of the vectors $\vec{v}_c$ corresponding to the content words that occur in C ($c \in C$). Context vectors are computed for each word in a given corpus and then clustered into a predetermined number of clusters (context groups) using the Expectation Maximization (EM) algorithm [Dempster et al., 1977]. Context groups for a word are taken as representations of its different senses. Despite its simplicity, the clustering-based approach of Schütze [1998] constitutes the basis for many of the subsequent techniques, which mainly differ in their representation of context or the underlying clustering algorithm. Figure 5.2 depicts the general procedure followed by the two-stage unsupervised sense representation techniques.

Given its requirement for computing independent representations for all individual contexts of a given word, the context-group discrimination approach is not easily scalable to large corpora. Reisinger and Mooney [2010] addressed this by directly clustering the contexts, represented as feature vectors of unigrams, instead of modeling individual contexts as vectors. The approach can be considered as the first new-generation sense representation technique, which is often referred to as *multi-prototype*. In this specific work, contexts were clustered using the Mixtures of von Mises-Fisher distributions (movMF) algorithm [Banerjee et al., 2005]. The algorithm is similar to k-means but permits to control the semantic breadth using a per-cluster concentration parameter which would better model skewed distributions of cluster sizes.

Similarly, Huang et al. [2012] proposed a clustering-based sense representation technique with three differences: (1) context vectors are obtained by a idf-weighted averaging of their word vectors; (2) spherical k-means is used for clustering; and (3) most importantly, occurrences of a word are labeled with their cluster and a second pass is used to learn sense representations. The idea of two-pass learning has also been employed by Vu and Parker [2016] for another sense representation modeling architecture.

Sense representations can also be obtained from semantic networks. For instance, Pelevina et al. [2016] constructed a semantic graph by connecting each word to the set of its semantically similar words. Nodes in this network are clustered using the Chinese Whispers algorithm [Biemann, 2006] and senses are induced as a weighted average of words in each cluster. A similar sense induction technique was employed by Sense-aware Semantic Analysis (SaSA) [Wu and Giles, 2015]. SaSA follows Explicit Semantic Analysis (ESA) [Gabrilovich and Markovitch, 2007] by representing a word using Wikipedia concepts. Instead of constructing a nearest neighbor graph, a graph of Wikipedia articles is built by gathering all related articles to a word w and clustering them. The sense induction step is then performed on the semantic space of Wikipedia articles.

Joint Models

The clustering-based approach to sense representation suffers from the limitation that clustering and sense representation are done independently from each other and, as a result, the two stages do not take advantage from their inherent similarities. The introduction of embedding models was one of the most revolutionary changes to vector space models of word meaning. As a closely related field, sense representations did not remain unaffected. Many researchers have proposed various extensions to the Skip-gram model [Mikolov et al., 2013a] which would enable to capture sense-specific distinctions. A major limitation of the two-stage models is their computational expensiveness.[3] Thanks to the convenience of embedding algorithms and their unified nature (as opposed to the two-phase nature of more conventional techniques) these techniques are generally efficient. Hence, many of the recent techniques have relied on embedding models as their base framework.

Neelakantan et al. [2014] was the first to propose a multi-prototype extension of the Skip-gram model. Their model, called Multiple-Sense Skip-Gram (MSSG), is similar to earlier work in that it represents the context of a word as the centroid of its words' vectors and clusters them to form the target word's sense representation. The fundamental difference is that clustering and sense embedding learning are performed jointly. During training, the intended sense for each word is dynamically selected as the closest sense to the context and weights are updated only for that sense. In a concurrent work, Tian et al. [2014] proposed a Skip-gram based sense representation technique that significantly reduced the number of parameters with respect to

---

[3]For instance, the model of Huang et al. [2012] took around one week to learn sense embeddings for a 6,000 subset of the 100,000 vocabulary on a corpus of one billion tokens [Neelakantan et al., 2014].

the model of Huang et al. [2012]. In this case, word embeddings in the Skip-gram model are replaced with a finite mixture model in which each mixture corresponds to a prototype of the word. The EM algorithm was adopted for the training of this multi-prototype Skip-gram model.

Liu et al. [2015b] argued that the above techniques are limited in that they consider only the local context of a word for inducing its sense representations. To address this limitation, they proposed Topical Word Embeddings (TWE) in which each word is allowed to have different embeddings under different topics, where topics are computed globally using latent topic modeling [Blei et al., 2003]. Three variants of the model were proposed: (1) TWE-1, which regards each topic as a pseudo word, and learns topic embeddings and word embeddings separately; (2) TWE-2, which considers each word-topic as a pseudo word, and learns topical word embeddings directly; and (3) TWE-3, which assigns distinct embeddings for each word and each topic and builds the embedding of each word-topic pair by concatenating the corresponding word and topic embeddings. Various extensions of the TWE model have been proposed. The Neural Tensor Skip-gram (NTSG) model [Liu et al., 2015a] applies the same idea of topic modeling for sense representation but introduces a tensor to better learn the interactions between words and topics. Another extension is MSWE [Nguyen et al., 2017], which argues that multiple senses might be triggered for a word in a given context and replaces the selection of the most suitable sense in TWE by a mixture of weights that reflect different association degrees of the word to multiple senses in the context.

These joint unsupervised models, however, suffer from two limitations. First, for ease of implementation, most unsupervised sense representation techniques assume a fixed number of senses per word. This assumption is far from being realistic. Words tend to have a highly variant number of senses, from one (monosemous) to dozens, a number that also depends on the underlying corpus [Kilgarriff, 1997]. In a given sense inventory, usually, most words are monosemous. For instance, around 80% of words in WordNet 3.0 are monosemous, with less than 5% having more than three senses. However, polysemous words tend to occur more frequently in a real text, which slightly smooths the highly skewed distribution of words across polysemy [Curtis, 1987, Fenk-Oczlon et al., 2010, Hernández-Fernández et al., 2016]. Table 5.1 shows the distribution of word types by their number of senses in SemCor [Miller et al., 1993], one of the largest available sense-annotated datasets which comprises around 235,000 semantic annotations for thousands of words. The skewed distribution clearly shows that word types tend to have a varying number of senses in naturally produced text, as also discussed in other studies [Bennett et al., 2016, Pasini and Navigli, 2018, Piantadosi, 2014]. In general, deciding the number of senses is an open problem for both unsupervised and knowledge-based models. In addition to the varying number of senses per word, the distinction between polysemy and ambiguity also plays an important role. Polysemous words include senses that are related, and in some settings it may not be a good idea to induce clusters for all senses [Erk et al., 2013, Jurgens and Klapaftis, 2013, McCarthy et al., 2016].

Table 5.1: Distribution of words per number of senses in the SemCor dataset (words with frequency < 10 were pruned)

#Senses	2	3	4	5	6	7	8	9	10	11	12	>12
Nouns	22%	17%	14%	13%	9%	7%	4%	4%	3%	3%	1%	3%
Verbs	15%	16%	14%	13%	9%	7%	5%	4%	4%	3%	1%	9%
Adjectives	23%	19%	15%	12%	8%	5%	2%	3%	3%	1%	2%	6%

Second, a common strand of most unsupervised models is that they extend the Skip-gram model by replacing the conditioning of a word to its context (as in the original model) with an additional conditioning on the intended senses. However, the context words in these models are not disambiguated. Hence, a sense embedding is conditioned on the embeddings of potentially ambiguous words in its context.

In the following, we review some of the approaches that are directly targeted at addressing these two limitations of the joint unsupervised models described above.

1. **Dynamic polysemy.** A direct solution to the fixed number of senses issue of previous models would be to set the number of senses of a word as defined in an external sense inventory. The Skip-gram extension of Nieto Piña and Johansson [2015] follows this procedure. However, by taking external lexicons as ground truth the approach suffers from two main limitations. First, the model is unable to handle words that are not present in the lexicon. Second, the model assumes that the sense distinctions found in text corpora match those specified in the lexicon, which might not be necessarily true. In other words, not all senses of a word might have occurred in a corpus, or the lexicon might not cover all the different intended senses of a word in the underlying corpus. A solution to this issue would involve a dynamic induction of senses from text corpora. Such a model was first implemented in the nonparametric MSSG (NP-MSSG) system of Neelakantan et al. [2014]. The model applies the online non-parametric clustering procedure of Meyerson [2001] to the task by creating a new sense for a word type only if its similarity (as computed using the current context) to existing senses for the word is less than a parameter λ. AdaGram [Bartunov et al., 2016] improves this dynamic behavior by a more principled nonparametric Bayesian approach. The model, which similarly to previous works builds on Skip-gram, assumes that the polysemy of a word is proportional to its frequency (more frequent words are probably more polysemous).

2. **Pure sense-based models.** Ideally, a model would consider the dependency between sense choices in order to address the ambiguity of context words. Qiu et al. [2016] addressed this problem by proposing a pure sense-based model. The model also expands the disambiguation context from a small window (as in previous work) to the whole sentence. MUSE [Lee

and Chen, 2017] is another Skip-gram extension that proposes pure sense representations using reinforcement learning. Thanks to a linear-time sense sequence decoding module, the approach provides a more efficient way for searching sense combinations.

5.1.2 SENSE REPRESENTATIONS EXPLOITING MULTILINGUAL CORPORA

Sense distinctions defined by a sense inventory such as WordNet might not be optimal for some downstream applications, such as MT. Given that ambiguity does not necessarily transfer across languages, sense distinctions for MT could be defined based on the translational divergences within a specific language pair [Dyvik, 2004, Resnik and Yarowsky, 1999]. The usual approach to do this is to cluster possible translations of a source word in the target language, with each cluster denoting a specific sense of the source word. For example, the English word *crane* can be translated to *grúa* or *grulla* in Spanish depending on the context. These different translations can give a hint on that indeed these two words represent two distinct senses.

Such translation-specific sense inventories have been used extensively in the MT literature [Bansal et al., 2012, Carpuat and Wu, 2007, Ide et al., 2002, Liu et al., 2018]. Similar inventories can be used for the creation of sense distinctions that are suitable for MT [Apidianaki, 2009]. Guo et al. [2014] induced a sense inventory in the same manner by clustering words' translations in parallel corpora. Words in the source language were tagged with their corresponding senses and the automatically annotated data was used to compute sense embeddings using standard word embedding techniques. Ettinger et al. [2016] followed the same sense induction procedure but used the retrofitting-based sense representation of Jauhar et al. [2015],[4] by replacing the standard sense inventory used in the original model (WordNet) with a translation-specific inventory.

Similarly, Šuster et al. [2016] exploited translation distinctions as supervisory signal in an autoencoder for inducing sense representations. At the encoding stage, the discrete-state autoencoder assigns a sense to the target word and during decoding recovers the context given the word and its sense. At training time, the encoder uses words as well as their translations (from aligned corpora). This bilingual model was extended by Upadhyay et al. [2017] to a multilingual setting, in order to better benefit from multilingual distributional information.

5.2   KNOWLEDGE-BASED SENSE EMBEDDINGS

This section provides an overview of the field of knowledge-based sense representation. These representations are usually obtained as a result of *de-conflating* a word into its individual sense representations, as defined by an external sense inventory. In the following we briefly explain the task of Word Sense Disambiguation, as it is closely related to how these representations are learned.

---

[4]See Section 5.2 for more details on this model.

Word Sense Disambiguation.   Word Sense Disambiguation (WSD) has been a long-standing task in NLP and AI [Navigli, 2009], dating back to the first half of the 20th century where it was viewed as a key intermediate task for machine translation [Weaver, 1955]. Given a word in context, the task of WSD consists in associating the word with its most appropriate meaning among those defined by a sense inventory. For example, in the sentence "My *mouse* was broken, so I bought a new one yesterday", *mouse* would be associated with its *computer device* meaning, assuming an entry for such sense exists in the pre-defined sense inventory.

WSD has been cataloged as an AI-complete problem [Mallery, 1988, Navigli, 2009] and its challenges (still present nowadays) are manifold: sense granularity, domain variability or the representation of word senses (topic addressed in this survey), to name a few. In addition, the fact that WSD relies on knowledge resources poses additional challenges such as the creation of such resources and the construction of sense-annotated corpora. All of these represent a very expensive and time-consuming effort, which needs to be repeated for different resources and languages, and updated over time. This causes the so-called knowledge-acquisition bottleneck [Gale et al., 1992].

The knowledge resources and sense inventories traditionally used in WSD have been associated with entries in a standard dictionary, with WordNet [Miller et al., 1993] being the de-facto sense inventory for WSD. Nevertheless, other machine-readable structures can be (and are) considered in practice. For example, Wikipedia, which is constantly being updated, can be viewed as a sense inventory where each entry corresponds to a different concept or entity [Mihalcea and Csomai, 2007]. As seen in Section 5.1, senses can even be induced automatically from a corpus using unsupervised methods, a task known as word sense induction or discrimination.

Methods to perform WSD can be roughly divided into two classes: supervised [Iacobacci et al., 2016, Luo et al., 2018, Raganato et al., 2017b, Yuan et al., 2016, Zhong and Ng, 2010] and knowledge-based [Agirre et al., 2014, Banerjee and Pedersen, 2002, Chaplot and Salakhutdinov, 2018, Lesk, 1986, Moro et al., 2014, Tripodi and Pelillo, 2017]. While supervised methods make use of sense-annotated corpora, knowledge-based methods exploit the structure and content of the underlying knowledge resource (e.g., sense definitions or a semantic network).[a] Currently, supervised methods clearly outperform knowledge-based systems [Raganato et al., 2017a], especially after the introduction of transformer-based contextualized embeddings [Loureiro and Jorge, 2019, Vial et al., 2019].[b] However, as mentioned earlier, supervised models heavily rely on the availability of sense-annotated corpora, which are generally scarce.

In this book, we will not go into further details about WSD. For a comprehensive historical survey of WSD we would recommend Navigli [2009], and more recent overviews of current methods can be found in the empirical comparison of Raganato et al. [2017a]

```
1. cell#1 (jail_cell, prison_cell): a
   room where a prisoner is kept.
2. cell#2 the basic structural and
   functional unit of all organisms.
3. cell#3 (cellphone, mobile_phone):
   a hand-held mobile radiotelephone.
4. cell#4 (electric_cell): a device
   that delivers an electric current.
5. cell#5 (cubicle): small room in
   which a monk or nun lives.
```

(1) Get senses as defined by a
sense inventory (e.g., WordNet)

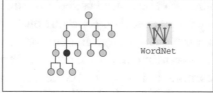

(2) Gather information for each sense
(e.g., by exploiting the structural properties
of sense inventory's semantic network,
and (optionally) then from text corpora)

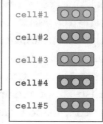

(3) Compute sense
representation

Figure 5.3: Knowledge-based sense representation techniques take sense distinctions for a word as defined by an external lexical resource (sense inventory). For each sense, relevant information is gathered and a representation is computed.

and the qualitative analysis of Loureiro et al. [2020], the latter focused on methods based on language models.

[a]Some methods can also be categorized as hybrid, as they make use of both sense-annotated corpora and knowledge resources, e.g., the gloss-augmented model of Luo et al. [2018].
[b]Transformer-based language models and contextualized embeddings will be studied in-depth in Chapter 6.

Figure 5.3 depicts the main workflow for knowledge-based sense representation techniques. The learning signal for these techniques varies, but in the main two different types of information available in lexical resources are leveraged: textual definitions (or *glosses*) and semantic networks.

Textual definitions are used as main signal for initializing sense embeddings by several approaches. Chen et al. [2014] proposed an initialization of word sense embeddings by averaging word embeddings pre-trained on text corpora. Then, these initialized sense representations are utilized to disambiguate a large corpus. Finally, the training objective of Skip-gram from Word2vec [Mikolov et al., 2013a] is modified in order to learn both word and sense embeddings from the disambiguated corpus. In contrast, Chen et al. [2015] exploited a convolutional neural network architecture for initializing sense embeddings using textual definitions from lexical resources. Then, these initialized sense embeddings are fed into a variant of the Multi-sense Skip-gram Model of Neelakantan et al. [2014] (see Section 5.1.1) for learning knowledge-based sense embeddings. Finally, in Yang and Mao [2016] word sense embeddings are learned by exploiting an adapted Lesk[5] algorithm [Vasilescu et al., 2004] over short contexts of word pairs.

A different line of research has experimented with the graph structure of lexical resources for learning knowledge-based sense representations. As explained in Section 2.3, many of the

[5]The original Lesk algorithm [Lesk, 1986] and its variants exploit the similarity between textual definitions and a target word's context for disambiguation.

existing lexical resources can be viewed as **semantic networks** in which nodes are concepts and edges represent the relations between concepts. Semantic networks constitute suitable knowledge resources for disambiguating large amounts of text [Agirre et al., 2014, Moro et al., 2014]. Therefore, a straightforward method to learn sense representations would be to automatically disambiguate text corpora and apply a word representation learning method on the resulting sense-annotated text [Iacobacci et al., 2015]. Following this direction, Mancini et al. [2017] proposed a shallow graph-based disambiguation procedure and modified the objective functions of Word2vec in order to simultaneously learn word and sense embeddings in a shared vector space. The objective function is in essence similar to the objective function proposed by Chen et al. [2014] explained above, which also learns both word and sense embeddings in the last step of the learning process.

Similarly to the post-processing of word embeddings by using knowledge resources (see Section 3.4), recent works have made use of pre-trained word embeddings not only for improving them but also de-conflating them into senses. Approaches that **post-process pre-trained word embeddings** for learning sense embeddings are listed below.

1. One way to obtain sense representations from a semantic network is to directly apply the Personalized PageRank algorithm [Haveliwala, 2002], as done by Pilehvar and Navigli [2015]. The algorithm carries out a set of random graph walks to compute a vector representation for each WordNet synset (node in the network). Using a similar random walk-based procedure, Pilehvar and Collier [2016] extracted for each WordNet word sense a set of *sense biasing words*, which are intended to be the most representative words for characterizing a given sense. Based on these, they put forward an approach, called DeConf, which takes a pre-trained word embedding space as input and adds a set of sense embeddings (as defined by WordNet) to the same space. DeConf achieves this by pushing a word's embedding in the space to the region occupied by its corresponding sense biasing words (for a specific sense of the word). Figure 5.4 shows the word *digit* and its induced *hand* and *number* senses in the vector space.

2. Jauhar et al. [2015] proposed an extension of *retrofitting*[6] [Faruqui et al., 2015] for learning representations for the senses of the underlying sense inventory (e.g., WordNet). They additionally presented a second approach which adapts the training objective of Word2vec to include senses within the learning process. The training objective is optimized using EM.

3. Johansson and Piña [2015] post-processed pre-trained word embeddings through an optimization formulation with two main constraints: polysemous word embeddings can be decomposed as combinations of their corresponding sense embeddings and sense embeddings should be close to their neighbors in the semantic network. A Swedish semantic

---

[6]See Section 3.4 for more information on retrofitting.

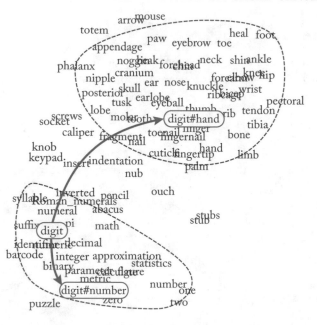

Figure 5.4: A mixed semantic space of words and word senses. DeConf [Pilehvar and Collier, 2016] introduces two new points in the word embedding space, for the *mathematical* and *body part* senses of the word *digit*, resulting in the mixed space.

network, SALDO [Borin et al., 2013], was used in their experiments, although their approach may be directly extensible to different semantic networks as well.

4. Finally, AutoExtend [Rothe and Schütze, 2015] is another method using pre-trained word embeddings as input. AutoExtend is based on an autoencoder architecture with two main constraints: a word vector corresponds to the sum of its sense vectors and a synset to the sum of its lexicalizations (senses). For example, the vector of the word *crane* would correspond to the sum of the vectors for its senses $crane_n^1$, $crane_n^2$, and $crane_v^1$ (using WordNet as reference). Similarly, the vector of the synset defined as "arrange for and reserve (something for someone else) in advance" in WordNet would be equal to the sum of the vectors of its corresponding senses *reserve*, *hold*, and *book*. Equation 5.1 displays these constraints mathematically:

$$\vec{w} = \sum_{s \in S(w)} \vec{s} \,; \; \vec{y} = \sum_{s \in L(y)} \vec{s}. \tag{5.1}$$

In Equation 5.1, $S(w)$ is the set all senses whose wordform is w and $L(y)$ is the set of all senses (or lexicalizations) of synset y.

Concept and Entity Representations.   In addition to these methods representing senses present in a sense inventory, other models combine cues from text corpora and knowledge resources to learn representations for concepts and entities (e.g., WordNet synsets or Wikipedia entities).[a] Given its semi-structured nature and the textual content provided, Wikipedia has been the main source for this kind of representation. While most approaches make use of Wikipedia-annotated corpora as their main source to learn representations for Wikipedia concepts and entities [Cao et al., 2017, Sherkat and Milios, 2017, Wang et al., 2014a], the combination of knowledge from heterogeneous resources like Wikipedia and WordNet has also been explored [Camacho-Collados et al., 2016].[b]

Given their hybrid nature, these models can easily be used in textual applications as well. A straightforward application is word or named entity disambiguation, where the embeddings can be used as initialization in the embedding layer of a neural network architecture [Eshel et al., 2017, Fang et al., 2016] or used directly as a knowledge-based disambiguation system exploiting semantic similarity [Camacho-Collados et al., 2016].

[a]For those methods that rely solely on the relational information of knowledge bases, please refer to Section 4.1.

[b]The combination of Wikipedia and WordNet relies on the multilingual mapping provided by BabelNet (see Section 2.3.3 for more information about BabelNet).

5.3   EVALUATION AND APPLICATION

The main motivation for sense representations is that they offer a solution to the meaning conflation deficiency of word representations. Given that sense representations are often considered as a specialized form of word embeddings, the sense representation models have often been evaluated on intrinsic benchmarks designed for words (see Section 3.6 for an overview). This has also been driven by scarcity of reliable intrinsic benchmarks for evaluating sense representations.

In order to adapt intrinsic word similarity benchmarks to evaluating sense embeddings, various strategies have been proposed [Reisinger and Mooney, 2010]. Among these, the most popular one is to take the most similar pair of senses across two words [Mancini et al., 2017, Pilehvar and Navigli, 2015, Resnik, 1995], also known as *MaxSim*:

$$sim(w_1, w_2) = \max_{s_1 \in S_{w_1}, s_2 \in S_{w_2}} \cos(\vec{s}_1, \vec{s}_2), \qquad (5.2)$$

where S_{w_i} is a set including all senses of w_i and $\vec{s}_i$ represents the sense vector representation of the sense s_i. Another strategy, known as *AvgSim*, simply averages the pairwise similarities of all possible senses of w_1 and w_2. Cosine similarity (cos) is the most prominent metric for computing the similarity between sense vectors.

In all these benchmarks, words are paired in isolation, i.e., out of context. However, we know that for a specific meaning of an ambiguous word to be triggered, the word needs to appear in particular contexts. In fact, Kilgarriff [1997] argued that representing a word with a fixed set of senses may not be the best way for modeling word senses but instead, word senses should be defined according to a given context. To this end, Huang et al. [2012] presented a different kind of similarity dataset in which words are provided in specific contexts. The task consists of assessing the similarity of two words by taking into consideration the contexts in which they occur. The dataset is known as Stanford Contextual Word Similarity (SCWS) and has been established as one of the main intrinsic evaluations for sense representations. A pre-disambiguation step is required to leverage sense representations in the contextual word similarity task. Simple similarity measures such as *MaxSim* or *AvgSim* can be used; however, they cannot incorporate the context of words. The more suitable choice of strategy for this setting is either *MaxSimC* and *AvgSimC*, which allow entering context into the similarity computation. First, the confidence for selecting the most appropriate sense within the sentence is computed (for instance by computing the average of word embeddings from the context and selecting the sense which is closest to the average context vector in terms of cosine similarity). Then, the final score corresponds to the similarity between the closest sense embeddings (i.e., *MaxSimC*) or to a weighted average among all sense embeddings (i.e., *AvgSimC*). However, even though sense representations have generally outperformed word-based models on intrinsic evaluations, the simple strategies used to disambiguate the input text may not have been optimal. In fact, it has been recently shown that the improvements of sense-based models in word similarity tasks using *AvgSim* may not be due to accurate meaning modeling but to related artifacts such as sub-sampling, which had not been controlled for [Dubossarsky et al., 2018].

A similar similarity benchmark to SCWS is Usim [Erk et al., 2009]. In Usim (Usage similarity), the same word is provided in two different contexts and the similarity is assessed by human annotators. Therefore, an appropriate modeling of the sense is required to solve this task. Following this idea, CoSimLex [Armendariz et al., 2020] is a dataset where the similarity of two different words needs to be estimated in two different contexts. The dataset is also available in languages other than English such as Croatian, Estonian, Finnish, and Slovene.

Finally, the Word-in-Context (WiC) dataset [Pilehvar and Camacho-Collados, 2019] is one of the very few existing intrinsic benchmarks specifically designed for evaluating sense representations not focused on similarity. WiC is framed as a binary classification task which alleviates the dependency on specific sense inventories. Each instance in WiC has a target word w, either a verb or a noun, for which two contexts are provided. Each of these contexts triggers a specific meaning of w. The task is to identify if the occurrences of w in the two contexts correspond to the same meaning or not.[7] In fact, the dataset can also be viewed as an application of Word Sense Disambiguation that alleviates dependency on specific sense inventories. In addition to English, the dataset has been extended to 12 different languages by Raganato et al. [2020].

---

[7]The original WiC dataset was constructed based on WordNet sense distinctions, integrating Wiktionary and Verb-Net [Schuler, 2005], but with post-processing step removing the most fine-grained instances.

Extrinsic evaluation of sense representations is very similar to that for word representations (cf. Section 3.6.2). The main distinguishing difference is that in the former, the input needs to be disambiguated to allow the integration of sense representations. This introduces another source of uncontrolled noise especially given the non-optimality of disambiguation techniques. Some of the most common tasks that have been used as extrinsic evaluation are text categorization and sentiment analysis [Li and Jurafsky, 2015, Liu et al., 2015b, Pilehvar et al., 2017], document similarity [Wu and Giles, 2015], and word sense induction [Panchenko et al., 2017, Pelevina et al., 2016] and disambiguation [Camacho-Collados et al., 2016, Chen et al., 2014, Peters et al., 2018, Rothe and Schütze, 2015].

CHAPTER 6

Contextualized Embeddings

This chapter provides an introduction to *contextualized word embeddings* which can be considered the new generation of word (and sense) embeddings. The distinguishing factor here is the sensitivity of a word's representation to the context: a target word's embedding can change depending on the context in which it appears. These *dynamic* embeddings alleviate many of the issues associated with *static* word embeddings and provide reliable means for capturing semantic and syntactic properties of word usage in context. Despite their young age, contextualized word embeddings have provided significant gains in almost any downstream NLP task to which they have been applied.

6.1 THE NEED FOR CONTEXTUALIZATION

Since their introduction, pretrained word embeddings have dominated the field of semantic representation. They have been a key component in most neural NLP systems. Usually, an NLP system is provided with a large set of pretrained word embeddings for all words in the vocabulary of a language.[1] At the input layer, the system looks up the embedding for a given word and feeds it to the subsequent layers. Figure 6.1a depicts the general architecture for such a system. Moving from hard-coded one-hot representations to a continuous word embedding space usually results in improved generalization power of the system, hence improved performance.

However, pretrained word embeddings, such as Word2vec and GloVe, compute a single *static* representation for each word. The representation is fixed and independent from the context in which the word appears. In our example in Figure 6.1a, the same embedding would be used for *cell* at the input layer even if the word is used in contexts that trigger its other meanings, e.g., "the cells of a honeycomb", "mobile cell", or "prison cell".

Static semantic representations suffer from two important limitations: (1) ignoring the role of context in triggering specific meanings of words is certainly an oversimplification of the way humans interpret meanings of words in texts; and (2) due to restricting the barriers to individual words, it is difficult for the model to capture higher-order semantic phenomena, such as compositionality and long-term dependencies. Therefore, the static representation of words can substantially hamper the ability of NLP systems to understand the semantics of the input text. In this setting, all the load of deriving meaning from a sequence of words is on the shoulders

---

[1]For instance, the widely used Google News Word2vec embeddings has a vocabulary of three million words: https://code.google.com/archive/p/word2vec/.

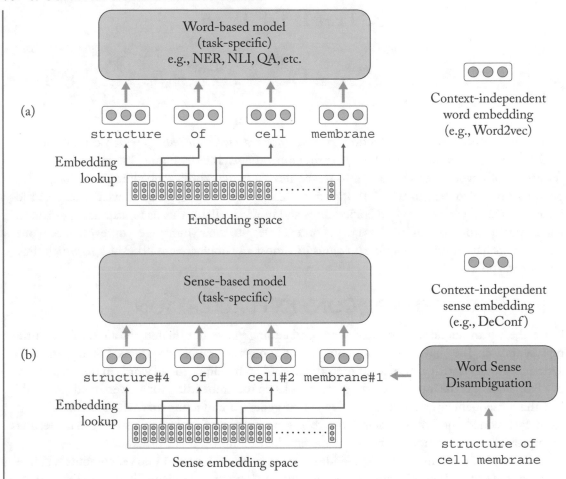

Figure 6.1: Context-independent (static) embeddings are fixed points in the semantic space: they do not change, irrespective of the context in which the target word appears. In the word-based model (a) for each input word, the static embedding is retrieved from a pretrained semantic space. Embeddings are introduced as features, usually in the input layer. In the sense-based model (b), words are first disambiguated before being input to the system, and the corresponding sense embeddings are passed to the model.

of the main system, which has to deal with ambiguity, syntactic nuances, agreement, negation, etc.

Knowledge-based sense representations (discussed in Chapter 5) can partly address the first issue. The distinct representations they provide for individual meanings of polysemous words enable the model to have a clear interpretation of the intended meaning for a word in a specific context. Swapping word embeddings with sense embeddings requires the system to carry out an additional step: a word sense disambiguation module has to identify the intended meaning of ambiguous words (e.g., *cell*). Having identified the intended sense, the system can swap the word embedding with the corresponding sense embedding. This swapping coupled with the disambiguation step can be regarded as a way of adapting each word's representation to the semantics of its surrounding context.

However, there are multiple factors that limit the efficacy of sense embeddings. First, word sense disambiguation is far from being optimal; hence, the initial stage of mapping words to word senses introduces inevitable noise to the pipeline [Pilehvar et al., 2017]. Second, it is not straightforward to benefit from raw texts, which are available at scale, to directly improve these representations. Hence, their coverage and semantic depth is limited to the knowledge encoded in lexical resources, which can be too restrictive. Third, these representations are still not fully contextualized. The intended sense of a word in a given context is assumed to fully align with that defined in the target inventory, which might not be always true. For instance, for the noun *watch* in the context "how do you pair your watch with headphones?", the closest concepts in WordNet are *digital watch*, defined as "a watch with a digital display" or *wristwatch*, defined as "a watch that is worn strapped to the wrist". Indeed, neither of the two concepts fully align with the intended meaning, i.e., *smart watch*. Even worse, the intended meaning of the word, or the word itself, might not be covered in the underlying sense inventory (for instance, the noun *embedding*, as it is widely used in NLP, is not defined in WordNet).

Unsupervised sense representations can be adapted to specific text domains; hence, they might not suffer as much in terms of coverage. However, a disambiguation step is still needed in this case, which is not as straightforward as that for knowledge-based counterparts. Given that these representations are often produced as a result of clustering, their semantic distinctions are unclear and their mapping to well-defined concepts is not simple. Hence, a more complicated word sense disambiguation step would be required, one that also needs to handle the mapping of disambiguated senses to the inventory. Given that such a technique cannot easily benefit from rich sense-specific information available in existing lexical resources, it is usually not that effective. Finally, another limitation of sense representation models lies in their difficult integration into downstream tasks [Li and Jurafsky, 2015].

6.2   BACKGROUND: TRANSFORMER MODEL

Given that most of the recent literature on contextualized embeddings is based on a novel model called Transformer, in this section, we provide a brief overview of the Transformer architecture. Figure 6.2 provides a high-level illustration of the Transformer model. The model is an auto-regressive sequence transducer: the goal is to convert an input sequence to an output sequence, while the predictions are done one part at a time, consuming the previously generated parts as additional input. Similarly to most other sequence to sequence (Seq2Seq) models (cf. Section 2.2.2), the Transformer employs an encoder-decoder structure. However, unlike previ-

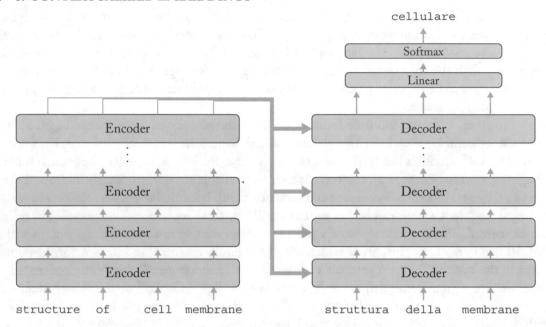

Figure 6.2: A high-level illustration of the Transformer model used for translation. The model is auto-regressive and has an encoder-decoder structure. The encoder and decoder have six identical encoders and decoders, respectively (only four shown here).

ous models which conventionally used a recurrent network (e.g., LSTM) for their encoder and decoder, the Transformer model is based on self-attention only with no recurrence. The Transformer forgoes the recurrence of RNNs for a fully feedforward attention-based architecture.

The main idea behind the Transformer model is self-attention. Self-attention, also known as intra-attention, is a mechanism that enables the sequence encoder to *attend* to specific parts of the sequence while processing a specific word.

6.2.1   SELF-ATTENTION

We saw in Section 2.2.2 the intuition behind the attention mechanism in sequence transduction models. The basic idea was to focus the attention of the model on the part of input for which the decoder is currently trying to generate the corresponding output (for instance, translation). The same idea can be applied to the process of reading and understanding natural language text.

Figure 6.3 shows an example of self-attention for two semantically ambiguous words, *mosaic* and *cell*. Consider the word *cell*. Even for a human reading this sentence, it would be almost impossible to identify the intended meaning of the word before accessing the succeeding word (i.e., *membrane*). In fact, to be able to get a clear grasp of the meaning of a sentence, humans often require to scan the context or finish reading the sentence.

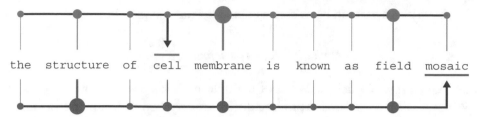

Figure 6.3: An illustration of self attention for the words *cell* (top) and *mosaic* (bottom). By attending to the context, particularly *membrane*, the interpretation of *cell* gets adapted to this specific usage and to the biological meaning. The same applies for *mosaic*, with a self attention mostly toward *structure*, *membrane*, and *fluid*. In the Transformer model, there are multiple spaces for self-attention (multi-head attention) that allows the model to have different interpretations in multiple representation sub-spaces.

Self-attention, also known as intra-attention, is a special attention mechanism that tries to mimic this process. Instead of relating positions across two different sequences, self-attention looks for relations between positions in the same sequence. The goal of self-attention is to allow the model to consider the context while reading a word. For the case of our example, while *reading* the target word *cell* the self-attention mechanism focuses the attention to the word *membrane* in order to better represent the target word, according to its biological meaning. Note that, similarly to the Seq2Seq attention mechanism, self-attention is a *soft* measure: multiple words can be attended to varying degrees.

Consider the input sequence $x_1, ..., x_n$. The self-attention mechanism maps the input embeddings for this sequence to an adapted output sequence $z_1, ..., z_n$. For an input *token*[2] x_t, the process of computing the self-attention vector z_t in the Transformer model can be summarized as follows:

1. For every input x_i, compute three different vectors: query q_i, key k_i, and value v_i. This is done by multiplying the input vector x_i with the corresponding matrices W^q, W^k, and W^v. The weights of these matrices are among the parameters that are learned during training.

2. Compute a score s_i for every input x_i. The score is computed as the dot product of the query vector q_t and the corresponding key vectors for every x_i (i.e., all k_i).

3. Normalize the scores by $\sqrt{d_k}$, where d_k is the dimensionality of the key (and query) vector.

4. Compute a weighted average of all value vectors (v_i), weighted by their corresponding scores s_i. The resulting vector is z_t.

[2]Usually, in Transformer-based models, input words are split into multiple subword units [Vaswani et al., 2017, Wu et al., 2016], which we will refer to as *tokens*; for instance, *membrane* can be split into *mem*, *bra*, and *ne_*. Therefore, the input to the model is a sequence of tokens (rather than words).

The above procedure can be written as the following equation in matrix form:

$$Attention(Q, K, V) = softmax(\frac{QK^T}{\sqrt{d_k}})V. \tag{6.1}$$

The Transformer model makes use of multiple attention *heads*. In other words, multiple sets of W matrices are considered to produce different query, key, and value vectors for the same word. This allows the model to have access to multiple representation sub-spaces to focus on different positions.

6.2.2   ENCODER

The original Transformer model [Vaswani et al., 2017] makes use of six identical encoder layers. Figure 6.4 (left) shows the stack of three of these encoders (for one of them, we are showing more details of its internal structure). Each encoder layer has two sub-layers: self-attention and feedforward. We saw in the previous section how the self-attention layer can help the model to look at the context words while *reading*, in order to get a clearer understanding of the semantics of individual tokens and, in turn, the meaning of the sentence. As explained before, each attention layer is coupled with multiple *heads* with the hope of enabling the model to attend to different parts, and to have multiple independent representation subspaces for capturing distinct patterns of the input.

The z_i outputs of the self-attention sub-layer are fed to the feedforward sub-layer which is in fact a fully-connected network. The feedforward layer is *point-wise*, i.e., the same feedforward network is applied independently to individual z_i vectors.

6.2.3   DECODER

Similarly to the encoder, the decoder of the Transformer model also consists of a stack of six identical decoder layers. Each decoder is very similar to encoder in architecture with the slight difference that it has a third sub-layer which performs a cross-attention between encoder's output and decoder's state.[3] Also, it is necessary to modify the self-attention sub-layer in the decoder in order to prevent the model from attending to subsequent positions. Transformer achieves this by means of masking the subsequent positions. This masking is to ensure that the predictions at any position can depend only on the outputs generated so far (and not future outputs).

6.2.4   POSITIONAL ENCODING

As explained above, the Transformer model does not involve any recurrence (or convolution) to capture the relative positioning of tokens in the sequence. However, we know that word order is crucial to semantics; ignoring this would diminish the model to a simple bag-of-words. The

---

[3]Both decoder and encoder involve other small architectural details, such as residual connections around sub-layers and normalization. We skip these for simplicity.

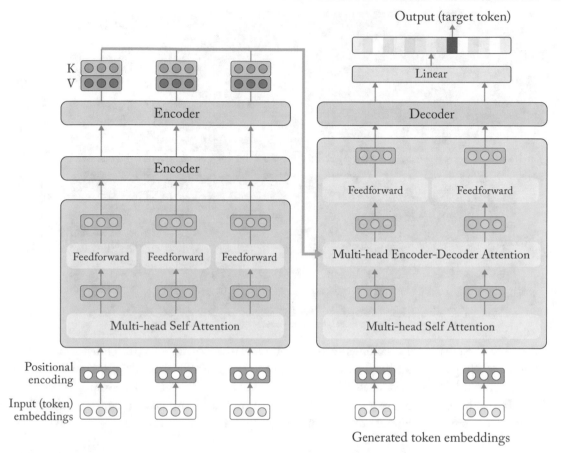

Figure 6.4: Encoders and decoders have similar internal structure, except for an encoder-decoder attention sub-layer added to the decoder. Input word embeddings are summed up with positional encodings and are fed to the bottom encoder. Decoders receive the outputs generated so far (as well as signal from the encoder) and predict the next token. Prediction is done via a fully connected layer that generates the scores over the vocabulary (logits vector), followed by a softmax (to make the scores probability-like).

authors of the Transformer model made use of a mechanism called positional encoding in order to inject information about token positions and hence making the model sensitive to word order.

To this end, each input embedding to the encoder and decoder is added with a positional embedding which denotes the position of each input word with respect to the rest of the sequence. To facilitate the summation, positional encodings are of the same size as the input token embeddings. There can be different ways of encoding the position; Transformer makes

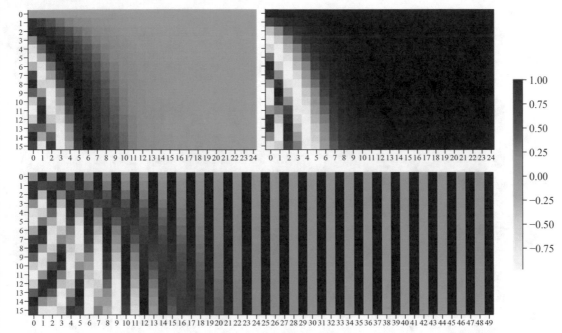

Figure 6.5: The positional encodings used to capture relative positions in the Transformer model. Sixteen encodings are visualized (rows), enough to encode a sequence of 16 tokens (10,000 in the original model). The model also makes use of 512-d encodings but, for simplicity, we show 50-d. Two sub-encodings are generated using sin() (top, left) and cos() (top, right) functions. The two are merged to generate the full encoding, shown at the bottom.

use of a sinosuidal function. Specifically, the positional encoding P for the tth token (starting from 0) is computed as follows:

$$D_i = \frac{1}{10000^{\frac{2i}{d}}}$$
$$P(t, 2i) = \sin(tD_i)$$
$$P(t, 2i + 1) = \cos(tD_i)$$

$$(6.2)$$

where $i \in \{0, .., d - 1\}$ is the encoding index, and d is the dimensionality of the positional encodings which is the same as input token embedding size (512 in the original model). An example is shown in Figure 6.5. Note that the final encoding is a merger of the two sub-encodings from sin() and cos() functions, where the former fills the even positions and the latter the odd ones.

6.3 CONTEXTUALIZED WORD EMBEDDINGS

Unlike static word embeddings, contextualized embeddings are representations of words in context. They can circumvent many of the limitations associated with word and sense embeddings, bringing in multiple advantages among which their seamless integration into most neural language processing models.

Unlike knowledge-based sense representations, these embeddings do not rely on annotated data or external lexical resources, and can be learned in an unsupervised manner. More importantly, their introduction to neural models does not require additional efforts (such as word sense disambiguation) as they function at the level of words. Interestingly, contextualized embeddings not only can capture various semantic roles of a word, but also its syntactic properties [Goldberg, 2019, Hewitt and Manning, 2019].

In contrast to static word embeddings which are fixed, contextualized word embeddings are *dynamic* in that the same word can be assigned different embeddings if it appears in different contexts. Therefore, unlike static word embeddings, contextualized embeddings are assigned to tokens as opposed to types. Instead of receiving words as distinct units and providing independent word embeddings for each, contextualized models receive the whole text span (the target word along with its context) and provide specialized embeddings for individual words which are adjusted to their context. Figure 6.6 provides an illustration: to produce a dynamic embedding for the target word (*cell*), the contextualized model analyzes the whole context. The following sections will provide more information on the specifics of the model in the figure.

6.3.1 EARLIER METHODS

The sequence tagger of Li and McCallum [2005] is one of the pioneering works that employ contextualized representations. The model infers context sensitive latent variables for each word based on a soft word clustering and integrates them, as additional features, to a CRF sequence tagger. The clustering technique enabled them to associate the same word with different features in different contexts.

With the introduction of word embeddings [Collobert et al., 2011, Mikolov et al., 2013c] and the efficacy of neural networks, and in the light of the meaning conflation deficiency of word embeddings, context-sensitive models have once again garnered research attention. **Context2vec** [Melamud et al., 2016] is one of the first proposals in the new branch of contextualized representations. Context2vec's initial goal was to compute a better representation for the context of a given target word. The widely practiced, and usually competitive, baseline approach for computing a representation for multiple words (a word seuqnce) is to simply average their embeddings. This baseline is unable to capture important properties of natural language, such as word order or semantic prominence. Instead, context2vec makes use of a bidirectional LSTM language model to better encode these properties. Figure 6.7 shows the architecture of context2vec and illustrates its different context modeling approach compared to Word2vec CBOW. Context2vec embeds sentential contexts and target words in the same semantic space.

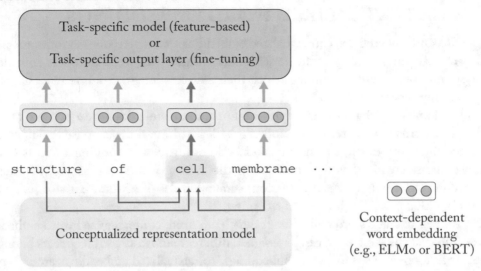

Figure 6.6: Unlike static (context independent) word embeddings, contextualized (dynamic) embeddings are not fixed: they adapt the representation of a word to its context of use. The contextualized representation model processes the context of the target word (*cell* in the figure) and generates its dynamic embedding. Similarly to static word embeddings, the contextualized counterparts can be used in a feature extraction setting where they are input as features to a task specific model. However, what makes them more interesting is that they can be efficiently adapted to perform a wide range of NLP tasks, through a process called "finetuning". We will discuss this in Section 6.6.

The encoded representation for the context of a target word can serve as its *contextualized* embedding. Hence, though the authors of context2vec did not explicitly view the approach as a means for computing dynamic word embeddings, it is highly similar to subsequent works in contextualized representations and constitutes one of the bases for this field of research. The most important distinguishing factor to subsequent techniques is that context2vec ignores the target word while computing the contextualized representation, which turns out to be crucial.

6.3.2 LANGUAGE MODELS FOR WORD REPRESENTATION

As discussed in Chapter 2, Language Models (LMs) aim at predicting the next word in a sentence given the preceding words. To be able to accurately predict a word in a sequence, LMs need encode both the semantic and syntactic roles of words in context. This makes them suitable candidates for word representation. In fact, nowadays, LMs are key components not only in NLG, but also in NLU. Additionally, the knowledge acquisition bottleneck is not an issue for LMs, since they can be trained on a multitude of raw texts in an unsupervised manner. In fact, extensive models can be trained with LM objectives and then transferred to specific tasks.

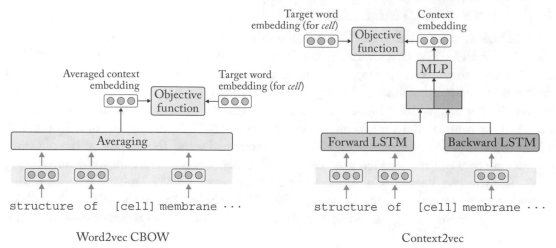

Figure 6.7: Architecture of context2vec and how it differs from Word2vec CBOW: instead of modeling the context by naively averaging embeddings of words in the context window (as in CBOW), context2vec models the context using a bidirectional LSTM. To represent the context of a target word in a sentence, context2vec first concatenates the LSTM output vector representations of the contexts in the two directions, and then feeds the concatenated vector to a multi-layer perceptron which in turn computes the *context* embedding.

Although still at early stages, this technique has been shown to be a promising direction [Radford et al., 2018], reminiscent of the pretraining procedure in Computer Vision which involves training an initial model on ImageNet or other large image datasets and then transferring the knowledge to new tasks [Pan and Yang, 2010].

Figure 6.6 provides a high-level illustration of the integration of contextualized word embeddings into an NLP model. At training time, for each word (e.g., *cell* in the figure) in a given input text, the language model unit is responsible for analyzing the context (usually using sequence-based neural networks) and adjusting the target word's representation by contextualising (adapting) it to the context. These context-sensitive embeddings are in fact the internal states of a deep neural network which is trained with language modeling objectives either in an *unsupervised* manner [Peters et al., 2018, Peters et al., 2017] or on a *supervised* task, such as a bilingual translation configuration [McCann et al., 2017]. The training of contextualized embeddings is carried out at a pretraining stage, independently from the main task, on a large unlabeled (or differently labeled) text corpus. The trained model can then generate contextualised representations for all the words in the given text. Depending on the sequence encoder used in language modeling, these models can be put into two broad categories: **RNN** (mostly LSTM) and **Transformer**.

6.3.3   RNN-BASED MODELS

For this branch of techniques, the "Contextualized representation model" in Figure 6.6 is on the shoulders of an LSTM-based encoder, usually a multi-layer bidirectional LSTM (BiLSTM). LSTMs are known to be able to capture word order to a good extend. Also, unlike the word embedding averaging baseline, LSTMs are capable of combining word representations in a more reasonable manner, assigning higher weights to words that are semantically more important than others in the context. The TagLM model of Peters et al. [2017] is an example of this approach which trains a BiLSTM sequence encoder on monolingual texts. The outputs of the sequence encoder are concatenated and fed to a neural CRF sequence tagger as additional features.

The Context Vectors (CoVe) model of McCann et al. [2017] similarly computes contextualized representations using a two-layer biLSTM network, but in the MT setting. CoVe vectors are pretrained using an LSTM encoder from an attentional sequence-to-sequence MT model.[4]

The prominent **ELMo** (Embeddings from Language Models) technique [Peters et al., 2018] is similar in principle. A multi-layer (two in the original model) BiLSTM sequence encoder is responsible for capturing the semantics of the context. The main difference between TagLM and ELMo lies in the fact that in the latter some weights are shared between the two directions of the language modeling unit. Figure 6.8 provides a high-level illustration of how ELMo embeddings are constructed. A residual connection between the LSTM layers enables the deeper layer(s) to have a better look at the original input and to allow the gradients to better backpropagate to the initial layers. The model is trained on large amounts of texts with the language modeling objective: given a sequence of tokens, predict the next token. The trained model is then used to derive contextualized embeddings that can be used as input into various NLP systems.

There can be multiple ways for combining the outputs of the ELMo model, i.e., the hidden states of the two BiLSTM layers, h_{k_1} and h_{k_2}, and the context-independent representation x_k. One may take only the top layer output or concatenate the representations from the top-n layers to have long vectors for each token, to be fed as inputs to an NLP system. One can also learn a weighted combination of these layers, based on the target task, or concatenate other static word embeddings with ELMo embeddings. ELMo makes use of a character-based technique (based on Convolution Neural Networks) for computing x_k embeddings. Therefore, it benefits from all the characteristics of character-based representations (cf. Section 3.3), such as robustness to unseen words.

---

[4]In general, the pretraining property of contextualized embeddings makes them closely related to transfer learning [Pratt, 1993], which is out of the scope of this book. For more detailed information on transfer learning for NLP, we would refer the reader to Ruder [2019].

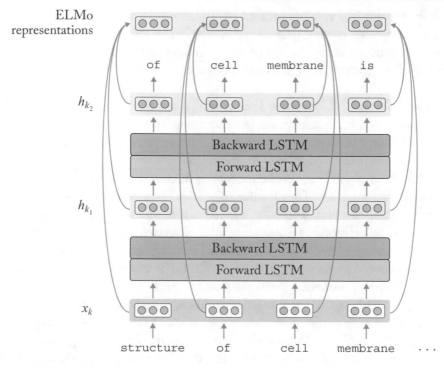

Figure 6.8: ELMo makes use of a two-layer bidirectional LSTM to encode the context. The ELMo representation for the target word is a combination of the hidden states of two BiLSTM layers, i.e., h_{k_1} and h_{k_2}, which encode the context-sensitive representation of each word, and the context-independent (static) representation of the word, i.e., x_k, which is character-based. ELMo uses some residual connections across LSTMs which are not shown in the figure for simplicity.

6.4   TRANSFORMER-BASED MODELS: BERT

The introduction of **Transformers** [Vaswani et al., 2017] and their immense potential in encoding text sequences resulted in another boost to the already fast-moving field of LM-based contextualized representations. Transformers come with two main advantages over recurrent neural networks (which were previously the dominant role players): (1) compared to RNNs which process the input sequentially, Transformers are parallel which makes them suitable for GPUs and TPUs which excel at massive parallel computation; and (2) unlike RNNs which have memory limitations and tend to process the input in one direction, the Transformer has access to distant parts of a sentence, on both sides of the target word, enabling a better understanding of the word without any locality bias. The long-distant access is enabled by the self-attention mechanism (cf. Section 6.2.1) of this model. For instance, the word *cell* in Figure 6.8 can be disambiguated by looking at the next word in the context, *membrane*.

The impressive initial results obtained by Transformers on sequence to sequence tasks, such as MT and syntactic parsing [Kitaev and Klein, 2018], suggested a potential replacement for LSTMs for sequence encoding. As of now, Transformers are dominantly exceeding the performance levels of conventional recurrent models on most NLP tasks that involve sequence encoding.

The OpenAI's **GPT** (Generative Pretrained Transformer) model [Radford, 2018] was one of the first attempts at representation learning using Transformers. Moving from LSTMs to Transformers resulted in a significant performance improvement and enabled a more effective way for finetuning the pretrained models to specific tasks.

The architecture of the Transformer model was discussed in Section 6.2. The GPT model is based on a modified version of Transformer, called the Transformer Decoder [Li et al., 2018], which discards the encoder part. Therefore, instead of having a source and a target sentence for the sequence transduction model, a single sentence is given to the decoder. Instead of generating a target sequence, the objective is set as a standard language modeling task where the goal is to predict the next word given a sequence of words. GPT was also one of the first works to popularize the finetuning procedure (to be discussed in Section 6.6).

However, like ELMo, GPT was based on unidirectional language modeling. While reading a token, GPT can only attend to previously seen tokens in the self-attention layers. This can be very limiting for encoding sentences, since understanding a word might require processing future words in the sentence. This is despite the fact that Transformers are characterized by their self-attention layer and the capability to receive the input sequence in parallel. What hindered a bidirectional Transformer approach was that bidirectional conditioning would result in a word indirectly *seeing* itself in a multi-layered context.

BERT.   BERT, short for Bidirectional Encoder Representations from Transformers [Devlin et al., 2019], revolutionized the NLP field in 2018/2019. Similarly to GPT, BERT is based on the Transformer architecture; however, BERT makes use of the encoder architecture (see Section 6.2 for more details).

The essential improvement over GPT is that BERT provides a solution for making Transformers bidirectional. This addition enables BERT to perform a joint conditioning on both left and right contexts in all layers. This is achieved by changing the conventional next-word prediction objective of language modeling to a new version, called Masked Language Modeling.

6.4.1   MASKED LANGUAGE MODELING

Before BERT, the commonly practiced language modeling objective was to predict the next token (given a sequence of tokens). Inspired by the cloze test [Taylor, 1953], BERT introduced an alternative language modeling objective to be used during the training of the model. According to this objective, instead of predicting the next token, the model is expected to guess a *masked* token; hence, the name Masked Language Modeling (MLM). MLM randomly masks some of the tokens from the input sequence (15% for example), by replacing them with a special token (e.g., "[MASK]").

For instance, the sequence "the structure of cell membrane is known as fluid mosaic" is changed to "the structure of cell [MASK] is known [MASK] fluid mosaic". The goal is to predict the masked (missing) tokens based on the information provided by unmasked tokens in the sequence. This allows the model to condition not only on the right side (next token prediction) or the left side (previous token prediction), but on context from both sides of the token to be predicted.

To be more precise, given that the [MASK] token only appears during the training phase, BERT employs a more comprehensive masking strategy. Instead of always replacing the token with the special [MASK] token (that has 80% chance), BERT sometimes replaces the word with a random word (10% chance) or with the same word (10%).

It is important to note that the model is not provided with information on missing words (or the specific words that have been replaced). The only information is the proportion of the input text that has been affected (e.g., 15% of the input size). It is on the model to make predictions or to suggest replacements. The objective enables BERT to capture both the left and right contexts, and to alleviate the unidirectional limitation of earlier models.

6.4.2   NEXT SENTENCE PREDICTION

In addition to the MLM objective, BERT also uses a Next Sentence Prediction (NSP) task for training where the model has to predict whether a given sentence is the subsequent sentence to the current one or not. This is motivated by the fact that in order to perform well in some tasks, the model needs to encode relationships between sentences or to resort to information that is beyond the boundary of the sentence.

The task is a binary classification one. For each sentence A the model is presented with a second sentence B, and is asked if B is the next sentence for A? To make a balanced self-training dataset, the actual next sentence is replaced with a random sentence 50% of the time. This objective helps the model learn the relationship between sentences and has been shown to be beneficial in tasks such as Natural Language Inference and Question Answering [Devlin et al., 2019].

6.4.3   TRAINING

The training objective of BERT is to minimize a combined loss function of MLM and NSP. Note that the training of BERT is carried out on pairs of sentences (given the NSP objective). In order to distinguish the two input sentences, BERT makes use of two special tokens: [CLS] and [SEP]. The [CLS] token is inserted at the beginning of the sequence and the [SEP] token between the two sentences. The entire sequence is then fed to the encoder. The output of the

[CLS] token encodes the information about the NSP objective and is used in a softmax layer for this classification.

The original BERT is trained in two settings: Base and Large. The two versions differ in their number of encoder layers, representation size and number of attention heads. BERT has given rise to several subsequent models, many of which are in fact variations of the original BERT in terms of the training objective or the number of parameters.

Subword tokenization. Unlike conventional word embedding algorithms, such as Word2vec and GloVe, which view whole words as individual tokens and generate an embedding for each token, usually resulting in hundreds of thousands or millions of token embeddings, more recent models, such as BERT and GPT, segment words into subword tokens and embed these units. In practice, different tokenization algorithms are used in order to split words into subword units.

Subword tokenization presents multiple advantages: (1) it drastically reduces the vocabulary size, from millions of tokens to dozens of thousands; (2) it provides a solution for handling out-of-vocabulary (OOV) words since any unseen word can theoretically be re-constructed based on its subword units (for which embeddings are available); and (3) it allows the model to share knowledge among words that have similar surface forms (look similar) with the hope that they share semantics, for instance, cognates across different languages or inflected forms of words in the same language.

The most commonly used tokenizers are Byte-Pair Encoding (BPE) and WordPiece tokenizer. Both tokenizers leverage a similar iterative algorithm: the vocabulary is initialized with all the characters (symbols) in a given text corpus. Then in each iteration, the vocabulary is updated with the most likely pairs of existing symbols in the vocabulary. BPE [Witten et al., 1994] takes the most frequent pair as the most *likely* one, whereas WordPiece [Schuster and Nakajima, 2012] considers likelihood on the training data.

6.5   EXTENSIONS

BERT is undoubtedly a revolutionary proposal that has changed the landscape of NLP. Therefore, it is natural to expect massive waves of research on improving the model, or on applying the ideas from the model (or the model itself) to various other tasks in NLP.

Many of the extensions to BERT mainly rely on changing hyperparameters, either increasing the amount of training data or model capacity, with the hope of pushing the performance barriers on various benchmarks. For instance, **RoBERTa** [Liu et al., 2019b] removes BERT's next-sentence pretraining objective which was shown to be non-optimal. RoBERTa trains with much larger mini-batches and learning rates on an order of magnitude more data than BERT, and for longer sequences of input. This results in a boost in the model's performance, for instance, around 15% on the SuperGLUE benchmark.

It is important to note that the recent trend has been to pretrain larger and larger[5] models on bigger datasets, in order to investigate the limits of transfer learning [Raffel et al., 2019]. However, not all extensions to BERT can be reduced to sole modifications of hyperparameters or to pushing model size. In the following sections, we will briefly overview some of the limitations of BERT and how different extensions have tried to address these.

6.5.1   TRANSLATION LANGUAGE MODELING

XLM [Lample and Conneau, 2019] modifies the training objective of BERT to achieve a better multi-lingual model. XLM introduces a cross-lingual training objective. Similarly to BERT, the objective is to predict the masked token but in the case of XLNet the model is asked to use the context from one language to predict tokens in another language. This multi-lingual objective was shown to result in representations that are significantly better than BERT in tasks that involve cross-lingual transfer of knowledge obtained during training, to allow for zero-shot application in an unseen language.

Moreover, XLM makes use of Byte-Pair Encoding (BPE), instead of working on words and tokens. BPE splits the tokens into the most common sub-tokens across all languages, allowing XLM to have a larger shared vocabulary between languages.

6.5.2   CONTEXT FRAGMENTATION

Dai et al. [2019] point out an issue with the Transformer architectures. The limitation, which they refer to as *context fragmentation*, is the result of inputting fixed length text segments to models such as BERT. These segments are usually fixed in size and do not take into account sentence boundary or any other semantic criteria. Therefore, the model cannot learn long-term dependencies that do not fit within the pre-defined context. In addition, there is no information flow across segments in these models. This leaves the model with no contextual information to predict the first few tokens.

Dai et al. [2019] proposed a model, called **Transformer-XL** (extra long), which allows the Transformer architecture to learn long-term dependencies across segments, hence addressing the segment fragmentation issue. This is achieved by adding a recurrence across segments, i.e., consecutive sequences of computation. This way, at any computation, the model is provided with information from the previous segments which can be used for generating the starting tokens, and allows the model to look for dependencies that go beyond segment boundaries.

In order to give a "temporal clue" to the model for distinguishing among positions in different segments, they also upgraded the positional encoding mechanism. The positional encoding, as explained in Section 6.2.4, is unable to distinguish the positional difference between tokens in different segments at different layers. Therefore, Dai et al. [2019] also put forward the

---

[5]For instance, Megatron-LM (NVidia) and Turing-NLG (Microsoft Research) push the 340M parameters of BERT-large to the astronomical 8B and 17B parameters, respectively.

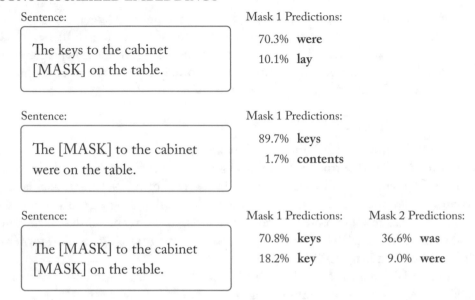

Figure 6.9: The parallel independent prediction in Masked Language Modeling of BERT prevents the model from taking into account dependencies between masked words which are to be predicted. Screenshot from AllenNLP's BERT MLM demo.[6]

relative positional encoding in order avoid temporal confusion in the recurrence mechanism of the model.

6.5.3   PERMUTATION LANGUAGE MODELING

As was mentioned in Section 6.2, the original Transformer model is autoregressive: the generated outputs until timestep t will be used as additional input to generate the $t + 1^{th}$ output. BERT proposes an autoencoder model based on the MLM objective (Section 6.4.1) which allows the language model to be conditioned on both directions to *see* context from both sides of the word to predict.

Despite the desirable property of enabling the model to see *future* context, autoencoder models have their own disadvantages. Importantly, BERT uses the [MASK] symbol during pretraining, but this artificial symbol is absent from the data used at finetuning time, resulting in a *pretrain-finetune discrepancy*. Another main disadvantage of BERT's autoencoder model is that it assumes that the masked tokens can be predicted only based on the other given unmasked tokens, and independently from each other. This can be essentially incorrect as masked words constitute around 15% of the context; hence, taking into account the correlations among them can be crucial for accurate prediction. Figure 6.9 shows an example for cases that the independence assumption of MLM can cause syntactic discrepancies.

XLNet [Yang et al., 2019] addresses the pretrain-finetune discrepancy and the parallel independent predictions issue of BERT's MLM by proposing a new objective called *Permutation Language Modeling* (PLM). PLM is similar in objective to traditional language models: predict one token given context. However, instead of receiving the context in a sequential order, as is the case for traditional language models, PLM predicts tokens in a random order. In other words, the task in PLM is to predict a missing token in a sequence using any combination of other words in that sequence (irrespective of their position). This forces the PLM to model the more difficult task of learning the dependencies between all combinations of tokens, in contrast to the traditional language models that only model dependencies in one direction.

XLNet is based on the Transformer-XL architecture and benefits from the recurrence across segments. The main contribution is the PLM objective which provides a reformulation of language modeling. In order to make PLM work and integrate it into the Transformer architecture, the authors had to address some other technical details (not discussed here), such as modifying the positional information through *Two-stream Self-attention*.

6.5.4   REDUCING MODEL SIZE

As was explained above, the general trend has been to push the models in size in order to investigate the limits of transformers in capturing complexities of natural language. However, a recent trend has started to move in the opposite direction: reducing model size while retaining the performance.

ALBERT [Lan et al., 2019] is one of the most recent Transformer-based models in this category. The model introduces some innovations that allow increasing the hidden layer size and the depth of the network, without increasing the overall number of parameters. Except from changing the NSP objective of BERT for a Sentence-Order Prediction (SOP) objective, which showed effective in multi-sentence encoding tasks, ALBERT introduces two parameter reduction techniques to lower memory requirements and speed up training. One is the cross-layer parameter sharing: the same set of parameters are used across layers. This prevents the number of parameters from growing along with the depth of the network, making the model significantly smaller in size. The other technique is to decompose the vocabulary matrix into two smaller matrices, which allows the hidden size to grow without significantly increasing the parameter size of the vocabulary embedding.

DistilBERT [Sanh et al., 2019] is another model in this trend that leverages knowledge distillation [Bucila et al., 2006, Hinton et al., 2015] during the pretraining phase to construct lighter models that can perform competitively.

6.6   FEATURE EXTRACTION AND FINETUNING

One of the distinguishing features of recent pretraining work (such as GPT, BERT, and GPT-2) is the possibility to leverage the language model directly for an end task. Contextualized word embeddings can be utilized in two different ways.

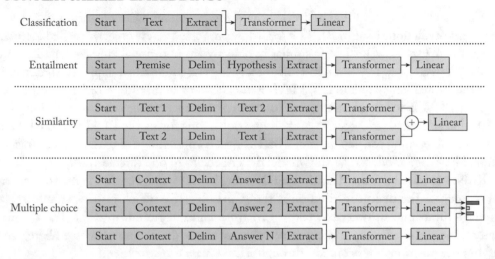

Figure 6.10: Finetuning of GPT to four different tasks. This setting involves minimal modifications to the pretrained (language) model, usually in the form of changing the last layer, in order to make it task specific (Image from Radford [2018]).

Feature extraction.   In this setting, the contextualized embeddings are fed as pretrained *features* to a task-specific model. The model has a task-specific architecture (the weights of which are randomly initialized) and the embeddings are integrated as additional features to this model. This setting usually requires large amounts of task-specific training data to be effective given that all weights of the main model need to be trained from scratch. The contextualized model is used as a feature extractor which is able to encode semantic and syntactic information of the input into a vector.

Finetuning.   This approach, first popularized by GPT and ULMFiT [Howard and Ruder, 2018], gets closer to the *one system for all tasks* setting. Finetuning mitigates the need for having task-specific models by transferring a pretrained language model directly to a distant task through minimal modifications (usually in terms of changes in the last layer).

Figure 6.10 shows an illustration of the finetuning used in GPT. All structured inputs are converted into token sequences which are input to the pretrained model, followed by a shallow linear+softmax layer. Peters et al. [2019] provides an experimental analysis of feature extraction and finetuning, which are the two most common ways of adapting the pretrained model to a given target task.

GPT-2 takes this setting to the extreme and alleviates the requirement for supervised learning on task-specific datasets (zero-shot task transfer). One interesting finding of the article is to show that reasonable results can be gained with no task specific finetuning, and by just framing the task as predicting conditional probabilities.

6.7   ANALYSIS AND EVALUATION

Contextualized models have shown great potential in a wide range of NLP applications, either semantic or syntactic. Moreover, the possibility to finetune and directly utilize these models in a diverse set of downstream NLP tasks suggests that they encode various sorts of syntactic and semantic knowledge.

In terms of semantics, despite the young age, BERT and its derivatives are now dominating the top rows in many benchmarks, including GLUE [Wang et al., 2019b] and Super-GLUE[7] [Wang et al., 2019a].

However, similarly to most other deep learning methods, the underlying procedure followed to achieve these cannot be unveiled unless some network analysis experiments are used to expose the hidden aspects, such as analytical studies performed for visualizing CNNs [Qin et al., 2018] or for understanding capabilities of LSTMs [Gulordava et al., 2018, Linzen et al., 2016].

In this line, many researchers have proposed *probing* experiments to explain the effectiveness of Transformer-based models in various NLP tasks. Probing usually involves checking if a linear model is able to correctly predict a linguistic property, syntactic or semantic, based on the representations. High performance in this prediction is often taken as evidence for the fact that relevant information for the task is encoded in the representation.

Given that this is an active area of research with dozens of papers, sometimes with contradicting conclusions, it is not possible to cover all the relevant work. In the following, we briefly describe few of the more prominent works in this direction.

6.7.1   SELF ATTENTION PATTERNS

Self-attention is a key feature to Transformer-based models. Therefore, analyzing its behavior constitutes an interesting research question, the answer to which would be crucial for understanding Transformer-based models and would allow us to better identify possible ways for improving the efficiency and capacity of these models.

One focus of this analysis has been on the semantic or syntactic patterns self-attention captures. Clark et al. [2019] carried out an experiment to check the attention distribution across attention heads. The findings suggested that heads within the same layer often have similar distributions, suggesting possible redundancy across attention patterns. Kovaleva et al. [2019] further analyzed the possibility of different attention heads encoding redundant information. The general finding was that even the smaller pretrained BERT model (i.e., *base*) is heavily overparametrized. The conclusion is based on the observation that there are many repeated self-attention patterns across different heads. This is also supported by the observation that disabling some heads, or even whole layers, does not necessarily result in performance drop, and some-

---

[7]For instance, on the Word-in-Context dataset [Pilehvar and Camacho-Collados, 2019], a simple binary classifier based on BERT without any task-specific tuning, significantly improves all existing sense representation techniques which explicitly model various word senses.

times can even lead to improvements. This observation corroborates the redundancy suggested by Clark et al. [2019] and is in line with the findings of Michel et al. [2019] and Voita et al. [2019] that a small subset of trained heads in each layer (sometimes a single one) might be enough for preserving the same level of performance at test time, in tasks such as translation.

Kovaleva et al. [2019] also investigated how the self-attention patterns change after fine-tuning a pretrained model. For most tasks in the GLUE benchmark, they concluded that it is the last one or two layers of the Transformer that encode most of the task-specific information during finetuning.

6.7.2   SYNTACTIC PROPERTIES

As for syntactic abilities, Clark et al. [2019] investigated BERT's attention mechanism and found that certain attention heads encode accurate information about syntax-related phenomena, such as direct objects of verbs, determiners of nouns, objects of prepositions, and coreferent mentions. The subject-verb agreement was also investigated by Goldberg [2019]. Specifically, it was shown that BERT assigns higher scores to the correct verb forms as opposed to the incorrect one in a masked language modeling task. This is despite the fact that, by design, Transformers do not have an explicit means for capturing word order, beyond a simple tagging of each word with its absolute-position embedding.

In the same spirit, Hewitt and Manning [2019] proposed a probe in order to investigate the extent to which contextualized models encode human-like parse trees. For this purpose, given a phrase or sentence, they learn a linear transformation of the contextualized embeddings of the words. Then, a minimum spanning tree is obtained for the transformed representations which is taken as the estimated parse tree. The results were surprising. The authors showed that the obtained tree matches the syntactic parse to a good extent.

The results clearly indicated that even though the contextualized models are trained with a language modeling objective, they implicitly encode the syntax of the language since it might indirectly help them in fulfilling the objective. Linzen et al. [2016] provided an analysis on how capturing syntactic information can be crucial for accurate language modeling. The sentence in Figure 6.9 is from the same authors and clearly indicates an example of this.

Figure 6.11 shows an example for the sentence "the chef who ran to the store was out of food". The minimum spanning tree estimated by the above procedure (shown on the left) closely resembles the syntactic parse tree shown on the right.

On the contrary, Ettinger [2020] showed that BERT falls short of effectively encoding the meaning of *negation*, as highlighted by a complete inability to prefer true over false completions for negative sentences. They also showed that, to a large extent, BERT is insensitive to malformed inputs as the predictions did not change when the input was truncated or the word order was shuffled. The same observation was made by Wallace et al. [2019], suggesting that BERT's encoding of syntactic structure does not necessarily indicate that it actually relies on that knowledge.

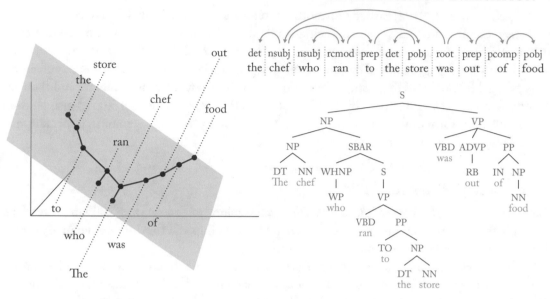

Figure 6.11: Hewitt and Manning [2019] showed that the minimum spanning tree over a linearly transformed space of contextualized embeddings (left) can estimate the dependency parse tree (top right) of a sentence or phrase to a good degree of accuracy. Illustration courtesy of the original work. The syntactic parse tree is generated using the Stanford Parser and the dependency parse is produced by Google NL API.

6.7.3   DEPTH-WISE INFORMATION PROGRESSION

Peters et al. [2018] performed an empirical study to see how the choice of neural structure (LSTM, CNN, or Transformer) influences the accuracy of learned representations in different NLP tasks. Additionally, they showed that the learned representations differ in their properties at different depths of the network. Initial layers tend to encode only high-level morphological information, middle layers encode local syntactic properties, and top layers encode long-range semantic relations such as co-reference. Similar findings are reported by Jawahar et al. [2019] on a number of semantic and syntactic probing tasks, and by Raganato and Tiedemann [2018] on the task of translation. Also, the prevalence of syntactic information in the middle layers is shown by other researchers, such as Vig and Belinkov [2019], Liu et al. [2019a], and Tenney et al. [2019a].

Lin et al. [2019] further studied the hierarchical organization of a sentence in BERT representations. They found that the hierarchical information in representations increases as we move to deeper layers, while the prevalence of linear/sequential information decreases. This suggests that in deeper layers, BERT replaces positional information with hierarchical features of increasing complexity.

Tenney et al. [2019a] carried out another interesting analysis of BERT's layers and showed that they resemble an NLP pipeline. Their analysis showed that the layers encode different tasks in a natural progression from basic syntactic information to high-level semantic information: part of speech tagging, followed by constituents, dependencies, semantic roles, and coreference. This gradual hierarchy of linguistic information from surface features to syntactic and then semantic features was also shown by Jawahar et al. [2019]. Tenney et al. [2019a] also showed that syntactic information tends to concentrate on a few layers while semantic information is generally spread across the network.

6.7.4   MULTILINGUALITY

The authors of BERT have released a *multilingual* version trained on over 100 languages. The model is trained on monolingual corpora derived from Wikipedia for different languages, tokenized by the WordPiece tokenizer (cf. Section 6.4.3).

The model is shown to perform surprisingly well at zero-shot cross-lingual model transfer in which task-specific data in a (resource-rich) language is used in fine-tuning for evaluation in other languages even with different scripts [Wu and Dredze, 2019]. The results are surprising given that the pretraining of multilingual BERT (M-BERT) does not involve any cross-lingual objective to encourage learning a unified multilingual representation. Moreover, M-BERT does not make use of aligned data, but only uses monolingual data in different languages.

One key question that can be asked with respect to the multilinguality of M-BERT is the extent to which these representations resemble an interlingua, i.e., a common multilingual space in which semantically similar words across languages are placed in proximity. Singh et al. [2019] is one of the first works that investigates this question. Using a set of probing experiments based on Canonical Correlation Analysis (CCA), they showed that the representations tend to partition across different languages rather than sharing a common interlingual space. The partitioning effect was shown to be magnified in deeper layers, suggesting that the model does not progressively abstract semantic content while disregarding languages. They also showed that the choice of tokenizer can significantly influence the structure of the multilingual space built by M-BERT and the commonalities across representations in different languages. For instance, the subword tokenizer was shown to have a strong bias toward the structure of phylogenetic tree of languages.

Another question that might arise is the impact of the WordPiece tokenizer and of the resulting subword overlap on the multilingual abilities of M-BERT. Is the effectiveness of M-BERT in zero-shot cross lingual transfer due to the vocabulary memorization performed by the model? Is the representation power of M-BERT transferrable across languages with no lexical overlap? Pires et al. [2019] provided an analysis of the same question. They opted for Named Entity Recognition (NER) as the target task, given that entities are often similar across languages and hence a basic vocabulary memorization would allow the model to perform well across similar languages, but fail for languages with small lexical overlap. They showed that M-

BERT can obtain high performance even across languages with no lexical overlap, suggesting that the multilingual representational capacity of M-BERT is deeper than simple vocabulary memorization.

Artetxe et al. [2020] carried out a different probing experiment on zero-shot cross-lingual transfer benchmarks with similar observations: monolingual models indeed learn some abstractions that can be generalized across languages. They showed that the multilingual representations in M-BERT do not necessarily rely on the shared vocabulary, and that joint pretraining is necessary for comparable performance to cross-lingual models.

For their probing experiment, Artetxe et al. [2020] proposed a simple methodology for transferring a pretrained monolingual model to a new language by just learning a new embedding matrix. To this end, they first pretrain BERT on data for language L_1, then freeze the transformer layers and continue training on monolingual data from a second language L_2 in order to learn a new token embedding matrix for L_2. The obtained model is fine-tuned on task-specific data in L_1 and then the embedding matrix of the model is swapped for the embedding matrix of L_2. The process involves no joint training and there is no shared vocabulary given that separate subword vocabularies are used for the two languages (each learned from the corresponding monolingual data).

The importance of lexical overlap was also investigated by Karthikeyan K. [2020]. The authors drew a similar conclusion that lexical overlap between languages plays a negligible role in cross-lingual success. They, however, showed that grammatical word order similarity across languages is quite important for the transferability of linguistic knowledge. A similar analysis was carried out by Pires et al. [2019], suggesting that effective transfer of structural knowledge across grammatically-divergent languages would require the model to incorporate an explicit multilingual training objective, such as the one used by Artetxe and Schwenk [2019] and Conneau and Lample [2019].

6.7.5 LEXICAL CONTEXTUALIZATION

Despite not having any specific objective to encourage the encoding of sense-level information, contextualized representations have proved their power in capturing deep lexical semantic information. This is highlighted by their effectiveness in various NLP tasks that require sense-specific information.

For instance, on the Word-in-Context dataset which is a test bed for evaluating the abilities of a model in capturing sense-specific information (see Section 6.7.6), BERT-based models significantly outperform classic sense representation techniques (discussed in Chapter 5). Moreover, state-of-the-art Word Sense Disambiguation models are currently powered by contextualized embeddings [Bevilacqua and Navigli, 2020, Loureiro and Jorge, 2019, Vial et al., 2019].

To explain the effectiveness of contextualized embeddings in encoding sense-specific information, Reif et al. [2019] carried out an analysis on the semantic properties of contextualized

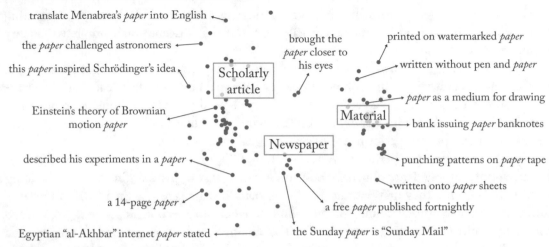

Figure 6.12: BERT contextualized embeddings for the word *paper* are clearly separated into different clusters depending on the intended meaning of the word.

BERT representations for ambiguous words. Figure 6.12 shows an example for the target word *paper*, with possible meanings "paper material", "scholarly article", and "newspaper".[8] The three meanings are clearly separated in the dimensionality reduced semantic space.

As it is clear from the figure, unlike classic sense embeddings, contextualized embeddings do not assign a finite number of senses to each word. Instead, the same word can be theoretically placed in an infinite number of different positions in the semantic space, depending on the context in which it appears. Ethayarajh [2019] carried out a comprehensive analysis on this property of contextualized lexical representations, specifically for ELMo, BERT, and GPT-2. He showed that the extent of variation in a word's contextualized representations is highly determined by the variety of contexts in which that word appears. This is not surprising as variety of contexts and polysemy are tightly connected. This observation was based on the fact that the contextualized representations for stopwords, such as *the*, *of*, and *to*, were among the most context-specific ones with low self-similarity across different contexts (as measured by the pairwise cosine similarity of their in-context instances).

Another finding of Ethayarajh [2019] was that contextualized representations are anisotropic rather than isotropic.[9] He showed that the contextualized word representations are not uniformly distributed in the semantic space (i.e., isotropic); instead, they occupy a narrow

---

[8]Illustration generated using Tensorflow's Projector; dimensionality reduction using T-SNE.
[9]Ethayarajh [2019] defines isotropy/anisotropy as follows. If word representations from a particular layer were isotropic (i.e., directionally uniform), then the average cosine similarity between uniformly randomly sampled words would be 0. The closer this average is to 1, the more anisotropic the representations. The geometric interpretation of anisotropy is that the word representations all occupy a narrow cone in the vector space rather than being uniform in all directions; the greater the anisotropy, the narrower this cone.

cone (i.e., anisotropic). Also, the extent of the anisotropy is magnified in deeper layers, especially for GPT-2 where the last layer's representations for any two random words would be almost equal to 1.0 according to cosine similarity.

6.7.6   EVALUATION

Similar to other types of embeddings, contextualized embeddings can be evaluated in two different settings: extrinsic or *in vitro* in which an explicit test is carried out to verify their quality, and, intrinsic or *in vivo* which checks for their impact when integrated into a downstream NLP application. Given their desirable finetuning property, most evaluations have focused on the *in-vivo* setting.

An example is the GLUE benchmark [Wang et al., 2019b] which mostly focuses on sentence-level representations, with tasks such as sentence similarity, sentiment analysis, grammatical acceptability, question answering, and inference. Not long after the introduction of the benchmark, contextualized models surpassed human level performance on these tasks. As an effort to making a more challenging dataset, the SuperGLUE [Wang et al., 2019a] benchmark was introduced, with tasks such as multi-sentence reading comprehension, common sense reasoning, and the Winograd Schema Challenge [Levesque et al., 2012]. SuperGLUE is currently one of the most widely accepted benchmarks for evaluating contextualized models.

The Word-in-Context dataset (WiC) is the only subtask in SuperGLUE that focuses on lexical semantics. As it was also discussed in Section 5.3, a system's task on the WiC dataset is to identify the intended meaning of words in context. WiC is framed as a binary classification task. Each instance in WiC has a target word w, either a verb or a noun, for which two contexts are provided. Each of these contexts triggers a specific meaning of w. The task is to identify if the occurrences of w in the two contexts correspond to the same meaning. Table 6.1 shows a few sample instances from WiC.

The key difference between the WiC task and standard Word Sense Disambiguation is that in the former there is no need to recourse to a predefined lexical resource or sense inventory. This enables seamless evaluation of a wide range of models. The Usim dataset [Erk et al., 2013] was constructed based on the same motivation. Here, the task is to measure the graded similarity of a word in different usages (contexts). Unlike the binary classification of WiC, the task in Usim is a regression one: judge the similarity of usages of a word on a similarity scale from 1 (completely different) to 5 (identical).

Table 6.1: Sample positive (T) and negative (F) pairs from the WiC dataset

Label	Target	Contents
F	bed	There's a lot of trash on the *bed* of the river
		I keep a glass of water next to my *bed* when I sleep
F	justify	*Justify* the margins
		The end *justifies* the means
F	land	The pilot managed to *land* the airplane safely
		The enemy *landed* several of our aircrafts
T	air	*Air* pollution
		Open a window and let in some *air*
T	beat	We *beat* the competition
		Agassi *beat* Becker in the tennis championship
F	window	The expanded *window* will give us time to catch the thieves
		You have a two-hour *window* of clear weather to finish working on the lawn

CHAPTER 7

Sentence and Document Embeddings

In the first part of the book, we focused on some of the smallest units in language, mostly those at the word-level. However, in most applications dealing with natural language, understanding longer units of meaning such as sentences[1] and documents is crucial. While this chapter is not covered as exhaustively as the other chapters, we still provide a basic overview and pointers so the reader can delve into these topics on their own.

In particular, we cover sentence embeddigs both in its unsupervised (Section 7.1) and supervised (Section 7.2) variants, document embeddings (Section 7.3), and their main applications and evaluation protocols (Section 7.4).

7.1 UNSUPERVISED SENTENCE EMBEDDINGS

In this section, we focus on sentence representation approaches that make use of unannotated text corpora as only source for building their sentence embeddings. This is similar to conventional word embedding models (see Section 3.2), which only need a large corpus in order to build their vector representations.

7.1.1 BAG OF WORDS

The traditional method for representing long pieces of texts has been through word-level features. Early methods in vector space models combined one-hot vector representations of words (see Section 1.2 for more details on these early methods). While this can lead to reasonable representations, their high dimensionality and sparsity has motivated researchers to explore other alternatives for combining word units. The process of representing sentences or documents through the composition of lower-level units such as words is known as compositionality.

Compositionality. Compositionality is a key concept in language understanding. How to combine small units (e.g., words) into a longer unit (e.g., a phrase or a sentence) has

---

[1]For a more casual survey on sentence embeddings, we would recommend the following two blog posts which have be taken as a reference for writing this chapter: (1) *The Current Best of Universal Word Embeddings and Sentence Embeddings*—https://medium.com/huggingface/universal-word-sentence-embeddings-ce48ddc8fc3a (last visited on September 2020); and (2) *On sentence representations, pt. 1: what can you fit into a single #$!%&% blog post?*—https://supernlp.github.io/2018/11/26/sentreps/ (last visited on September 2020).

been a long-studied topic in NLP. This became especially relevant since the introduction of high-quality vector representations of short units like words, as we studied in previous chapters. One of the first extensive analyses in this area is that of Mitchell and Lapata [2008]. Different arithmetic operations such as multiplication and addition were compared, with the results pointing out to a complementarity of these operations. Later works were also inspired by linguistically motivated vector spaces for composition. For instance, adjectives have been represented as functions that alter the meaning of nouns, which are represented as vectors [Baroni and Zamparelli, 2010]. Similar mathematical frameworks where nouns are modeled differently from verbs and adjectives have also been proposed [Coecke and Clark, 2010, Grefenstette et al., 2011].

More recently, approaches based on neural networks have been employed as compositional functions. For instance, recursive neural networks over parse trees [Socher et al., 2012] have been proved useful compositional functions in various NLP tasks such as sentiment analysis [Socher et al., 2013b].

In addition to these complex methods, interestingly, a simple method based on word embedding averaging was shown to be a strong alternative [Arora et al., 2017]. This average can be weighted (e.g., tf-idf or lexical specificity) or unweighted (i.e., weights are determined by word frequency in a sentence). Postprocessing techniques such as Principal Component Analysis (PCA) are often also employed.

In Bag of Words (BoW) methods, compositionality often disregards word order. This makes these methods (including those based on vector averaging) unsuitable for hard language understanding tasks on which word order is an important component. For instance, sentiment analysis or language inference are tasks where not capturing word order can be clearly detrimental. Moreover, tasks involving a generation component (e.g., MT) are also affected by this limitation. In the following section, we present methods that aim at learning sentence representations directly as part of the training process.

7.1.2 SENTENCE-LEVEL TRAINING

Direct training on sentences has been proposed as a way to overcome the insensitivity of bag-of-word models to word order. The main underlying idea behind these models is their capacity to predict surrounding sentences (often the following sentence) given an input sentence. This feature helps models understand the meaning of isolated sentences without having to rely solely on their components (like the models presented in the previous section). In a sense, this goal is similar to standard word embedding models (see Chapter 3). In the Skip-gram model of Word2Vec [Mikolov et al., 2013a], for example, given a word the goal is to predict the words in its immediate context. In this case, what is predicted is the following sentence and not words, but the underlying idea remains quite similar.

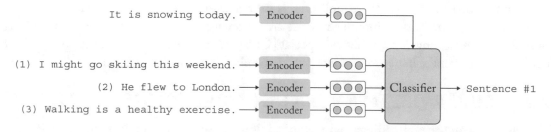

Figure 7.1: High-level overview of unsupervised sentence embedding techniques. On the top an approach based on generation and at the bottom an approach based on classification.

This motivation has led to several specific models with small variations. A popular example of this kind of model is **Skip-Thought** vectors [Kiros et al., 2015]. In this model, an RNN is employed as part of a standard sequence to sequence (seq2seq) architecture, similar to that used for MT [Sutskever et al., 2014]. The training workflow of this model is as follows.

1. A sentence (e.g., "The kids were playing with a ball in the garden.") is given as input. The goal is to predict the next sentence (e.g., "The ball fell into a flower pot."), which we will refer to as the output sentence.

2. Using the RNN-based seq2seq architecture, the input sentence is encoded into an intermediate representation.

3. The output sentence is generated by decoding this intermediate representation.

This process is repeated for all sentence pairs in the training data, which usually sum to a large number, in the order of millions.

Alternatively, **Quick-thoughts** vectors [Logeswaran and Lee, 2018] propose to treat the problem as a classification, rather than a prediction, task. The main difference between these two types of model is illustrated in Figure 7.1. Instead of having an encoder-decoder architecture which attempts to generate the output sentence, this model will just select the output sentence from a set of sentences sampled from the reference corpus. One of the main advantages of this method is the speed, as the generation step, which is quite costly, is replaced by a faster classification procedure. This makes Quick-thoughts vectors more scalable and suitable to train on a large corpus.

Finally, it is important to highlight that recent high-quality sentence representations are built by relying on **pre-trained language models** and contextualized embeddings (cf. Chapter 6). In this case, given a pre-trained language model it is straightforward to obtain a representation for a given sentence. Reducing the complexity of pre-trained language models to obtaining one embedding per sentence has obvious advantages in similarity, clustering and retrieval tasks that would require heavy computations otherwise. Reimers and Gurevych [2019] discuss several strategies to retrieve such sentence embeddings from a pre-trained language model like BERT (see Chapter 6). The most common strategies are retrieving a single contextualized embedding as sentence embedding (e.g., using the special [CLS] token as explained in Section 6.4.3), or performing an average between all contextualized embeddings of the sentence.

7.2 SUPERVISED SENTENCE EMBEDDINGS

This class of sentence embeddings make use of additional resources in addition to unlabeled text corpora. Training on unlabeled corpora can be limiting and these approaches exploit diverse sources aiming at improving the quality of unsupervised representations.

1. **Language Inference data.** Natural Language Inference[2] (NLI) is the task of determining whether a statement (called premise) entails, contradicts, or is neutral with respect to another statement (called hypothesis). NLI has often been considered an important proxy to language understanding and large-scale benchmarks such as SNLI [Bowman et al., 2015] or MultiNLI [Williams et al., 2018] have been developed. In the context of sentence embeddings, Conneau et al. [2017] developed a bidirectional LSTM encoder that takes the sentence pairs from the SNLI corpus as external supervision.

2. **Machine Translation.** An external task that has been used to learn sentence embeddings is Neural Machine Translation (NMT). The signal of sentence translation has been found to be complementary to unsupervised methods for training sentence representations from an unlabeled corpus. For instance, McCann et al. [2017] incorporate a network that updates the weights of sentence embeddings during training, which are then combined with their CoVe contextualized word representations (cf. Chapter 6).

3. **Vision.** In some cases, language comes together with different modalities, such as acoustic or visual features. For instance, images are frequently accompanied with captions, which encourages the development of systems which take advantage of both modalities for language understanding. As an example, Kiela et al. [2018] propose a sentence embedding model that aims at predicting visual features from the image associated with a caption (sentence). In this case, the sentences are encoded with a bidirectional LSTM which are then enriched with the visual features.

---

[2]Natural Language Inference has also been refered to as Textual Entailment [Dagan et al., 2005].

Multi-task learning.   In general, different aspects of the same sentence can be encoded into a multi-task learning (MTL) framework [Caruana, 1997]. MTL is a machine learning framework where training signals of related tasks are used as an inductive bias or are trained jointly within the main end task. In NLP, MTL has been popularized since the early work of Collobert and Weston [2008] and has subsequently shown improvements in NLP tasks by leveraging similar tasks where data is available [Peng et al., 2017, Ruder, 2017]. For an overview, the following studies discuss the settings in which MTL can be helpful in the context of NLP [Alonso and Plank, 2017, Bingel and Søgaard, 2017]. In the context of sentence embeddings, Subramanian et al. [2018] leveraged several NLP tasks (including language inference and machine translation) into a unified MTL framework to learn general purpose sentence representations. Similarly, Cer et al. [2018] encode sentences into a transformer-based architecture that integrates a variety of language understanding tasks.

7.3   DOCUMENT EMBEDDINGS

In this section, we discuss specific approaches for modeling units longer than sentences, mainly documents.[3] While some of the approaches mentioned in the previous sections can also be used to model documents, this setting usually needs lighter models—approaches based on neural networks can be quite expensive to represent documents. For this reason, BoW models tend to be a popular technique for learning representations of longer units of text such as documents. As with sentence embedding BoW techniques (cf. Section 7.1.1), these approaches are often suboptimal as word order is not taken into account. However, this limitation is less pronounced for documents as context is larger.

A popular technique to induce topics from documents, which can then be used as a document representation, is based on Latent Dirichlet Allocation (LDA) [Blei et al., 2003]. This method relies on a generative probabilistic model that employs a hierarchical Bayesian structure to infer the latent topics within text corpora. More recently, and similarly to word embedding techniques such as Word2Vec (cf. Chapter 3), approaches going beyond count-based bag of word methods often involve some kind of predictive behavior. Le and Mikolov [2014] proposed a language model-based architecture to predict the words occurring in a given document (or paragraph). Kusner et al. [2015] also showed that the word embeddings of a given document are in most cases enough for inferring a reliable semantic similarity metric among documents.

7.4   APPLICATION AND EVALUATION

One of the main advantages of encoding portions of texts into fixed-length vectors is the flexibility of the approach. Sentence and document embeddings can be applied to any task involving

---

[3]Some approaches also model paragraphs but the distinction is often not clear, and approaches for either unit (paragraph or document) may be applied interchangeably in some settings.

these linguistic units, with the added benefit of being computationally cheaper than other methods involving supervised classifiers such as neural networks. In particular, they are particularly attractive for applications involving large amounts of computation such as information retrieval or document clustering.

Sentence level.   The spectrum of application for sentence level tasks is immense. As mentioned earlier, many NLP tasks involve some kind of sentence processing in one way or another. Tasks such as sentiment analysis or language inference, to name but a few, can often be framed as sentence classification tasks. Therefore, the evaluation of sentence embedding models is often difficult given the large number of tasks and domains for which they can be applied. In order to provide a unified framework for different tasks, two efforts have been presented. First, SentEval [Conneau and Kiela, 2018] contains a variety of sentence-level tasks including sentiment analysis, sentence similarity, language inference and image caption retrieval. Supervised classifiers are provided as part of the framework so as to compare the underlying sentence representations directly. Second, the language understanding benchmarks GLUE [Wang et al., 2019b] and SuperGLUE [Wang et al., 2019a] are mostly composed of sentence-level tasks (cf. Section 6.7), and hence are suitable for testing sentence embeddings. Finally, semantic and syntactic probing tasks have also been proposed as a way for a more linguistically grounded evaluation of sentence embedding techniques [Conneau et al., 2018a]. Perone et al. [2018] provide an extensive empirical comparison involving both downstream and linguistic probing tasks.

Document level.   Evaluation at the document level has been almost exclusively focused on text categorization. In text categorization, various categories are pre-defined and the task consists in associating a given input document with the most appropriate category. This task is often framed as supervised classification, where documents with their gold categories as given as training data. The most usual domain for the evaluation is newswire [Greene and Cunningham, 2006, Lang, 1995, Lewis et al., 2004], while text categorization datasets for specialized domains are also available, e.g., Ohsumed [Hersh et al., 1994] for the medical domain.

CHAPTER 8

Ethics and Bias

Most current Machine Learning models are data-driven: they learn from the data to which they are exposed. Therefore, they inevitably encode all the implicit stereotyped biases, such as gender, racial, or ideological biases, present in the data, unless specific measures are undertaken to prevent this. This raises concerns over the use of these techniques in real-world situations, which would lead in perpetuating the prejudice and stereotyped biases that unfortunately reflect everyday human culture. In a seminal study, Caliskan et al. [2017] showed that text corpora usually contain imprints of our various historic biases: "morally neutral as toward insects or flowers, problematic as toward race or gender, or even simply veridical, reflecting the status quo distribution of gender with respect to careers or first names".

Addressing harmful biases is crucial because machine learning models have now passed the *experimental* stage and have directly entered people's lives in different areas, such as criminal justice, online advertising, and medical testing. Having such societal biases in models can have serious implications, not only for their direct applications in real life but also for their role in reproduction and propagation of ideas about discrimination.

An example is a study by MIT Media Lab on gender and skin type performance disparities in commercial facial recognition models [Raji and Buolamwini, 2019]. Initial results of this study revealed a strong bias against women and darker skins in gender classification, and resulted in a sequence of updates to these models for addressing the bias. Another example is ProPublica's study[1] on a risk assessment tool that was widely used in criminal justice in the U.S. The tool was being used to predict the probability of a defendant to commit a crime in the future. The study found that risk estimates had a strong bias against African-American defendants.

In fact, during the past few years, with the widespread use of data hungry deep learning models, the ethical aspect in predictive models has been raised as an important concern which is worthy of more attention and investigation [Zhao et al., 2017]. Public sensitivity to this topic is very much highlighted by the wide objection over the "emotional contagion" experiment of Facebook [Kramer et al., 2014]. Despite being legal according to Facebook's Data Use Policy, the study resulted in a lot of ethical discussion inside and outside academia [Jouhki et al., 2016].

Facebook's *emotional contagion* experiment was a massive psychological experiment conducted in January 2012. The goal of this study was to see if emotional states can be transferred across individuals. For this, Kramer et al. [2014] manipulated Facebook's news feed

---

[1]https://www.propublica.org/article/machine-bias-risk-assessments-in-criminal-sentencing

for around 700K Facebook users, by tweaking the amount of positive and negative contents shown. After a week, manipulated users were more likely to post especially positive or negative updates. They concluded that "emotional states can be transferred to others via emotional contagion, leading people to experience the same emotions without their awareness".

Analyzing bias in NLP systems has recently garnered a lot of attention, with ACL 2020 dedicating a new track to "Ethics and NLP". Work on bias in NLP expand over many areas, including language modeling [Bordia and Bowman, 2019, Qian et al., 2019], coreference resolution [Rudinger et al., 2018], MT [Stanovsky et al., 2019], sentiment analysis [Kiritchenko and Mohammad, 2018], and semantic representation (discussed in detail in Section 8.1). Bender and Friedman [2018] focused on bias from the dataset point of view, highlighting the importance of having knowledge about characterization of a dataset we use for training a model. They argued that having this knowledge would allow us to better understand the potential biases reflected in the model and to have an idea about the extent to which the results may generalize to other domains. To this end, they also proposed a "data statement" schema which involves various types of information, such as source of texts used, language variety, and annotator demographics.

Hovy and Spruit [2016] overviewed the social impact of NLP research and discussed various implications of bias in NLP, including: (1) demographic misrepresentation and *exclusion* of the language used by minority groups making the technology less suitable for them, hence reinforcing demographic differences; (2) *overgeneralization* which is a modeling side-effect and a consequence of negligence over false positives; and (3) topic *overexposure*, which is particularly relevant for the choice of languages under research which is mostly centered around a few languages only, directly impacting typological variety.

8.1 BIAS IN WORD EMBEDDINGS

Given what was described above, it is natural for word embeddings to encode implicit bias in human-generated text. In a seminal work, Bolukbasi et al. [2016] studied the existence of gender bias in word embeddings. The results pinpointed female/male gender stereotypes to a disturbing extent. This was surprising as the studied word embeddings were the standard Word2vec embeddings trained on Google News articles which are written by professional journalists.[2]

Moreover, Bolukbasi et al. [2016] extracted the closest occupation words in the embedding space to the gender pronouns *he* and *she*. The results, shown in Table 8.1, have strong indications of gender stereotypicality. They observed similar unwanted gender biases in an analogy test. They extracted from the embedding space the set of analogous word pairs to *he-she* with the condition that words in a pair are semantically similar to each other. Many of the identified pairs were found to exhibit gender stereotypes. Sample pairs are shown in Table 8.2.

---

[2]Similar results were observed using GloVe embeddings trained on the Common Crawl corpus.

Table 8.1: The closest occupations (words) to the gender pronouns *she* and *he* in the embedding space of Word2vec Google News (from Bolukbasi et al. [2016])

he	she
maestro, skipper, protege, philosopher, captain, architect, financier, warrior, broadcaster, magician	homemaker, nurse, receptionist, librarian, socialite, hairdresser, nanny, bookkeeper, stylist, housekeeper

Table 8.2: Analogous pairs to the *he-she* relation, identified by Bolukbasi et al. [2016]

Gender stereotype analogies	Gender appropriate analogies
sewing-carpentry, registered nurse-physician, housewife-shopkeeper, nurse-surgeon, interior designer-architect, softball-baseball, blond-burly, feminism-conservatism, cosmetics-pharmaceuticals, giggle-chuckle, vocalist-guitarist, petite-lanky sassy-snappy, diva-superstar, charming-affable, volleyball-football, cupcakes-pizzas, lovely-brilliant	queen-king, sister-brother, mother-father, waitress-waiter, ovarian cancer-prostate cancer, convent-monastery

8.2   DEBIASING WORD EMBEDDINGS

The existence of gender-specific stereotypes in word embeddings is particularly important since they can potentially amplify the bias in societies given their widespread use. Therefore, it is crucial to seek techniques for reducing or discarding bias from word embeddings. Recently, there have been many efforts to mitigate gender bias in word embeddings either at a post-processing stage [Bolukbasi et al., 2016] or as part of the training procedure [Zhang et al., 2018, Zhao et al., 2018]. Sun et al. [2019] provide a review of the literature on mitigating gender bias in NLP. One of the first attempts at debiasing word embeddings was carried out by Bolukbasi et al. [2016]. The authors quantified bias for a word w based on its relative distance to pairs of gender specific words (such as *brother*, *sister*, *actress*, and *actor*). The word w is said to possess gender bias, if the distances of w to the gender specific words in pairs are unequal. In other words, to compute gender bias for w, they projected the embedding of w to "the gender direction". The value of this projection was taken as the extent of bias for w. The gender direction is computed by combining[3] the differences of ten gender-specific word pairs.

Bolukbasi et al. [2016] used a post-processing technique for debiasing word embeddings. For each word in a word embeddings space, they neutralize the projection on the "gender direction". They also make sure that all these words are equi-distant from the predefined gender-specific pairs. Zhang et al. [2018] used the gender direction of Bolukbasi et al. [2016] and learned

---

[3]More specifically, gender direction is computed as the principal component of the ten gender pair difference vectors.

a transformation from the biased embedding space to a debiased one using adversarial training. Zhao et al. [2018] took a different approach and proposed training debiased embeddings by changing the loss function in the GloVe model. The change aims at concentrating all the gender information to a specific dimension which they can discard to produce gender-debiased word embeddings.

The above works differ in their methodology but share a similar definition of debiasing: being neutral with respect to the gender direction. However, Gonen and Goldberg [2019] showed through a set of experiments that this definition is insufficient for determining bias, and the bias reflecting world stereotypes is much more subtle in the embeddings. Specifically, they observed that there exists a systematic bias in the embeddings which is independent of the gender direction. For instance, it was shown that the gender subspace is spanned by dozens to hundreds of orthogonal directions in the space, and a mere selection of a few (or a single) intuitive directions (such as *he-she*) is not enough for addressing the bias. Therefore, removing this "remaining" bias in other directions requires scrutinizing embeddings at much deeper levels.

In a follow-up work, Ravfogel et al. [2020] addressed some of these limitations by an approach called Interative Null-space Projection (INLP). Using repeated training of a linear classifier, INLP automatically learns directions in which specific properties are encoded (such as gender) in the latent space, as opposed to the manual selection of these directions that was often done in previous techniques. The authors show that automatically learned directions are more suitable as there are many subtle ways in which properties, such as gender, can be encoded. Moreover, the automatic identification enables the model to learn many directions which alleviates the limitation of previous projection-based methods that usually had to resort to one or a few intuitive directions. Figure 8.1 shows an illustration of the impact of INLP's debiasing for profession words on BERT representations.

Debiasing is closely related to the task of disentanglement of representations, i.e., identifying (and removing) different kinds of information encoded in neural representations [Mathieu et al., 2016, Peng et al., 2019]. Disentanglement process is necessary in scenarios such as transfer learning, in which specific type of information, such as domain or style, is intended to be removed from representations in order to improve generalizability to new arbitrary settings. This is usually achieved through modifying the training objective function by adding an adversarial [Goodfellow et al., 2014, Wang et al., 2019c, Xie et al., 2017] regularization component that competes with the main objective to avoid encoding specific information.

In a critical survey of the literature on bias in NLP, Blodgett et al. [2020] highlight that most works in the area lack clear motivations and normative reasoning. In terms of motivation, they differentiate works into various categories, such as allocational harms,[4] stereotyping, and questionable correlations. As for normative reasoning, they point out that many works make

---

[4]Harms of allocation arise when an automated system allocates opportunities (e.g., jobs and education) or resources (e.g., loans) in an unjust manner to different social groups.

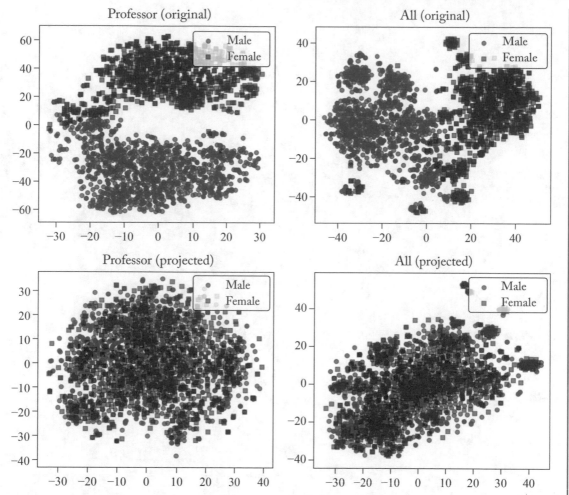

Figure 8.1: A 2D visualization of BERT representations for the profession "professor" (left) and for a random sample of all professions (right), before and after debiasing by INLP [Ravfogel et al., 2020]. Illustration is taken from their work.

unstated assumptions about how and why NLP systems can have harmful behaviors, and at what groups are these targeted. They also find that many papers do not present any apparent normative concerns, and instead focus on issues with system performance. Based on these observations, they propose recommendations for guiding work on analyzing bias, including explicit statement of motivations and grounding the analysis in the relevant literature outside NLP that explores relationships between language and social hierarchies.

CHAPTER 9

Conclusions

In this book, we aimed at providing a high-level introduction to various types of embeddings used in NLP. We covered early works in word embeddings and more recent contextualized embeddings based on large pre-trained language models. The currently celebrated contextualized embeddings are the product of a long path of evolution. Since early works on lexical semantics, the distributional hypothesis has been the dominating basis for the field of semantic representation and prevailed even for recent models, however, the way of constructing representations has gone under a lot of change. The initial stage of this path is characterized by models that explicitly collected co-occurrence statistics, an approach that often required a subsequent dimensionality reduction step (Chapter 3). Together with the revival of neural networks and deep learning, the field of semantic representation experienced a massive boost. Neural networks provided an efficient way for processing large amounts of texts and for directly computing dense compact representations. Since then, the term *representation* has been almost fully substituted by their dense version, called *embeddings*. This development path has revolutionalized other fields of research such as graph embedding (Chapter 4) or resulted in the emergence of other fields of research, such as sense embedding (Chapter 5) and sentence embedding (Chapter 7).

An important evolution to note is the rapid pace of development in the field of semantic representation. For instance, upon its introduction in early 2018, ELMo (Chapter 6) occupied the top of most NLP benchmarks. However, in less than a year, BERT significantly outperformed all previous (feature extraction-based) models, including ELMo. The development has not stopped though with several new contextualized models giving further boosts in model performance. These models currently approach (or even pass) human-level performance in many of the standard NLP benchmarks, such as SuperGLUE [Wang et al., 2019a]. However, it is clear that in many fields, such as question answering with common sense reasoning, MT, or summarization, to name a few, there is still a big room for improvement.[1] In other words, "true" NLU is far from reached. While progress has been indisputable, an explanation of the high performance in certain tasks comes from certain biases and artefacts present in these datasets. This is often inevitable, and highlights the need for the introduction of new datasets or benchmarks for a more rigorous evaluation and for measuring our progress toward concrete goals [Linzen, 2020].

---

[1]For example, question answering requiring sentence composition [Khot et al., 2020] or the Winograd Scheme Challenge [Levesque et al., 2012], which requires referential disambiguation, are two tasks where humans perform considerably better than machines.

Another point of concern is that NLP research has mostly focused on the English language and on settings where abundant data is available. Extending these tools and knowledge to languages other than English, especially resource-poor languages, and to domains where little data is available, is another problem which is open for research. Also, almost all these techniques are purely text-based. Integrating semi-structured knowledge, such as knowledge encoded in lexical resources and semantic or syntactic priors of a given language constitutes another research challenge. It is also noteworthy to mention that due to the deep learning hype, the current research in NLP is getting dismissive of the importance of linguistic aspects, ignoring the decades of methodological and linguistic insights. This is also relevant to semantics, which is the main topic of this book. It is necessary to step back and rethink in order to achieve true language understanding.

Last but not least, deep learning models are known to be blackboxes. It is difficult to ask models to reason or to analyze the reasons behind their decisions. With respect to semantic representation, embeddings are generally not interpretable. An existing research area investigates the problem of explaining these representations and what they (do not) capture, especially in relation to syntax and the structure of language [Ettinger, 2020, Hewitt and Manning, 2019, Jawahar et al., 2019, Saphra and Lopez, 2019, Tenney et al., 2019b], but there are many areas that should be further explored.

Bibliography

Eneko Agirre and Aitor Soroa. Personalizing PageRank for word sense disambiguation. In *Proc. of the Conference of the European Chapter of the Association for Computational Linguistics*, pages 33–41, 2009. DOI: 10.3115/1609067.1609070 54

Eneko Agirre, Enrique Alfonseca, Keith Hall, Jana Kravalova, Marius Paşca, and Aitor Soroa. A study on similarity and relatedness using distributional and WordNet-based approaches. In *Proc. of the Conference of the North American Chapter of the Association for Computational Linguistics*, pages 19–27, 2009. DOI: 10.3115/1620754.1620758 37

Eneko Agirre, Oier Lopez de Lacalle, and Aitor Soroa. Random walks for knowledge-based word sense disambiguation. *Computational Linguistics*, 40(1):57–84, 2014. DOI: 10.1162/coli_a_00164 62, 64

Amr Ahmed, Nino Shervashidze, Shravan Narayanamurthy, Vanja Josifovski, and Alexander J. Smola. Distributed large-scale natural graph factorization. In *Proc. of the 22nd International Conference on World Wide Web, WWW'13*, pages 37–48, ACM, New York, 2013. DOI: 10.1145/2488388.2488393 43

Carl Allen and Timothy Hospedales. Analogies explained: Towards understanding word embeddings. In *International Conference on Machine Learning*, pages 223–231, 2019. 51

Carl Allen, Ivana Balazevic, and Timothy Hospedales. What the vec? towards probabilistically grounded embeddings. In H. Wallach, H. Larochelle, A. Beygelzimer, F. d'Alché-Buc, E. Fox, and R. Garnett, Eds., *Advances in Neural Information Processing Systems 32*, pages 7467–7477. Curran Associates, Inc., 2019. http://papers.nips.cc/paper/8965-what-the-vec-towards-probabilistically-grounded-embeddings.pdf 51

Héctor Martínez Alonso and Barbara Plank. When is multitask learning effective? semantic sequence prediction under varying data conditions. In *Proc. of the 15th Conference of the European Chapter of the Association for Computational Linguistics: Volume 1, Long Papers*, pages 44–53, 2017. DOI: 10.18653/v1/e17-1005 101

David Alvarez-Melis and Tommi Jaakkola. Gromov-Wasserstein alignment of word embedding spaces. In *Proc. of the Conference on Empirical Methods in Natural Language Processing*, pages 1881–1890, Association for Computational Linguistics, Brussels, Belgium, October–November 2018. https://www.aclweb.org/anthology/D18-1214 DOI: 10.18653/v1/d18-1214 37

112   BIBLIOGRAPHY

Waleed Ammar, George Mulcaire, Yulia Tsvetkov, Guillaume Lample, Chris Dyer, and Noah A. Smith. Massively multilingual word embeddings. *ArXiv Preprint ArXiv:1602.01925*, 2016. 33

Marianna Apidianaki. Data-driven semantic analysis for multilingual WSD and lexical selection in translation. In *Proc. of the 12th Conference of the European Chapter of the ACL (EACL)*, pages 77–85, 2009. DOI: 10.3115/1609067.1609075 61

Carlos Santos Armendariz, Matthew Purver, Matej Ulčar, Senja Pollak, Nikola Ljubešić, and Mark Granroth-Wilding. Cosimlex: A resource for evaluating graded word similarity in context. In *Proc. of The 12th Language Resources and Evaluation Conference*, pages 5878–5886, 2020. 67

Sanjeev Arora, Yingyu Liang, and Tengyu Ma. A simple but tough-to-beat baseline for sentence embeddings. In *Proc. of the International Conference on Learning Representations*, 2017. 98

Mikel Artetxe and Holger Schwenk. Massively multilingual sentence embeddings for zero-shot cross-lingual transfer and beyond. *Transactions of the Association of Computational Linguistics*, 7:597–610, 2019. https://transacl.org/ojs/index.php/tacl/article/view/1742 DOI: 10.1162/tacl_a_00288 93

Mikel Artetxe, Gorka Labaka, and Eneko Agirre. Learning principled bilingual mappings of word embeddings while preserving monolingual invariance. In *Proc. of the Conference on Empirical Methods in Natural Language Processing*, pages 2289–2294, 2016. DOI: 10.18653/v1/d16-1250 33

Mikel Artetxe, Gorka Labaka, and Eneko Agirre. Learning bilingual word embeddings with (almost) no bilingual data. In *Proc. of the 55th Annual Meeting of the Association for Computational Linguistics (Volume 1: Long Papers)*, pages 451–462, Vancouver, Canada, July 2017. http://aclweb.org/anthology/P17-1042 DOI: 10.18653/v1/p17-1042 36

Mikel Artetxe, Gorka Labaka, and Eneko Agirre. Generalizing and improving bilingual word embedding mappings with a multi-step framework of linear transformations. In *Proc. of the 32nd AAAI Conference on Artificial Intelligence (AAAI-18)*, pages 5012–5019, 2018a. 35, 36

Mikel Artetxe, Gorka Labaka, and Eneko Agirre. A robust self-learning method for fully unsupervised cross-lingual mappings of word embeddings. In *Proc. of the Annual Meeting of the Association for Computational Linguistics*, pages 789–798, 2018b. DOI: 10.18653/v1/p18-1073 31, 37

Mikel Artetxe, Sebastian Ruder, and Dani Yogatama. On the cross-lingual transferability of monolingual representations. In *Proc. of the Annual Meeting of the Association of Computational Linguistics (ACL)*, 2020. DOI: 10.18653/v1/2020.acl-main.421 93

Ben Athiwaratkun and Andrew Wilson. Multimodal word distributions. In *Proc. of the 55th Annual Meeting of the Association for Computational Linguistics (Volume 1: Long Papers)*, 1:1645–1656, 2017. DOI: 10.18653/v1/p17-1151 31

Ben Athiwaratkun, Andrew Wilson, and Anima Anandkumar. Probabilistic FastText for multi-sense word embeddings. In *Proc. of the 56th Annual Meeting of the Association for Computational Linguistics (Volume 1: Long Papers)*, pages 1–11, 2018. DOI: 10.18653/v1/p18-1001 31

Dzmitry Bahdanau, Kyunghyun Cho, and Yoshua Bengio. Neural machine translation by jointly learning to align and translate. In Yoshua Bengio and Yann LeCun, Eds., *3rd International Conference on Learning Representations ICLR, Conference Track Proceedings*, San Diego, May 7–9, 2015. http://arxiv.org/abs/1409.0473 19, 20

Dzmitry Bahdanau, Tom Bosc, Stanislaw Jastrzebski, Edward Grefenstette, Pascal Vincent, and Yoshua Bengio. Learning to compute word embeddings on the fly. *CoRR*, 2017. 32

Amir Bakarov. A survey of word embeddings evaluation methods. In *Proc. of the Joint Conference on Lexical and Computational Semantics (*SEM)*, 2018. 38

Collin F. Baker, Charles J. Fillmore, and John B. Lowe. The Berkeley FrameNet project. In *Proc. of the 17th International Conference on Computational Linguistics, Volume 1*, pages 86–90, Association for Computational Linguistics, 1998. DOI: 10.3115/980451.980860 32

Livio Baldini Soares, Nicholas FitzGerald, Jeffrey Ling, and Tom Kwiatkowski. Matching the blanks: Distributional similarity for relation learning. In *Proc. of the 57th Annual Meeting of the Association for Computational Linguistics*, pages 2895–2905, Florence, Italy, July 2019. https://www.aclweb.org/anthology/P19-1279 DOI: 10.18653/v1/p19-1279 54

Miguel Ballesteros, Chris Dyer, and Noah A. Smith. Improved transition-based parsing by modeling characters instead of words with LSTMs. In *Proc. of the Conference on Empirical Methods in Natural Language Processing*, pages 349–359, 2015. DOI: 10.18653/v1/d15-1041 32

Arindam Banerjee, Inderjit S. Dhillon, Joydeep Ghosh, and Suvrit Sra. Clustering on the unit hypersphere using von Mises-Fisher distributions. *Journal of Machine Learning Research*, 6(Sep):1345–1382, 2005. 57

Satanjeev Banerjee and Ted Pedersen. An adapted Lesk algorithm for Word Sense Disambiguation using WordNet. In *Proc. of the 3rd International Conference on Computational Linguistics and Intelligent Text Processing, CICLing'02*, pages 136–145, Mexico City, 2002. DOI: 10.1007/3-540-45715-1_11 62

Mohit Bansal, John Denero, and Dekang Lin. Unsupervised translation sense clustering. In *Proc. of the Conference of the North American Chapter of the Association for Computational Linguistics: Human Language Technologies, NAACL HLT'12*, pages 773–782, Stroudsburg, PA, 2012. 61

Antonio Valerio Miceli Barone. Towards cross-lingual distributed representations without parallel text trained with adversarial autoencoders. In *Proc. of the 1st Workshop on Representation Learning for NLP*, pages 121–126, 2016. DOI: 10.18653/v1/w16-1614 36

Marco Baroni and Alessandro Lenci. Distributional memory: A general framework for corpus-based semantics. *Computational Linguistics*, 36(4):673–721, 2010. DOI: 10.1162/coli_a_00016 27

Marco Baroni and Roberto Zamparelli. Nouns are vectors, adjectives are matrices: Representing adjective-noun constructions in semantic space. In *Proc. of the Conference on Empirical Methods in Natural Language Processing*, pages 1183–1193, Association for Computational Linguistics, Cambridge, MA, October 2010. https://www.aclweb.org/anthology/D10-1115 98

Marco Baroni, Georgiana Dinu, and Germán Kruszewski. Don't count, predict! a systematic comparison of context-counting vs. context-predicting semantic vectors. In *Proc. of the Annual Meeting of the Association for Computational Linguistics*, pages 238–247, 2014. DOI: 10.3115/v1/p14-1023 8, 38

Sergey Bartunov, Dmitry Kondrashkin, Anton Osokin, and Dmitry Vetrov. Breaking sticks and ambiguities with adaptive skip-gram. In *Proc. of the 19th International Conference on Artificial Intelligence and Statistics*, volume 51 of *Proc. of Machine Learning Research, PMLR*, pages 130–138, Cadiz, Spain, May 09–11, 2016. 60

Mikhail Belkin and Partha Niyogi. Laplacian eigenmaps for dimensionality reduction and data representation. *Neural Computation*, 15(6):1373–1396, 2003. DOI: 10.1162/089976603321780317 43

Emily M. Bender. Linguistic fundamentals for natural language processing: 100 essentials from morphology and syntax. *Synthesis lectures on human language technologies*, 6(3):1–184, 2013. DOI: 10.2200/s00493ed1v01y201303hlt020 9

Emily M. Bender and Batya Friedman. Data statements for Natural Language Processing: Toward mitigating system bias and enabling better science. *Transactions of the Association for Computational Linguistics*, 6:587–604, 2018. https://www.aclweb.org/anthology/Q18-1041 DOI: 10.1162/tacl_a_00041 104

Emily M. Bender and Alex Lascarides. Linguistic fundamentals for natural language processing II: 100 essentials from semantics and pragmatics. *Synthesis Lectures on Human Language Technologies*, pages 1–268, 2019. DOI: 10.2200/s00935ed1v02y201907hlt043 9

Y. Bengio, P. Simard, and P. Frasconi. Learning long-term dependencies with gradient descent is difficult. *IEEE Transactions on Neural Networks*, 5(2):157–166, March 1994. DOI: 10.1109/72.279181 15

Yoshua Bengio, Réjean Ducharme, Pascal Vincent, and Christian Janvin. A neural probabilistic language model. *The Journal of Machine Learning Research*, 3:1137–1155, 2003. 29

Andrew Bennett, Timothy Baldwin, Jey Han Lau, Diana McCarthy, and Francis Bond. Lexsemtm: A semantic dataset based on all-words unsupervised sense distribution learning. In *Proc. of the Annual Meeting of the Association for Computational Linguistics*, pages 1513–1524, 2016. DOI: 10.18653/v1/p16-1143 59

Michele Bevilacqua and Roberto Navigli. Breaking through the 80% glass ceiling: Raising the state of the art in word sense disambiguation by incorporating knowledge graph information. In *Proc. of the 58th Annual Meeting of the Association for Computational Linguistics*, pages 2854–2864, 2020. DOI: 10.18653/v1/2020.acl-main.255 93

Chris Biemann. Chinese whispers: An efficient graph clustering algorithm and its application to natural language processing problems. In *Proc. of the 1st workshop on graph based methods for natural language processing*, pages 73–80, Association for Computational Linguistics, 2006. DOI: 10.3115/1654758.1654774 58

Joachim Bingel and Anders Søgaard. Identifying beneficial task relations for multi-task learning in deep neural networks. In *Proc. of the 15th Conference of the European Chapter of the Association for Computational Linguistics: Volume 2, Short Papers*, pages 164–169, 2017. DOI: 10.18653/v1/e17-2026 101

Christian Bizer, Jens Lehmann, Georgi Kobilarov, Sören Auer, Christian Becker, Richard Cyganiak, and Sebastian Hellmann. DBpedia-a crystallization point for the Web of data. *Web Semantics: Science, Services and Agents on the World Wide Web*, 7(3):154–165, 2009. DOI: 10.1016/j.websem.2009.07.002 23

Philip Blair, Yuval Merhav, and Joel Barry. Automated generation of multilingual clusters for the evaluation of distributed representations. In *Proc. of the International Conference on Learning Representations (ICLR), Workshop*, 2016. 38

David M. Blei, Andrew Y. Ng, and Michael I. Jordan. Latent Dirichlet allocation. *The Journal of Machine Learning Research*, 3:993–1022, 2003. DOI: 10.1109/asru.2015.7404785 59, 101

Su Lin Blodgett, Solon Barocas, Hal Daumé III, and Hanna Wallach. Language (technology) is power: A critical survey of "bias" in NLP. In *Proc. of the 58th Annual Meeting of the Association for Computational Linguistics*, pages 5454–5476, July 2020. https://www.aclweb.org/anthology/2020.acl-main.485 DOI: 10.18653/v1/2020.acl-main.485 106

Piotr Bojanowski, Edouard Grave, Armand Joulin, and Tomas Mikolov. Enriching word vectors with subword information. *Transactions of the Association of Computational Linguistics*, 5(1):135–146, 2017. DOI: 10.1162/tacl_a_00051 31

Kurt Bollacker, Colin Evans, Praveen Paritosh, Tim Sturge, and Jamie Taylor. Freebase: A collaboratively created graph database for structuring human knowledge. In *Proc. of the ACM SIGMOD International Conference on Management of Data*, pages 1247–1250, 2008. DOI: 10.1145/1376616.1376746 23

Danushka Bollegala, Mohammed Alsuhaibani, Takanori Maehara, and Ken-ichi Kawarabayashi. Joint word representation learning using a corpus and a semantic lexicon. In *Proc. of the AAAI Conference on Artificial Intelligence*, pages 2690–2696, 2016. 33

Tolga Bolukbasi, Kai-Wei Chang, James Zou, Venkatesh Saligrama, and Adam Kalai. Man is to computer programmer as woman is to homemaker? debiasing word embeddings. In *Proc. of the 30th International Conference on Neural Information Processing Systems, NIPS'16*, pages 4356–4364, Curran Associates Inc., 2016. http://dl.acm.org/citation.cfm?id=3157382.3157584 104, 105

Francis Bond and Ryan Foster. Linking and extending an open multilingual WordNet. In *Proc. of the Annual Meeting of the Association of Computational Linguistics (ACL)*, pages 1352–1362, 2013. 23

Antoine Bordes, Nicolas Usunier, Alberto Garcia-Duran, Jason Weston, and Oksana Yakhnenko. Translating embeddings for modeling multi-relational data. In *Advances in Neural Information Processing Systems*, pages 2787–2795, 2013. 49, 50

Shikha Bordia and Samuel R. Bowman. Identifying and reducing gender bias in word-level language models. In *Proc. of the Conference of the North American Chapter of the Association for Computational Linguistics: Student Research Workshop*, pages 7–15, Association for Computational Linguistics, Minneapolis, MN, June 2019. https://www.aclweb.org/anthology/N19-3002 DOI: 10.18653/v1/n19-3002 104

Lars Borin, Markus Forsberg, and Lennart Lönngren. Saldo: A touch of yin to WordNet's yang. *Language Resources and Evaluation*, 47(4):1191–1211, 2013. DOI: 10.1007/s10579-013-9233-4 65

Jan A. Botha and Phil Blunsom. Compositional morphology for word representations and language modelling. In *Proc. of the International Conference on Machine Learning (ICML)*, pages 1899–1907, Beijing, China, 2014. 31

Zied Bouraoui, Shoaib Jameel, and Steven Schockaert. Relation induction in word embeddings revisited. In *Proc. of the International Conference on Computational Linguistics (COLING)*, pages 1627–1637, 2018. 51

Samuel R. Bowman, Gabor Angeli, Christopher Potts, and Christopher D. Manning. A large annotated corpus for learning natural language inference. In *Proc. of the Conference on Empirical Methods in Natural Language Processing*, pages 632–642, Association for Computational Linguistics, Lisbon, Portugal, September 2015. https://www.aclweb.org/anthology/D15-1075 DOI: 10.18653/v1/d15-1075 100

Ulrik Brandes, Daniel Delling, Marco Gaertler, Robert Gorke, Martin Hoefer, Zoran Nikoloski, and Dorothea Wagner. On modularity clustering. *IEEE Transactions on Knowledge and Data Engineering*, 20(2):172–188, February 2008. DOI: 10.1109/tkde.2007.190689 42

Cristian Bucila, Rich Caruana, and Alexandru Niculescu-Mizil. Model compression. In *Proc. of the International Conference on Knowledge Discovery and Data Mining (KDD)*, pages 535–541, 2006. DOI: 10.1145/1150402.1150464 87

Hongyun Cai, Vincent W. Zheng, and Kevin Chang. A comprehensive survey of graph embedding: Problems, techniques and applications. *IEEE Transactions on Knowledge and Data Engineering*, 2018. DOI: 10.1109/tkde.2018.2807452 50

Aylin Caliskan, Joanna J. Bryson, and Arvind Narayanan. Semantics derived automatically from language corpora contain human-like biases. *Science*, 356(6334):183–186, 2017. https://science.sciencemag.org/content/356/6334/183 DOI: 10.1126/science.aal4230 103

José Camacho-Collados and Roberto Navigli. Find the word that does not belong: A framework for an intrinsic evaluation of word vector representations. In *Proc. of the 1st Workshop on Evaluating Vector-Space Representations for NLP*, pages 43–50, 2016. DOI: 10.18653/v1/w16-2508 38

Jose Camacho-Collados and Mohammad Taher Pilehvar. From word to sense embeddings: A survey on vector representations of meaning. *Journal of Artificial Intelligence Research*, 63:743–788, 2018. DOI: 10.1613/jair.1.11259 xv, 55

José Camacho-Collados, Mohammad Taher Pilehvar, and Roberto Navigli. A framework for the construction of monolingual and cross-lingual word similarity datasets. In *Proc. of the 53rd Annual Meeting of the Association for Computational Linguistics and the 7th International Joint Conference on Natural Language Processing, Short Papers*, pages 1–7, Beijing, China, 2015. DOI: 10.3115/v1/p15-2001 38

José Camacho-Collados, Mohammad Taher Pilehvar, and Roberto Navigli. Nasari: Integrating explicit knowledge and corpus statistics for a multilingual representation of concepts and entities. *Artificial Intelligence*, 240:36–64, 2016. DOI: 10.1016/j.artint.2016.07.005 66, 68

Jose Camacho-Collados, Mohammad Taher Pilehvar, Nigel Collier, and Roberto Navigli. SemEval-2017 Task 2: Multilingual and cross-lingual semantic word similarity. In *Proc. of the 11th International Workshop on Semantic Evaluation (SemEval)*, pages 15–26, 2017. 38

Jose Camacho-Collados, Luis Espinosa-Anke, Shoaib Jameel, and Steven Schockaert. A latent variable model for learning distributional relation vectors. In *Proc. of the International Joint Conferences on Artificial Intelligence (IJCAI)*, 2019. DOI: 10.24963/ijcai.2019/682 52, 54

Shaosheng Cao, Wei Lu, and Qiongkai Xu. GraRep: Learning graph representations with global structural information. In *Proc. of the 24th ACM International on Conference on Information and Knowledge Management, CIKM'15*, pages 891–900, New York, 2015. DOI: 10.1145/2806416.2806512 43

Shaosheng Cao, Wei Lu, and Qiongkai Xu. Deep neural networks for learning graph representations. In *Proc. of the 30th AAAI Conference on Artificial Intelligence, AAAI'16*, pages 1145–1152, AAAI Press, 2016. http://dl.acm.org/citation.cfm?id=3015812.3015982 48

Yixin Cao, Lifu Huang, Heng Ji, Xu Chen, and Juanzi Li. Bridge text and knowledge by learning multi-prototype entity mention embedding. In *Proc. of the 55th Annual Meeting of the Association for Computational Linguistics (Volume 1: Long Papers)*, 1:1623–1633, 2017. DOI: 10.18653/v1/p17-1149 66

Marine Carpuat and Dekai Wu. Improving statistical machine translation using word sense disambiguation. In *Proc. of the Joint Conference on Empirical Methods in Natural Language Processing and Computational Natural Language Learning (EMNLP-CoNLL)*, 2007. 61

Rich Caruana. Multitask learning. *Machine Learning*, 28(1):41–75, 1997. DOI: 10.1016/b978-1-55860-307-3.50012-5 101

Daniel Cer, Yinfei Yang, Sheng-yi Kong, Nan Hua, Nicole Limtiaco, Rhomni St John, Noah Constant, Mario Guajardo-Cespedes, Steve Yuan, Chris Tar, et al. Universal sentence encoder. In *Proc. of the Conference on Empirical Methods in Natural Language Processing (EMNLP)*, 2018. DOI: 10.18653/v1/d18-2029 101

Devendra Singh Chaplot and Ruslan Salakhutdinov. Knowledge-based word sense disambiguation using topic models. In *Proc. of the AAAI Conference on Artificial Intelligence*, 2018. 62

Eugene Charniak. Natural language learning. *ACM Computing Surveys (CSUR)*, 27(3):317–319, 1995. DOI: 10.1145/212094.212108 11

Tao Chen, Ruifeng Xu, Yulan He, and Xuan Wang. Improving distributed representation of word sense via WordNet gloss composition and context clustering. In *Proc. of the 53rd Annual Meeting of the Association for Computational Linguistics and the 7th International Joint Conference on Natural Language Processing, Short Papers*, pages 15–20, Beijing, China, 2015. DOI: 10.3115/v1/p15-2003 63

Xinxiong Chen, Zhiyuan Liu, and Maosong Sun. A unified model for word sense representation and disambiguation. In *Proc. of the Conference on Empirical Methods in Natural Language Processing (EMNLP)*, pages 1025–1035, Doha, Qatar, 2014. DOI: 10.3115/v1/d14-1110 63, 64, 68

Billy Chiu, Anna Korhonen, and Sampo Pyysalo. Intrinsic evaluation of word vectors fails to predict extrinsic performance. In *Proc. of the ACL Workshop on Evaluating Vector Space Representations for NLP*, Berlin, Germany, 2016. DOI: 10.18653/v1/w16-2501 39

Kyunghyun Cho, Bart van Merriënboer, Dzmitry Bahdanau, and Yoshua Bengio. On the properties of neural machine translation: Encoder—decoder approaches. In *Proc. of SSST-8, 8th Workshop on Syntax, Semantics and Structure in Statistical Translation*, pages 103–111, Association for Computational Linguistics, Doha, Qatar, October 2014a. https://www.aclweb.org/anthology/W14-4012 DOI: 10.3115/v1/w14-4012 19

Kyunghyun Cho, Bart van Merriënboer, Caglar Gulcehre, Dzmitry Bahdanau, Fethi Bougares, Holger Schwenk, and Yoshua Bengio. Learning phrase representations using RNN encoder—decoder for statistical machine translation. In *Proc. of the Conference on Empirical Methods in Natural Language Processing (EMNLP)*, pages 1724–1734, Association for Computational Linguistics, Doha, Qatar, October 2014b. https://www.aclweb.org/anthology/D14-1179 DOI: 10.3115/v1/d14-1179 14, 17

Noam Chomsky. *Syntactic Structures*. Mouton & Co., The Hague, 1957. DOI: 10.1515/9783112316009 10

Kenneth Ward Church and Patrick Hanks. Word association norms, mutual information, and lexicography. *Computational Linguistics*, 16(1):22–29, 1990. DOI: 10.3115/981623.981633 27

Kevin Clark, Urvashi Khandelwal, Omer Levy, and Christopher D. Manning. What does BERT look at? An analysis of BERT's attention. In *Proc. of the ACL Workshop BlackboxNLP: Analyzing and Interpreting Neural Networks for NLP*, pages 276–286, Association for Computational Linguistics, Florence, Italy, August 2019. https://www.aclweb.org/anthology/W19-4828 DOI: 10.18653/v1/w19-4828 89, 90

Anne Cocos, Marianna Apidianaki, and Chris Callison-Burch. Comparing constraints for taxonomic organization. In *Proc. of the Conference of the North American Chapter of the Association for*

Computational Linguistics: Human Language Technologies, Volume 1 (Long Papers), pages 323–333, 2018. DOI: 10.18653/v1/n18-1030 51

B. Coecke, M. Sadrzadeh, and S. Clark. Mathematical foundations for a compositional distributed model of meaning. *Lambek Festschirft, Linguistic Analysis*, 36, 2010. 98

Ronan Collobert and Jason Weston. A unified architecture for natural language processing: Deep neural networks with multitask learning. In *Proc. of the International Conference on Machine Learning (ICML)*, pages 160–167, 2008. DOI: 10.1145/1390156.1390177 29, 101

Ronan Collobert, Jason Weston, Léon Bottou, Michael Karlen, Koray Kavukcuoglu, and Pavel Kuksa. Natural language processing (almost) from scratch. *Journal of Machine Learning Research*, 12:2493–2537, November 2011. 11, 29, 40, 77

Alexis Conneau and Douwe Kiela. SentEval: An Evaluation Toolkit for Universal Sentence Representations. In *Proc. of the 11th International Conference on Language Resources and Evaluation (LREC)*, European Language Resources Association (ELRA), Miyazaki, Japan, 2018. 102

Alexis Conneau and Guillaume Lample. Cross-lingual language model pretraining. In H. Wallach, H. Larochelle, A. Beygelzimer, F. d'Alché-Buc, E. Fox, and R. Garnett, Eds., *Advances in Neural Information Processing Systems 32*, pages 7059–7069. Curran Associates, Inc., 2019. http://papers.nips.cc/paper/8928-cross-lingual-language-model-pretraining.pdf 93

Alexis Conneau, Douwe Kiela, Holger Schwenk, Loïc Barrault, and Antoine Bordes. Supervised learning of universal sentence representations from natural language inference data. In *Proc. of the Conference on Empirical Methods in Natural Language Processing*, pages 670–680, Association for Computational Linguistics, Copenhagen, Denmark, September 2017. https://www.aclweb.org/anthology/D17-1070 DOI: 10.18653/v1/d17-1070 100

Alexis Conneau, German Kruszewski, Guillaume Lample, Loïc Barrault, and Marco Baroni. What you can cram into a single $&!#* vector: Probing sentence embeddings for linguistic properties. In *Proc. of the 56th Annual Meeting of the Association for Computational Linguistics (Volume 1: Long Papers)*, pages 2126–2136, Melbourne, Australia, July 2018a. https://www.aclweb.org/anthology/P18-1198 DOI: 10.18653/v1/p18-1198 102

Alexis Conneau, Guillaume Lample, Marc'Aurelio Ranzato, Ludovic Denoyer, and Hervé Jégou. Word translation without parallel data. In *Proc. of the International Conference on Learning Representations (ICLR)*, 2018b. 31, 36

Mary E. Curtis. Vocabulary testing and vocabulary instruction. *The Nature of Vocabulary Acquisition*, pages 37–51, 1987. 59

Ido Dagan, Oren Glickman, and Bernardo Magnini. The pascal recognising textual entailment challenge. In *Machine Learning Challenges Workshop*, pages 177–190. Springer, 2005. DOI: 10.1007/11736790_9 100

Zihang Dai, Zhilin Yang, Yiming Yang, Jaime Carbonell, Quoc Le, and Ruslan Salakhutdinov. Transformer-XL: Attentive language models beyond a fixed-length context. In *Proc. of the 57th Annual Meeting of the Association for Computational Linguistics*, pages 2978–2988, Florence, Italy, July 2019. https://www.aclweb.org/anthology/P19-1285 DOI: 10.18653/v1/p19-1285 85

Scott C. Deerwester, Susan T. Dumais, Thomas K. Landauer, George W. Furnas, and Richard A. Harshman. Indexing by latent semantic analysis. *Journal of American Society for Information Science*, 41(6):391–407, 1990. DOI: 10.1002/(sici)1097-4571(199009)41:6<391::aid-asi1>3.0.co;2-9 26

Arthur P. Dempster, Nan M. Laird, and Donald B. Rubin. Maximum likelihood from incomplete data via the EM algorithm. *Journal of the Royal Statistical Society. Series B (Methodological)*, pages 1–38, 1977. DOI: 10.1111/j.2517-6161.1977.tb01600.x 57

Jacob Devlin, Ming-Wei Chang, Kenton Lee, and Kristina Toutanova. Bert: Pre-training of deep bidirectional transformers for language understanding. In *Proc. of the Conference of the North American Chapter of the Association for Computational Linguistics: Human Language Technologies, Volume 1 (Long and Short Papers)*, pages 4171–4186, 2019. 82, 83

Claire Donnat, Marinka Zitnik, David Hallac, and Jure Leskovec. Learning structural node embeddings via diffusion wavelets. In *Proc. of the 24th ACM SIGKDD International Conference on Knowledge Discovery and Data Mining, KDD'18*, pages 1320–1329, New York, 2018. DOI: 10.1145/3219819.3220025 45

Cícero Nogueira Dos Santos and Bianca Zadrozny. Learning character-level representations for part-of-speech tagging. In *Proc. of the 31st International Conference on International Conference on Machine Learning*, pages II–1818–II–1826, 2014. 32

Yerai Doval, Jose Camacho-Collados, Luis Espinosa-Anke, and Steven Schockaert. Improving cross-lingual word embeddings by meeting in the middle. In *Proc. of the Conference on Empirical Methods in Natural Language Processing*, pages 294–304, 2018. DOI: 10.18653/v1/d18-1027 33, 36

Yerai Doval, Jose Camacho-Collados, Luis Espinosa-Anke, and Steven Schockaert. On the robustness of unsupervised and semi-supervised cross-lingual word embedding learning. In *Proc. of the International Conference on Language Resources and Evaluation (LREC)*, 2020. 36

Haim Dubossarsky, Eitan Grossman, and Daphna Weinshall. Coming to your senses: On controls and evaluation sets in polysemy research. In *Proc. of the Conference on Empirical*

Methods in Natural Language Processing, pages 1732–1740, Brussels, Belgium, 2018. DOI: 10.18653/v1/d18-1200 67

Helge Dyvik. Translations as semantic mirrors: From parallel corpus to WordNet. In *Advances in Corpus Linguistics*, pages 309–326. Brill Rodopi, 2004. DOI: 10.1163/9789004333710_019 61

Takuma Ebisu and Ryutaro Ichise. Toruse: Knowledge graph embedding on a lie group. In *Proc. of the AAAI Conference on Artificial Intelligence*, 2018. 50

Katrin Erk. A simple, similarity-based model for selectional preferences. In *Proc. of the Annual Meeting of the Association for Computational Linguistics*, Prague, Czech Republic, 2007. 7

Katrin Erk and Sebastian Padó. A structured vector space model for word meaning in context. In *Proc. of the Conference on Empirical Methods in Natural Language Processing*, pages 897–906, 2008. DOI: 10.3115/1613715.1613831 56

Katrin Erk, Diana McCarthy, and Nicholas Gaylord. Investigations on word senses and word usages. In *Proc. of the Joint Conference of the 47th Annual Meeting of the ACL and the 4th International Joint Conference on Natural Language Processing of the AFNLP*, pages 10–18, Association for Computational Linguistics, 2009. DOI: 10.3115/1687878.1687882 67

Katrin Erk, Diana McCarthy, and Nicholas Gaylord. Measuring word meaning in context. *Computational Linguistics*, 39(3):511–554, 2013. DOI: 10.1162/coli_a_00142 59, 95

Yotam Eshel, Noam Cohen, Kira Radinsky, Shaul Markovitch, Ikuya Yamada, and Omer Levy. Named entity disambiguation for noisy text. In *Proc. of the 21st Conference on Computational Natural Language Learning (CoNLL)*, pages 58–68, 2017. DOI: 10.18653/v1/k17-1008 66

Luis Espinosa-Anke and Steven Schockaert. SeVeN: Augmenting word embeddings with unsupervised relation vectors. In *Proc. of the International Conference on Computational Linguistics (COLING)*, pages 2653–2665, 2018. 52, 54

Luis Espinosa-Anke, Jose Camacho-Collados, Claudio Delli Bovi, and Horacio Saggion. Supervised distributional hypernym discovery via domain adaptation. In *Proc. of the Conference on Empirical Methods in Natural Language Processing (EMNLP)*, pages 424–435, 2016. DOI: 10.18653/v1/d16-1041 51

Kawin Ethayarajh. How contextual are contextualized word representations? comparing the geometry of BERT, ELMo, and GPT-2 embeddings. In *Proc. of the Conference on Empirical Methods in Natural Language Processing and the 9th International Joint Conference on Natural Language Processing (EMNLP-IJCNLP)*, pages 55–65, Association for Computational Linguistics, Hong Kong, China, November 2019. https://www.aclweb.org/anthology/D19-1006 DOI: 10.18653/v1/d19-1006 94

Allyson Ettinger. What BERT is not: Lessons from a new suite of psycholinguistic diagnostics for language models. *Transactions of the Association for Computational Linguistics*, 8:34–48, 2020. DOI: 10.1162/tacl_a_00298 90, 110

Allyson Ettinger, Philip Resnik, and Marine Carpuat. Retrofitting sense-specific word vectors using parallel text. In *Proc. of the Conference of the North American Chapter of the Association for Computational Linguistics: Human Language Technologies (HLT-NAACL)*, pages 1378–1383, San Diego, CA, June 2016. DOI: 10.18653/v1/n16-1163 61

Wei Fang, Jianwen Zhang, Dilin Wang, Zheng Chen, and Ming Li. Entity disambiguation by knowledge and text jointly embedding. In *Proc. of the Conference on Natural Language Learning (CoNLL)*, pages 260–269, 2016. DOI: 10.18653/v1/k16-1026 66

Manaal Faruqui and Chris Dyer. Improving vector space word representations using multilingual correlation. In *Proc. of the 14th Conference of the European Chapter of the Association for Computational Linguistics*, pages 462–471, 2014. DOI: 10.3115/v1/e14-1049 35

Manaal Faruqui, Jesse Dodge, Sujay K. Jauhar, Chris Dyer, Eduard Hovy, and Noah A. Smith. Retrofitting word vectors to semantic lexicons. In *Proc. of the Conference of the North American Chapter of the Association for Computational Linguistics*, pages 1606–1615, 2015. DOI: 10.3115/v1/n15-1184 32, 64

Manaal Faruqui, Yulia Tsvetkov, Pushpendre Rastogi, and Chris Dyer. Problems with evaluation of word embeddings using word similarity tasks. In *Proc. of the 1st Workshop on Evaluating Vector-Space Representations for NLP*, pages 30–35, Association for Computational Linguistics, 2016. DOI: 10.18653/v1/w16-2506 38

Gertraud Fenk-Oczlon, August Fenk, and Pamela Faber. Frequency effects on the emergence of polysemy and homophony. *International Journal of Information Technologies and Knowledge*, 4(2):103–109, 2010. 59

Lev Finkelstein, Gabrilovich Evgeniy, Matias Yossi, Rivlin Ehud, Solan Zach, Wolfman Gadi, and Ruppin Eytan. Placing search in context: The concept revisited. *ACM Transactions on Information Systems*, 20(1):116–131, 2002. DOI: 10.1145/371920.372094 37

John Rupert Firth. *A Synopsis of Linguistic Theory, 1930–1955*. Studies in Linguistic Analysis, Blackwell, Oxford, 1957. 8, 25

Evgeniy Gabrilovich and Shaul Markovitch. Computing semantic relatedness using Wikipedia-based explicit semantic analysis. In *Proc. of the International Joint Conferences on Artificial Intelligence (IJCAI)*, pages 1606–1611, Hyderabad, India, 2007. 58

Anna Gladkova, Alexsandr Drozd, and Satoshi Matsuoka. Analogy-based detection of morphological and semantic relations with word embeddings: what works and what doesn't. In

Proc. of the Student Research Workshop at NAACL, pages 8–15, 2016. DOI: 10.18653/v1/n16-2002 38

William A. Gale, Kenneth Church, and David Yarowsky. A method for disambiguating word senses in a corpus. *Computers and the Humanities*, 26:415–439, 1992. DOI: 10.1007/bf00136984 57, 62

Juri Ganitkevitch, Benjamin Van Durme, and Chris Callison-Burch. PPDB: The paraphrase database. In *Proc. of the Conference of the North American Chapter of the Association for Computational Linguistics: Human Language Technologies (HLT-NAACL)*, pages 758–764, 2013. 24, 32

Hongchang Gao and Heng Huang. Deep attributed network embedding. In *Proc. of the 27th International Joint Conference on Artificial Intelligence, IJCAI-18*, pages 3364–3370. International Joint Conferences on Artificial Intelligence Organization, July 2018. DOI: 10.24963/ijcai.2018/467 46

Peter Gärdenfors. *Conceptual Spaces: The Geometry of Thought*. MIT Press, 2004. DOI: 10.7551/mitpress/2076.001.0001 6

Felix A. Gers, Nicol N. Schraudolph, and Jürgen Schmidhuber. Learning precise timing with LSTM recurrent networks. *Journal of Machine Learning Research*, 3(null):115–143, March 2003. DOI: 10.1162/153244303768966139 17

Josu Goikoetxea, Aitor Soroa, and Eneko Agirre. Random walks and neural network language models on knowledge bases. In *Proc. of the Conference of the North American Chapter of the Association for Computational Linguistics (NAACL)*, pages 1434–1439, Denver, CO, 2015. DOI: 10.3115/v1/n15-1165 33

Josu Goikoetxea, Aitor Soroa, and Eneko Agirre. Bilingual embeddings with random walks over multilingual wordnets. *Knowledge-Based Systems*, 2018. DOI: 10.1016/j.knosys.2018.03.017 33

Yoav Goldberg. Neural network methods for natural language processing. *Synthesis Lectures on Human Language Technologies*, 10(1):1–309, 2017. DOI: 10.2200/s00762ed1v01y201703hlt037 11, 40

Yoav Goldberg. Assessing BERT's syntactic abilities. *CoRR*, 2019. http://arxiv.org/abs/1901.05287 10, 77, 90

Hila Gonen and Yoav Goldberg. Lipstick on a pig: Debiasing methods cover up systematic gender biases in word embeddings but do not remove them. In *Proc. of the Conference of the North American Chapter of the Association for Computational Linguistics: Human Language Technologies, Volume 1 (Long and Short Papers)*, pages 609–614, Minneapolis, MN, June 2019. https://www.aclweb.org/anthology/N19-1061 DOI: 10.1109/TNNLS.2016.2582924 106

Ian Goodfellow, Jean Pouget-Abadie, Mehdi Mirza, Bing Xu, David Warde-Farley, Sherjil Ozair, Aaron Courville, and Yoshua Bengio. Generative adversarial nets. In *Advances in Neural Information Processing Systems*, pages 2672–2680, 2014. 36, 106

Palash Goyal and Emilio Ferrara. Graph embedding techniques, applications, and performance: A survey. *Knowledge-Based Systems*, 151:78–94, 2018. DOI: 10.1016/j.knosys.2018.03.022 54

Roger Granada, Cassia Trojahn, and Renata Vieira. Comparing semantic relatedness between word pairs in Portuguese using Wikipedia. In *Computational Processing of the Portuguese Language*, pages 170–175, 2014. DOI: 10.1007/978-3-319-09761-9_17 38

Alex Graves. Generating sequences with recurrent neural networks. *CoRR*, 2013. 32

Derek Greene and Pádraig Cunningham. Practical solutions to the problem of diagonal dominance in kernel document clustering. In *Proc. of the 23rd International Conference on Machine Learning*, pages 377–384, ACM, 2006. DOI: 10.1145/1143844.1143892 102

Edward Grefenstette, Mehrnoosh Sadrzadeh, Stephen Clark, Bob Coecke, and Stephen Pulman. Concrete sentence spaces for compositional distributional models of meaning. In *Proc. of the 9th International Conference on Computational Semantics (IWCS)*, 2011. https://www.aclweb.org/anthology/W11-0114 DOI: 10.1007/978-94-007-7284-7_5 98

K. Greff, R. K. Srivastava, J. Koutník, B. R. Steunebrink, and J. Schmidhuber. LSTM: A search space odyssey. *IEEE Transactions on Neural Networks and Learning Systems*, 28(10):2222–2232, October 2017. DOI: 10.1109/tnnls.2016.2582924 17

Aditya Grover and Jure Leskovec. Node2Vec: Scalable feature learning for networks. In *Proc. of the 22nd ACM SIGKDD International Conference on Knowledge Discovery and Data Mining, KDD'16*, pages 855–864, New York, 2016. DOI: 10.1145/2939672.2939754 44

Kristina Gulordava, Piotr Bojanowski, Edouard Grave, Tal Linzen, and Marco Baroni. Colorless green recurrent networks dream hierarchically. In *Proc. of the Conference of the North American Chapter of the Association for Computational Linguistics: Human Language Technologies, Volume 1 (Long Papers)*, pages 1195–1205, New Orleans, LA, June 2018. https://www.aclweb.org/anthology/N18-1108 DOI: 10.18653/v1/n18-1108 89

Jiang Guo, Wanxiang Che, Haifeng Wang, and Ting Liu. Learning sense-specific word embeddings by exploiting bilingual resources. In *Proc. of the International Conference on Computational Linguistics (COLING)*, pages 497–507, 2014. 61

Iryna Gurevych. Using the structure of a conceptual network in computing semantic relatedness. In *Natural Language Processing, IJCNLP*, pages 767–778, Springer, 2005. DOI: 10.1007/11562214_67 38

Will Hamilton, Zhitao Ying, and Jure Leskovec. Inductive representation learning on large graphs. In I. Guyon, U. V. Luxburg, S. Bengio, H. Wallach, R. Fergus, S. Vishwanathan, and R. Garnett, Eds., *Advances in Neural Information Processing Systems 30*, pages 1024–1034, Curran Associates, Inc., 2017a. http://papers.nips.cc/paper/6703-inductive-representation-learning-on-large-graphs.pdf 48, 49

William L. Hamilton, Rex Ying, and Jure Leskovec. Inductive representation learning on large graphs. In *Proc. of the 31st International Conference on Neural Information Processing Systems*, *NIPS'17*, pages 1025–1035, Curran Associates Inc., 2017b. 49

Donna Harman. The history of IDF and its influences on IR and other fields. In *Charting a New Course: Natural Language Processing and Information Retrieval*, pages 69–79, Springer, 2005. DOI: 10.1007/1-4020-3467-9_5 27

Zellig Harris. Distributional structure. *Word*, 10:146–162, 1954. DOI: 10.1080/00437956.1954.11659520 8, 12, 27

Samer Hassan and Rada Mihalcea. Semantic relatedness using salient semantic analysis. In *Proc. of the AAAI Conference on Artificial Intelligence*, page 884–889, 2011. 38

Taher H. Haveliwala. Topic-sensitive PageRank. In *Proc. of the 11th International Conference on World Wide Web*, pages 517–526, Hawaii, 2002. DOI: 10.1145/511446.511513 33, 64

Xiaofei He and Partha Niyogi. Locality preserving projections. In S. Thrun, L. K. Saul, and B. Schölkopf, Eds., *Advances in Neural Information Processing Systems 16*, pages 153–160, MIT Press, 2004. http://papers.nips.cc/paper/2359-locality-preserving-projections.pdf 43

Marti A. Hearst. Automatic acquisition of hyponyms from large text corpora. In *Proc. of the International Conference on Computational Linguistics (COLING)*, pages 539–545, 1992. DOI: 10.3115/992133.992154 51

Mark Heimann, Haoming Shen, Tara Safavi, and Danai Koutra. Regal: Representation learning-based graph alignment. In *Proc. of the 27th ACM International Conference on Information and Knowledge Management, CIKM'18*, pages 117–126, New York, 2018. DOI: 10.1145/3269206.3271788 45

I. Herman, G. Melancon, and M. S. Marshall. Graph visualization and navigation in information visualization: A survey. *IEEE Transactions on Visualization and Computer Graphics*, 6(1):24–43, 2000. DOI: 10.1109/2945.841119 54

Karl Moritz Hermann and Phil Blunsom. Multilingual distributed representations without word alignment. In *Proc. of the International Conference on Learning Representations (ICLR)*, 2014. 34

Antoni Hernández-Fernández, Bernardino Casas, Ramon Ferrer-i Cancho, and Jaume Baix-eries. Testing the robustness of laws of polysemy and brevity versus frequency. In *International Conference on Statistical Language and Speech Processing*, pages 19–29, Springer, 2016. DOI: 10.1007/978-3-319-45925-7_2 59

William Hersh, Chris Buckley, T.J. Leone, and David Hickam. Ohsumed: An interactive retrieval evaluation and new large test collection for research. In *Proc. of the International ACM SIGIR Conference on Research and Development in Information Retrieval*, pages 192–201, Springer, 1994. DOI: 10.1007/978-1-4471-2099-5_20 102

John Hewitt and Christopher D. Manning. A structural probe for finding syntax in word rep-resentations. In *Proc. of the Conference of the North American Chapter of the Association for Computational Linguistics: Human Language Technologies, Volume 1 (Long and Short Papers)*, pages 4129–4138, Minneapolis, MN, June 2019. https://www.aclweb.org/anthology/N19-1419 DOI: 10.18653/v1/N19-1419 77, 90, 91, 110

Felix Hill, Roi Reichart, and Anna Korhonen. Simlex-999: Evaluating semantic models with (genuine) similarity estimation. *Computational Linguistics*, 2015. DOI: 10.1162/coli_a_00237 37, 39

Geoffrey E. Hinton, Oriol Vinyals, and Jeffrey Dean. Distilling the knowledge in a neural network. In *Proc. of the NIPS 2014 Deep Learning Workshop*, 2015. 87

Yedid Hoshen and Lior Wolf. Non-adversarial unsupervised word translation. In *Proc. of Empirical Methods in Natural Language Processing (EMNLP)*, Brussels, Belgium, 2018. https://www.aclweb.org/anthology/D18-1043 DOI: 10.18653/v1/d18-1043 37

Dirk Hovy and Shannon L. Spruit. The social impact of natural language processing. In *Proc. of the 54th Annual Meeting of the Association for Computational Linguistics (Volume 2: Short Papers)*, pages 591–598, Berlin, Germany, August 2016. https://www.aclweb.org/anthology/P16-2096 DOI: 10.18653/v1/p16-2096 104

Jeremy Howard and Sebastian Ruder. Universal language model fine-tuning for text classi-fication. In *Proc. of the 56th Annual Meeting of the Association for Computational Linguistics (Volume 1: Long Papers)*, pages 328–339, Melbourne, Australia, 2018. https://www.aclweb.org/anthology/P18-1031 DOI: 10.18653/v1/p18-1031 88

Eric H. Huang, Richard Socher, Christopher D. Manning, and Andrew Y. Ng. Improving word representations via global context and multiple word prototypes. In *Proc. of the Annual Meeting of the Association for Computational Linguistics*, pages 873–882, Jeju Island, Korea, 2012. 58, 59, 67

Thad Hughes and Daniel Ramage. Lexical semantic relatedness with random graph walks. In *Proc. of Empirical Methods in Natural Language Processing, CoNLL*, pages 581–589, 2007. 44

Ignacio Iacobacci, Mohammad Taher Pilehvar, and Roberto Navigli.   Sensembed: Learning sense embeddings for word and relational similarity.   In *Proc. of the Annual Meeting
of the Association for Computational Linguistics*, pages 95–105, Beijing, China, 2015. DOI:
10.3115/v1/p15-1010 64

Ignacio Iacobacci, Mohammad Taher Pilehvar, and Roberto Navigli.   Embeddings for word
sense disambiguation: An evaluation study. In *Proc. of the Annual Meeting of the Association for
Computational Linguistics*, pages 897–907, Berlin, Germany, 2016. DOI: 10.18653/v1/p16-
1085 62

N. Ide, T. Erjavec, and D. Tufis. Sense discrimination with parallel corpora. In *Proc. of ACL-
02 Workshop on WSD: Recent Successes and Future Directions*, pages 54–60, Philadelphia, 2002.
DOI: 10.3115/1118675.1118683 61

Shoaib Jameel, Zied Bouraoui, and Steven Schockaert. Unsupervised learning of distributional
relation vectors. In *Proc. of the Annual Meeting of the Association of Computational Linguistics
(ACL)*, 2018. DOI: 10.18653/v1/p18-1003 51

Mario Jarmasz and Stan Szpakowicz. Roget's thesaurus and semantic similarity. In *Proc. of
Recent Advances in Natural Language Processing*, pages 212–219, Borovets, Bulgaria, 2003.
DOI: 10.1075/cilt.260.12jar 38

Sujay Kumar Jauhar, Chris Dyer, and Eduard Hovy. Ontologically grounded multi-sense rep-
resentation learning for semantic vector space models. In *Proc. of the Conference of the North
American Chapter of the Association for Computational Linguistics*, pages 683–693, Denver, CO,
May–June 2015. DOI: 10.3115/v1/n15-1070 61, 64

Ganesh Jawahar, Benoît Sagot, and Djamé Seddah. What does BERT learn about the structure
of language? In *Proc. of the 57th Annual Meeting of the Association for Computational Linguistics*,
pages 3651–3657, Florence, Italy, July 2019. https://www.aclweb.org/anthology/P19-1356
DOI: 10.18653/v1/p19-1356 10, 91, 92, 110

Guoliang Ji, Shizhu He, Liheng Xu, Kang Liu, and Jun Zhao. Knowledge graph embedding
via dynamic mapping matrix. In *Proc. of the 53rd Annual Meeting of the Association for Computational Linguistics and the 7th International Joint Conference on Natural Language Processing
(Volume 1: Long Papers)*, 1:687–696, 2015. DOI: 10.3115/v1/p15-1067 50

Richard Johansson and Luis Nieto Piña. Embedding a semantic network in a word space.
In *Proc. of the Conference of the North American Chapter of the Association for Computational
Linguistics*, pages 1428–1433, Denver, CO, 2015. DOI: 10.3115/v1/n15-1164 64

I. T. Jolliffe. *Principal Component Analysis and Factor Analysis*, pages 115–128. Springer New
York, 1986. DOI: 10.1007/978-1-4757-1904-8_7 53

Karen Spärck Jones. A statistical interpretation of term specificity and its application in retrieval. *Journal of Documentation*, 28:11–21, 1972. 27

Michael P. Jones and James H. Martin. Contextual spelling correction using latent semantic analysis. In *Proc. of the 5th Conference on Applied Natural Language Processing, ANLC'97*, pages 166–173, 1997. DOI: 10.3115/974557.974582 7

Mandar Joshi, Eunsol Choi, Omer Levy, Daniel S. Weld, and Luke Zettlemoyer. Pair2vec: Compositional word-pair embeddings for cross-sentence inference. In *Proc. of the Conference of the North American Chapter of the Association for Computational Linguistics (NAACL)*, pages 3597–3608, 2019. DOI: 10.18653/v1/n19-1362 52, 53, 54

Colette Joubarne and Diana Inkpen. Comparison of semantic similarity for different languages using the Google n-gram corpus and second-order co-occurrence measures. In *Advances in Artificial Intelligence*, pages 216–221, 2011. DOI: 10.1007/978-3-642-21043-3_26 38

Jukka Jouhki, Epp Lauk, Maija Penttinen, Niina Sormanen, and Turo Uskali. Facebook's emotional contagion experiment as a challenge to research ethics. *Media and Communication*, 4(4):75–85, 2016. https://www.cogitatiopress.com/mediaandcommunication/article/view/579 DOI: 10.17645/mac.v4i4.579 103

David Jurgens and Ioannis Klapaftis. Semeval-2013 task 13: Word sense induction for graded and non-graded senses. In *2nd Joint Conference on Lexical and Computational Semantics (* SEM), Volume 2: Proceedings of the 7th International Workshop on Semantic Evaluation (SemEval)*, pages 290–299, 2013. 59

Nal Kalchbrenner, Lasse Espeholt, Karen Simonyan, Aäron van den Oord, Alex Graves, and Koray Kavukcuoglu. Neural machine translation in linear time. *CoRR*, 2016. http://arxiv.org/abs/1610.10099 32

Stephen Mayhew Dan Roth Karthikeyan K. and Zihan Wang. Cross-lingual ability of multilingual bert: An empirical study. In *International Conference on Learning Representations*, 2020. https://openreview.net/forum?id=HJeT3yrtDr 93

Dimitri Kartsaklis, Mohammad Taher Pilehvar, and Nigel Collier. Mapping text to knowledge graph entities using multi-sense LSTMs. In *Proc. of the Conference on Empirical Methods in Natural Language Processing*, pages 1959–1970, Brussels, Belgium, 2018. https://www.aclweb.org/anthology/D18-1221 DOI: 10.18653/v1/d18-1221 46

Mikhail Khodak, Andrej Risteski, Christiane Fellbaum, and Sanjeev Arora. Automated Word-Net construction using word embeddings. In *Proc. of the 1st Workshop on Sense, Concept and Entity Representations and their Applications*, pages 12–23, 2017. DOI: 10.18653/v1/w17-1902 22

Tushar Khot, Peter Clark, Michal Guerquin, Peter Jansen, and Ashish Sabharwal. Qasc: A dataset for question answering via sentence composition. In *Proc. of the AAAI Conference on Artificial Intelligence*, pages 8082–8090, 2020. DOI: 10.1609/aaai.v34i05.6319 109

Douwe Kiela, Felix Hill, and Stephen Clark. Specializing word embeddings for similarity or relatedness. In *Proc. of the Conference on Empirical Methods in Natural Language Processing*, pages 2044–2048, 2015. DOI: 10.18653/v1/d15-1242 33

Douwe Kiela, Alexis Conneau, Allan Jabri, and Maximilian Nickel. Learning visually grounded sentence representations. In *Proc. of the Conference of the North American Chapter of the Association for Computational Linguistics: Human Language Technologies, Volume 1 (Long Papers)*, pages 408–418, 2018. DOI: 10.18653/v1/n18-1038 100

Adam Kilgarriff. "I don't believe in word senses". *Computers and the Humanities*, 31(2):91–113, 1997. DOI: 10.1515/9783110895698.361 23, 59, 66

Yoon Kim, Yacine Jernite, David Sontag, and Alexander M. Rush. Character-aware neural language models. In *Proc. of the 30th AAAI Conference on Artificial Intelligence*, 2016. 32

Thomas N. Kipf and Max Welling. Semi-supervised classification with graph convolutional networks. In *Proc. of International Conference on Learning Representations (ICLR)*, 2017. 42, 49

Svetlana Kiritchenko and Saif Mohammad. Examining gender and race bias in two hundred sentiment analysis systems. In *Proc. of the 7th Joint Conference on Lexical and Computational Semantics*, pages 43–53, Association for Computational Linguistics, New Orleans, LA, June 2018. https://www.aclweb.org/anthology/S18-2005 DOI: 10.18653/v1/s18-2005 104

Ryan Kiros, Yukun Zhu, Ruslan R. Salakhutdinov, Richard Zemel, Raquel Urtasun, Antonio Torralba, and Sanja Fidler. Skip-thought vectors. In *Advances in Neural Information Processing Systems*, pages 3294–3302, 2015. 99

Nikita Kitaev and Dan Klein. Constituency parsing with a self-attentive encoder. In *Proc. of the 56th Annual Meeting of the Association for Computational Linguistics (Volume 1: Long Papers)*, pages 2676–2686, Melbourne, Australia, July 2018. https://www.aclweb.org/anthology/P18-1249 DOI: 10.18653/v1/p18-1249 82

Philipp Koehn. Europarl: A parallel corpus for statistical machine translation. In *Proc. of Machine Translation Summit X*, 2005. 34

Philipp Koehn. *Statistical Machine Translation*. Cambridge University Press, 2009. DOI: 10.1017/cbo9780511815829 10

Olga Kovaleva, Alexey Romanov, Anna Rogers, and Anna Rumshisky. Revealing the dark secrets of BERT. In *Proc. of the Conference on Empirical Methods in Natural Language Processing and the 9th International Joint Conference on Natural Language Processing (EMNLP-IJCNLP)*, pages 4365–4374, Association for Computational Linguistics, Hong Kong, China, November 2019. https://www.aclweb.org/anthology/D19-1445 DOI: 10.18653/v1/d19-1445 89, 90

Adam D. I. Kramer, Jamie E. Guillory, and Jeffrey T. Hancock. Experimental evidence of massive-scale emotional contagion through social networks. *Proc. of the National Academy of Sciences*, 111(24):8788–8790, 2014. https://www.pnas.org/content/111/24/8788 DOI: 10.1073/pnas.1320040111 103

Matt Kusner, Yu Sun, Nicholas Kolkin, and Kilian Weinberger. From word embeddings to document distances. In *International Conference on Machine Learning*, pages 957–966, 2015. 101

Alberto H. F. Laender, Berthier A. Ribeiro-Neto, Altigran S. da Silva, and Juliana S. Teixeira. A brief survey of Web data extraction tools. *SIGMOD Record*, 31(2):84–93, 2002. DOI: 10.1145/565117.565137 7

Guillaume Lample and Alexis Conneau. Cross-lingual language model pretraining. In *Advances in Neural Information Processing Systems*, 2019. 85

Zhenzhong Lan, Mingda Chen, Sebastian Goodman, Kevin Gimpel, Piyush Sharma, and Radu Soricut. ALBERT: A lite BERT for self-supervised learning of language representations. *ArXiv Preprint ArXiv:1909.11942*, 2019. 87

Thomas K. Landauer and Susan T. Dumais. A solution to Plato's problem: The latent semantic analysis theory of acquisition, induction, and representation of knowledge. *Psychological Review*, 104(2):211, 1997. DOI: 10.1037/0033-295x.104.2.211 7, 26, 38

Ken Lang. Newsweeder: Learning to filter netnews. In *Proc. of the 12th International Conference on Machine Learning*, pages 331–339, Tahoe City, CA, 1995. DOI: 10.1016/b978-1-55860-377-6.50048-7 102

Stanislas Lauly, Alex Boulanger, and Hugo Larochelle. Learning multilingual word representations using a bag-of-words autoencoder. In *Proc. of the NIPS Workshop on Deep Learning*, pages 1–8, 2014. 34

Angeliki Lazaridou, Marco Marelli, Roberto Zamparelli, and Marco Baroni. Compositionally derived representations of morphologically complex words in distributional semantics. In *Proc. of the Annual Meeting of the Association for Computational Linguistics (ACL)*, pages 1517–1526, Sofia, Bulgaria, 2013. 31

Angeliki Lazaridou, Georgiana Dinu, and Marco Baroni. Hubness and pollution: Delving into cross-space mapping for zero-shot learning. In *Proc. of the 53rd Annual Meeting of the Association for Computational Linguistics and the 7th International Joint Conference on Natural Language Processing (Volume 1: Long Papers)*, pages 270–280, Beijing, China, July 2015. https://www.aclweb.org/anthology/P15-1027 DOI: 10.3115/v1/p15-1027 35, 39

Quoc Le and Tomas Mikolov. Distributed representations of sentences and documents. In *International Conference on Machine Learning*, pages 1188–1196, 2014. 101

Dik L. Lee, Huei Chuang, and Kent Seamons. Document ranking and the vector-space model. *IEEE Software*, 14(2):67–75, 1997. DOI: 10.1109/52.582976 27

Guang-He Lee and Yun-Nung Chen. Muse: Modularizing unsupervised sense embeddings. In *Proc. of the Conference on Empirical Methods in Natural Language Processing (EMNLP)*, Copenhagen, Denmark, 2017. DOI: 10.18653/v1/d17-1034 60

Jason Lee, Kyunghyun Cho, and Thomas Hofmann. Fully character-level neural machine translation without explicit segmentation. *Transactions of the Association for Computational Linguistics*, 5:365–378, 2017. https://www.aclweb.org/anthology/Q17-1026 DOI: 10.1162/tacl_a_00067 32

Ben Lengerich, Andrew Maas, and Christopher Potts. Retrofitting distributional embeddings to knowledge graphs with functional relations. In *Proc. of the 27th International Conference on Computational Linguistics*, pages 2423–2436, Association for Computational Linguistics, Santa Fe, New Mexico, August 2018. https://www.aclweb.org/anthology/C18-1205 33

Michael Lesk. Automatic sense disambiguation using machine readable dictionaries: How to tell a pine cone from an ice cream cone. In *Proc. of the 5th Annual Conference on Systems Documentation*, pages 24–26, Toronto, Ontario, Canada 1986. DOI: 10.1145/318723.318728 62, 63

Hector J. Levesque, Ernest Davis, and Leora Morgenstern. The Winograd schema challenge. In *Proc. of the 13th International Conference on Principles of Knowledge Representation and Reasoning, KR'12*, pages 552–561. AAAI Press, 2012. http://dl.acm.org/citation.cfm?id=3031843.3031909 2, 95, 109

Ira Leviant and Roi Reichart. Separated by an un-common language: Towards judgment language informed vector space modeling. *ArXiv Preprint ArXiv:1508.00106*, 2015. 38

Omer Levy and Yoav Goldberg. Dependency-based word embeddings. In *ACL*, pages 302–308, 2014a. DOI: 10.3115/v1/p14-2050 31

Omer Levy and Yoav Goldberg. Neural word embedding as implicit matrix factorization. In *Advances in Neural Information Processing Systems*, pages 2177–2185, 2014b. 30

Omer Levy, Yoav Goldberg, and Israel Ramat-Gan. Linguistic regularities in sparse and explicit word representations. In *Proc. of the Conference on Natural Language Learning (CoNLL)*, pages 171–180, 2014. DOI: 10.3115/v1/w14-1618 51

Omer Levy, Yoav Goldberg, and Ido Dagan. Improving distributional similarity with lessons learned from word embeddings. *Transactions of the Association for Computational Linguistics*, 3:211–225, 2015. DOI: 10.1162/tacl_a_00134 30

David D. Lewis, Yiming Yang, Tony G. Rose, and Fan Li. Rcv1: A new benchmark collection for text categorization research. *Journal of Machine Learning Research*, 5(Apr):361–397, 2004. 102

Jiwei Li and Dan Jurafsky. Do multi-sense embeddings improve natural language understanding? In *Proc. of the Conference on Empirical Methods in Natural Language Processing (EMNLP)*, pages 683–693, Lisbon, Portugal, 2015. DOI: 10.18653/v1/d15-1200 56, 68, 71

Juzheng Li, Jun Zhu, and Bo Zhang. Discriminative deep random walk for network classification. In *Proc. of the 54th Annual Meeting of the Association for Computational Linguistics (Volume 1: Long Papers)*, pages 1004–1013, Berlin, Germany, August 2016. https://www.aclweb.org/anthology/P16-1095 DOI: 10.18653/v1/p16-1095 46

Peter J. Li, Mohammad Saleh, Etienne Pot, Ben Goodrich, Ryan Sepassi, Lukasz Kaiser, and Noam Shazeer. Generating Wikipedia by summarizing long sequences. In *International Conference on Learning Representations*, 2018. 82

Wei Li and Andrew McCallum. Semi-supervised sequence modeling with syntactic topic models. In *Proc. of the 20th National Conference on Artificial Intelligence, Volume 2*, pages 813–818, AAAI Press, 2005. 77

David Liben-Nowell and Jon Kleinberg. The link prediction problem for social networks. In *Proc. of the 12th International Conference on Information and Knowledge Management, CIKM'03*, pages 556–559, ACM, New York, 2003. DOI: 10.1145/956863.956972 42

Dekang Lin and Patrick Pantel. DIRT—discovery of inference rules from text. In *Proc. of the 7th ACM SIGKDD International Conference on Knowledge Discovery and Data Mining (KDD)*, pages 323–328, San Francisco, 2001. 26

Yankai Lin, Zhiyuan Liu, Maosong Sun, Yang Liu, and Xuan Zhu. Learning entity and relation embeddings for knowledge graph completion. In *Proc. of the AAAI Conference on Artificial Intelligence*, pages 2181–2187, 2015. 50

Yongjie Lin, Yi Chern Tan, and Robert Frank. Open sesame: Getting inside BERT's linguistic knowledge. In *Proc. of the ACL Workshop BlackboxNLP: Analyzing and Interpreting Neural Networks for NLP*, pages 241–253, Association for Computational Linguistics, Florence, Italy,

August 2019. https://www.aclweb.org/anthology/W19-4825 DOI: 10.18653/v1/w19-4825 91

Wang Ling, Chris Dyer, Alan W. Black, Isabel Trancoso, Ramon Fermandez, Silvio Amir, Luis Marujo, and Tiago Luis. Finding function in form: Compositional character models for open vocabulary word representation. In *Proc. of the Conference on Empirical Methods in Natural Language Processing*, pages 1520–1530, 2015. DOI: 10.18653/v1/d15-1176 32

Tal Linzen. Issues in evaluating semantic spaces using word analogies. In *Proc. of the 1st Workshop on Evaluating Vector-Space Representations for NLP*, pages 13–18, 2016. DOI: 10.18653/v1/w16-2503 38, 51

Tal Linzen. How can we accelerate progress towards human-like linguistic generalization? In *Proc. of the 58th Annual Meeting of the Association for Computational Linguistics*, pages 5210–5217, July 2020. https://www.aclweb.org/anthology/2020.acl-main.465 DOI: 10.18653/v1/2020.acl-main.465 109

Tal Linzen, Emmanuel Dupoux, and Yoav Goldberg. Assessing the ability of LSTMs to learn syntax-sensitive dependencies. *Transactions of the Association for Computational Linguistics*, 4:521–535, 2016. https://www.aclweb.org/anthology/Q16-1037 DOI: 10.1162/tacl_a_00115 89, 90

Frederick Liu, Han Lu, and Graham Neubig. Handling homographs in neural machine translation. In *Proc. of the Conference of the North American Chapter of the Association for Computational Linguistics*, New Orleans, LA, 2018. DOI: 10.18653/v1/n18-1121 61

Nelson F. Liu, Matt Gardner, Yonatan Belinkov, Matthew E. Peters, and Noah A. Smith. Linguistic knowledge and transferability of contextual representations. In *Proc. of the Conference of the North American Chapter of the Association for Computational Linguistics: Human Language Technologies*, pages 1073–1094, 2019a. DOI: 10.18653/v1/n19-1112 91

Pengfei Liu, Xipeng Qiu, and Xuanjing Huang. Learning context-sensitive word embeddings with neural tensor skip-gram model. In *Proc. of the 24th International Conference on Artificial Intelligence*, pages 1284–1290, 2015a. 56, 59

Yang Liu, Zhiyuan Liu, Tat-Seng Chua, and Maosong Sun. Topical word embeddings. In *Proc. of the 29th AAAI Conference on Artificial Intelligence*, pages 2418–2424, 2015b. 59, 68

Yinhan Liu, Myle Ott, Naman Goyal, Jingfei Du, Mandar Joshi, Danqi Chen, Omer Levy, Mike Lewis, Luke Zettlemoyer, and Veselin Stoyanov. Roberta: A robustly optimized BERT pretraining approach. *CoRR*, 2019b. http://arxiv.org/abs/1907.11692 84

Lajanugen Logeswaran and Honglak Lee. An efficient framework for learning sentence representations. In *International Conference on Learning Representations*, 2018. https://openreview.net/forum?id=rJvJXZb0W 99

Daniel Loureiro and Alípio Jorge. Language modelling makes sense: Propagating representations through WordNet for full-coverage word sense disambiguation. In *Proc. of the 57th Annual Meeting of the Association for Computational Linguistics*, pages 5682–5691, Florence, Italy, July 2019. https://www.aclweb.org/anthology/P19-1569 DOI: 10.18653/v1/p19-1569 62, 93

Daniel Loureiro, Kiamehr Rezaee, Mohammad Taher Pilehvar, and Jose Camacho-Collados. Language models and word sense disambiguation: An overview and analysis. *ArXiv Preprint ArXiv:2008.11608*, 2020. 63

Ang Lu, Weiran Wang, Mohit Bansal, Kevin Gimpel, and Karen Livescu. Deep multilingual correlation for improved word embeddings. In *Proc. of the Conference of the North American Chapter of the Association for Computational Linguistics: Human Language Technologies*, pages 250–256, Denver, CO, May–June 2015. https://www.aclweb.org/anthology/N15-1028 DOI: 10.3115/v1/n15-1028 35

Kevin Lund and Curt Burgess. Producing high-dimensional semantic spaces from lexical co-occurrence. *Behavior Research Methods, Instruments, and Computers*, 28(2):203–208, 1996. DOI: 10.3758/bf03204766 27

Kevin Lund, Curt Burgess, and Ruth Ann Atchley. Semantic and associative priming in high-dimensional semantic space. In *Proc. of the 17th Annual Conference of the Cognitive Science Society*, pages 660–665, 1995. 7

Fuli Luo, Tianyu Liu, Qiaolin Xia, Baobao Chang, and Zhifang Sui. Incorporating glosses into neural word sense disambiguation. In *Proc. of the 56th Annual Meeting of the Association for Computational Linguistics (Volume 1: Long Papers)*, pages 2473–2482, 2018. DOI: 10.18653/v1/p18-1230 62, 63

Yuanfei Luo, Quan Wang, Bin Wang, and Li Guo. Context-dependent knowledge graph embedding. In *Proc. of the Conference on Empirical Methods in Natural Language Processing*, pages 1656–1661, 2015. DOI: 10.18653/v1/d15-1191 50

Thang Luong, Hieu Pham, and Christopher D. Manning. Effective approaches to attention-based neural machine translation. In *Proc. of the Conference on Empirical Methods in Natural Language Processing*, pages 1412–1421, Association for Computational Linguistics, Lisbon, Portugal, September 2015. https://www.aclweb.org/anthology/D15-1166 DOI: 10.18653/v1/d15-1166 20

Laurens van der Maaten and Geoffrey Hinton. Visualizing data using t-SNE. *Journal of Machine Learning Research*, 9(Nov):2579–2605, 2008. 7, 54

J. C. Mallery. Thinking about foreign policy: Finding an appropriate role for artificial intelligence computers, Ph.D. Thesis, M.I.T. Political Science Department, Cambridge, MA, 1988. 62

Massimiliano Mancini, Jose Camacho-Collados, Ignacio Iacobacci, and Roberto Navigli. Embedding words and senses together via joint knowledge-enhanced training. In *Proc. of the Conference on Natural Language Learning (CoNLL)*, pages 100–111, Vancouver, Canada, 2017. DOI: 10.18653/v1/k17-1012 64, 66

Christopher D. Manning. Computational linguistics and deep learning. *Computational Linguistics*, 41(4):701–707, December 2015. DOI: 10.1162/coli_a_00239 8

Michael F. Mathieu, Junbo Jake Zhao, Junbo Zhao, Aditya Ramesh, Pablo Sprechmann, and Yann LeCun. Disentangling factors of variation in deep representation using adversarial training. In D. D. Lee, M. Sugiyama, U. V. Luxburg, I. Guyon, and R. Garnett, Eds., *Advances in Neural Information Processing Systems 29*, pages 5040–5048, Curran Associates, Inc., 2016. http://papers.nips.cc/paper/6051-disentangling-factors-of-variation-in-deep-representation-using-adversarial-training.pdf 106

Andrew Kachites McCallum, Kamal Nigam, Jason Rennie, and Kristie Seymore. Automating the construction of internet portals with machine learning. *Information Retrieval*, 3(2):127–163, July 2000. DOI: 10.1023/A:1009953814988 46

Bryan McCann, James Bradbury, Caiming Xiong, and Richard Socher. Learned in translation: Contextualized word vectors. In *Advances in Neural Information Processing Systems*, pages 6294–6305, 2017. 79, 80, 100

Diana McCarthy, Marianna Apidianaki, and Katrin Erk. Word sense clustering and clusterability. *Computational Linguistics*, 2016. DOI: 10.1162/coli_a_00247 59

John McCrae, Guadalupe Aguado-de Cea, Paul Buitelaar, Philipp Cimiano, Thierry Declerck, Asunción Gómez-Pérez, Jorge Gracia, Laura Hollink, Elena Montiel-Ponsoda, Dennis Spohr, et al. Interchanging lexical resources on the Semantic Web. *Language Resources and Evaluation*, 46(4):701–719, 2012. DOI: 10.1007/s10579-012-9182-3 24

Oren Melamud, Jacob Goldberger, and Ido Dagan. Context2vec: Learning generic context embedding with bidirectional LSTM. In *Proc. of The 20th SIGNLL Conference on Computational Natural Language Learning*, pages 51–61, Berlin, Germany, 2016. DOI: 10.18653/v1/k16-1006 77

A. Meyerson. Online facility location. In *Proc. of the 42nd IEEE Symposium on Foundations of Computer Science*, pages 426–432, IEEE Computer Society, Washington, DC, 2001. DOI: 10.1109/sfcs.2001.959917 60

Paul Michel, Omer Levy, and Graham Neubig. Are sixteen heads really better than one? In H. Wallach, H. Larochelle, A. Beygelzimer, F. d'Alché-Buc, E. Fox, and R. Garnett, Eds., *Advances in Neural Information Processing Systems 32*, pages 14014–14024. Curran Associates,

Inc., 2019. http://papers.nips.cc/paper/9551-are-sixteen-heads-really-better-than-one.pdf 90

Rada Mihalcea and Andras Csomai. Wikify! Linking documents to encyclopedic knowledge. In *Proc. of the 16th ACM Conference on Information and Knowledge Management*, pages 233–242, Lisbon, Portugal, 2007. DOI: 10.1145/1321440.1321475 62

Tomas Mikolov, Kai Chen, Greg Corrado, and Jeffrey Dean. Efficient estimation of word representations in vector space. *CoRR*, 2013a. 11, 29, 30, 58, 63, 98

Tomas Mikolov, Quoc V. Le, and Ilya Sutskever. Exploiting similarities among languages for machine translation. *ArXiv Preprint ArXiv:1309.4168*, 2013b. 33, 34

Tomas Mikolov, Ilya Sutskever, Kai Chen, Greg S. Corrado, and Jeff Dean. Distributed representations of words and phrases and their compositionality. In *Advances in Neural Information Processing Systems*, pages 3111–3119, 2013c. 8, 38, 52, 77

Tomas Mikolov, Wen-tau Yih, and Geoffrey Zweig. Linguistic regularities in continuous space word representations. In *Proc. of the Conference of the North American Chapter of the Association for Computational Linguistics: Human Language Technologies (HLT-NAACL)*, pages 746–751, 2013d. 29, 51

George A. Miller. WordNet: A lexical database for English. *Communications of the ACM*, 38(11):39–41, 1995. DOI: 10.1145/219717.219748 22

George A. Miller and Walter G. Charles. Contextual correlates of semantic similarity. *Language and Cognitive Processes*, 6(1):1–28, 1991. DOI: 10.1080/01690969108406936 37, 38

George A. Miller, Claudia Leacock, Randee Tengi, and Ross Bunker. A semantic concordance. In *Proc. of the 3rd DARPA Workshop on Human Language Technology*, pages 303–308, Plainsboro, NJ, 1993. DOI: 10.3115/1075671.1075742 39, 59, 62

R. Milo, S. Shen-Orr, S. Itzkovitz, N. Kashtan, D. Chklovskii, and U. Alon. Network motifs: Simple building blocks of complex networks. *Science*, 298(5594):824–827, 2002. https://science.sciencemag.org/content/298/5594/824 DOI: 10.1126/science.298.5594.824 42

Jeff Mitchell and Mirella Lapata. Vector-based models of semantic composition. In *Proc. of the Annual Meeting of the Association for Computational Linguistics*, pages 236–244, Columbus, OH, June 2008. https://www.aclweb.org/anthology/P08-1028 98

Andrea Moro, Alessandro Raganato, and Roberto Navigli. Entity linking meets word sense disambiguation: A unified approach. *Transactions of the Association for Computational Linguistics (TACL)*, 2:231–244, 2014. DOI: 10.1162/tacl_a_00179 62, 64

138 BIBLIOGRAPHY

Nikola Mrksic, Ivan Vulić, Diarmuid Ó Séaghdha, Ira Leviant, Roi Reichart, Milica Gašić, Anna Korhonen, and Steve Young. Semantic specialisation of distributional word vector spaces using monolingual and cross-lingual constraints. *Transactions of the Association for Computational Linguistics (TACL)*, 2017. DOI: 10.1162/tacl_a_00063 33

Brian Murphy, Partha Talukdar, and Tom Mitchell. Learning effective and interpretable semantic models using non-negative sparse embedding. In *Proc. of the International Conference on Computational Linguistics (COLING)*, pages 1933–1950, 2012. 38

Roberto Navigli. Word sense disambiguation: A survey. *ACM Computing Surveys*, 41(2):1–69, 2009. DOI: 10.1145/1459352.1459355 7, 62

Roberto Navigli and Simone Paolo Ponzetto. BabelNet: Building a very large multilingual semantic network. In *Proc. of the 48th Annual Meeting of the Association for Computational Linguistics (ACL)*, pages 216–225, Uppsala, Sweden, 2010. 48

Roberto Navigli and Simone Paolo Ponzetto. BabelNet: The automatic construction, evaluation and application of a wide-coverage multilingual semantic network. *Artificial Intelligence*, 193:217–250, 2012. DOI: 10.1016/j.artint.2012.07.001 24

Steven Neale. A survey on automatically-constructed WordNets and their evaluation: Lexical and word embedding-based approaches. In *Proc. of the 11th International Conference on Language Resources and Evaluation (LREC)*, European Language Resources Association (ELRA), Miyazaki, Japan, May 7–12, 2018. 22

Arvind Neelakantan, Jeevan Shankar, Alexandre Passos, and Andrew McCallum. Efficient non-parametric estimation of multiple embeddings per word in vector space. In *Proc. of Empirical Methods in Natural Language Processing*, pages 1059–1069, Doha, Qatar, 2014. DOI: 10.3115/v1/d14-1113 55, 58, 60, 63

Dai Quoc Nguyen, Dat Quoc Nguyen, Ashutosh Modi, Stefan Thater, and Manfred Pinkal. A mixture model for learning multi-sense word embeddings. In *Proc. of the Joint Conference on Lexical and Computational Semantics (*SEM)*, 2017. DOI: 10.18653/v1/s17-1015 59

Dat Quoc Nguyen. An overview of embedding models of entities and relationships for knowledge base completion. *ArXiv Preprint ArXiv:1703.08098*, 2017. 50

Maximillian Nickel and Douwe Kiela. Poincaré embeddings for learning hierarchical representations. In I. Guyon, U. V. Luxburg, S. Bengio, H. Wallach, R. Fergus, S. Vishwanathan, and R. Garnett, Eds., *Advances in Neural Information Processing Systems 30*, pages 6341–6350, Curran Associates, Inc., 2017. http://papers.nips.cc/paper/7213-poincare-embeddings-for-learning-hierarchical-representations.pdf 47

Elisabeth Niemann and Iryna Gurevych. The people's Web meets linguistic knowledge: Automatic sense alignment of Wikipedia and WordNet. In *Proc. of the 9th International Conference on Computational Semantics*, pages 205–214, 2011. 24

Luis Nieto Piña and Richard Johansson. A simple and efficient method to generate word sense representations. In *Proc. of Recent Advances in Natural Language Processing*, pages 465–472, Hissar, Bulgaria, 2015. 60

Malvina Nissim, Rik van Noord, and Rob van der Goot. Fair is better than sensational: Man is to doctor as woman is to doctor. *Computational Linguistics*, 46(2):487–497, June 2020. https://www.aclweb.org/anthology/2020.cl-2.7 DOI: 10.1162/coli_a_00379 51

Mingdong Ou, Peng Cui, Jian Pei, Ziwei Zhang, and Wenwu Zhu. Asymmetric transitivity preserving graph embedding. In *Proc. of the 22nd ACM SIGKDD International Conference on Knowledge Discovery and Data Mining, KDD'16*, pages 1105–1114, New York, 2016a. DOI: 10.1145/2939672.2939751 43

Mingdong Ou, Peng Cui, Jian Pei, Ziwei Zhang, and Wenwu Zhu. Asymmetric transitivity preserving graph embedding. In *Proc. of the 22nd ACM SIGKDD International Conference on Knowledge Discovery and Data Mining, KDD'16*, pages 1105–1114, 2016b. DOI: 10.1145/2939672.2939751 54

Shirui Pan, Jia Wu, Xingquan Zhu, Chengqi Zhang, and Yang Wang. Tri-party deep network representation. In *Proc. of the 25th International Joint Conference on Artificial Intelligence, IJCAI'16*, pages 1895–1901, AAAI Press, 2016. http://dl.acm.org/citation.cfm?id=3060832.3060886 46

Sinno Jialin Pan and Qiang Yang. A survey on transfer learning. *IEEE Transactions on Knowledge and Data Engineering*, 22(10):1345–1359, October 2010. DOI: 10.1109/tkde.2009.191 79

Alexander Panchenko, Eugen Ruppert, Stefano Faralli, Simone Paolo Ponzetto, and Chris Biemann. Unsupervised does not mean uninterpretable: The case for word sense induction and disambiguation. In *Proc. of the Conference of the European Chapter of the Association for Computational Linguistics*, pages 86–98, 2017. DOI: 10.18653/v1/e17-1009 68

Tommaso Pasini and Roberto Navigli. Two knowledge-based methods for high-performance sense distribution learning. In *Proc. of the AAAI Conference on Artificial Intelligence*, New Orleans, 2018. 59

Ellie Pavlick, Pushpendre Rastogi, Juri Ganitkevitch, Benjamin Van Durme, and Chris Callison-Burch. PPDB 2.0: Better paraphrase ranking, fine-grained entailment relations, word embeddings, and style classification. In *Proc. of the Annual Meeting of the Association for Computational Linguistics*, pages 425–430, Beijing, China, 2015. DOI: 10.3115/v1/p15-2070 24

Karl Pearson. On lines and planes of closest fit to systems of points in space. *The London, Edinburgh, and Dublin Philosophical Magazine and Journal of Science*, 2(11):559–572, 1901. DOI: 10.1080/14786440109462720. 43

Maria Pelevina, Nikolay Arefyev, Chris Biemann, and Alexander Panchenko. Making sense of word embeddings. In *Proc. of the 1st Workshop on Representation Learning for NLP*, pages 174–183, 2016. DOI: 10.18653/v1/w16-1620 58, 68

Hao Peng, Sam Thomson, and Noah A Smith. Deep multitask learning for semantic dependency parsing. In *Proc. of the 55th Annual Meeting of the Association for Computational Linguistics (Volume 1: Long Papers)*, pages 2037–2048, 2017. DOI: 10.18653/v1/p17-1186 101

Xingchao Peng, Zijun Huang, Ximeng Sun, and Kate Saenko. Domain agnostic learning with disentangled representations. In Kamalika Chaudhuri and Ruslan Salakhutdinov, Eds., *Proc. of the 36th International Conference on Machine Learning*, volume 97 of *Proc. of Machine Learning Research*, pages 5102–5112, PMLR, Long Beach, CA, June 09–15, 2019. http://proceedings.mlr.press/v97/peng19b.html 106

Jeffrey Pennington, Richard Socher, and Christopher D. Manning. GloVe: Global vectors for word representation. In *Proc. of the Conference on Empirical Methods in Natural Language Processing (EMNLP)*, pages 1532–1543, 2014. DOI: 10.3115/v1/d14-1162 30

Christian S. Perone, Roberto Silveira, and Thomas S. Paula. Evaluation of sentence embeddings in downstream and linguistic probing tasks. *ArXiv Preprint ArXiv:1806.06259*, 2018. 102

Bryan Perozzi, Rami Al-Rfou, and Steven Skiena. DeepWalk: Online learning of social representations. In *Proc. of the 20th ACM SIGKDD International Conference on Knowledge Discovery and Data Mining, KDD'14*, pages 701–710, 2014. DOI: 10.1145/2623330.2623732 44

Bryan Perozzi, Vivek Kulkarni, Haochen Chen, and Steven Skiena. Don't walk, skip!: Online learning of multi-scale network embeddings. In *Proc. of the IEEE/ACM International Conference on Advances in Social Networks Analysis and Mining, ASONAM'17*, pages 258–265, New York, 2017. DOI: 10.1145/3110025.3110086 47

M. E. Peters, M. Neumann, M. Iyyer, M. Gardner, C. Clark, K. Lee, and L. Zettlemoyer. Deep contextualized word representations. In *Proc. of the Conference of the North American Chapter of the Association for Computational Linguistics*, New Orleans, LA, 2018. DOI: 10.18653/v1/n18-1202 68, 79, 80

Matthew Peters, Waleed Ammar, Chandra Bhagavatula, and Russell Power. Semi-supervised sequence tagging with bidirectional language models. In *Proc. of the 55th Annual Meeting of the Association for Computational Linguistics (Volume 1: Long Papers)*, pages 1756–1765. 2017. DOI: 10.18653/v1/p17-1161 79, 80

Matthew Peters, Mark Neumann, Luke Zettlemoyer, and Wen-tau Yih. Dissecting contextual word embeddings: Architecture and representation. In *Proc. of the Conference on Empirical Methods in Natural Language Processing*, pages 1499–1509, Association for Computational Linguistics, Brussels, Belgium, October–November 2018. https://www.aclweb.org/anthology/D18-1179 DOI: 10.18653/v1/d18-1179 91

Matthew Peters, Sebastian Ruder, and Noah A. Smith. To tune or not to tune? adapting pretrained representations to diverse tasks. *CoRR*, 2019. http://arxiv.org/abs/1903.05987 DOI: 10.18653/v1/w19-4302 88

Steven T. Piantadosi. Zipf's word frequency law in natural language: A critical review and future directions. *Psychonomic Bulletin and Review*, 21(5):1112–1130, 2014. DOI: 10.3758/s13423-014-0585-6 59

Mohammad Taher Pilehvar and Jose Camacho-Collados. WiC: The word-in-context dataset for evaluating context-sensitive meaning representations. In *Proc. of the Conference of the North American Chapter of the Association for Computational Linguistics: Human Language Technologies, Volume 1 (Long and Short Papers)*, pages 1267–1273, Minneapolis, MN, June 2019. https://www.aclweb.org/anthology/N19-1128 67, 89

Mohammad Taher Pilehvar and Nigel Collier. De-conflated semantic representations. In *Proc. of the Conference on Empirical Methods in Natural Language Processing (EMNLP)*, pages 1680–1690, Austin, TX, 2016. DOI: 10.18653/v1/d16-1174 55, 64, 65

Mohammad Taher Pilehvar and Nigel Collier. Inducing embeddings for rare and unseen words by leveraging lexical resources. In *Proc. of the 15th Conference of the European Chapter of the Association for Computational Linguistics: Volume 2, Short Papers*, pages 388–393, Valencia, Spain, April 2017. https://www.aclweb.org/anthology/E17-2062 DOI: 10.18653/v1/e17-2062 32, 33

Mohammad Taher Pilehvar and Roberto Navigli. A robust approach to aligning heterogeneous lexical resources. In *Proc. of the Annual Meeting of the Association for Computational Linguistics*, pages 468–478, 2014. DOI: 10.3115/v1/p14-1044 24

Mohammad Taher Pilehvar and Roberto Navigli. From senses to texts: An all-in-one graph-based approach for measuring semantic similarity. *Artificial Intelligence*, 228:95–128, 2015. DOI: 10.1016/j.artint.2015.07.005 44, 64, 66

Mohammad Taher Pilehvar, David Jurgens, and Roberto Navigli. Align, disambiguate and walk: A unified approach for measuring semantic similarity. In *Proc. of the 51st Annual Meeting of the Association for Computational Linguistics*, pages 1341–1351, Sofia, Bulgaria, 2013. 44, 48, 54

Mohammad Taher Pilehvar, Jose Camacho-Collados, Roberto Navigli, and Nigel Collier. Towards a seamless integration of word senses into downstream NLP applications. In *Proc. of the Annual Meeting of the Association for Computational Linguistics*, Vancouver, Canada, 2017. DOI: 10.18653/v1/p17-1170 68, 71

Telmo Pires, Eva Schlinger, and Dan Garrette. How multilingual is multilingual BERT? In *Proc. of the 57th Annual Meeting of the Association for Computational Linguistics*, pages 4996–5001, Florence, Italy, July 2019. https://www.aclweb.org/anthology/P19-1493 DOI: 10.18653/v1/p19-1493 92, 93

Lorien Y. Pratt. Discriminability-based transfer between neural networks. In *Advances in Neural Information Processing Systems 5*, pages 204–211, 1993. 80

Yusu Qian, Urwa Muaz, Ben Zhang, and Jae Won Hyun. Reducing gender bias in word-level language models with a gender-equalizing loss function. In *Proc. of the 57th Annual Meeting of the Association for Computational Linguistics: Student Research Workshop*, pages 223–228, Florence, Italy, 2019. https://www.aclweb.org/anthology/P19-2031 DOI: 10.18653/v1/p19-2031 104

Zhuwei Qin, Fuxun Yu, Chenchen Liu, and Xiang Chen. How convolutional neural network see the world—A survey of convolutional neural network visualization methods. *CoRR*, 2018. http://arxiv.org/abs/1804.11191 89

Lin Qiu, Kewei Tu, and Yong Yu. Context-dependent sense embedding. In *Proc. of the Conference on Empirical Methods in Natural Language Processing*, pages 183–191, 2016. DOI: 10.18653/v1/d16-1018 56, 60

Alec Radford. Improving language understanding by generative pre-training. 2018. 82, 88

Alec Radford, Jeffrey Wu, Rewon Child, David Luan, Dario Amodei, and Ilya Sutskever. Language models are unsupervised multitask learners. 2018. 79

Kira Radinsky, Eugene Agichtein, Evgeniy Gabrilovich, and Shaul Markovitch. A word at a time: Computing word relatedness using temporal semantic analysis. In *Proc. of the 20th International Conference on World Wide Web, WWW'11*, pages 337–346, 2011. DOI: 10.1145/1963405.1963455 7

Colin Raffel, Noam Shazeer, Adam Roberts, Katherine Lee, Sharan Narang, Michael Matena, Yanqi Zhou, Wei Li, and Peter J. Liu. Exploring the limits of transfer learning with a unified text-to-text transformer. *CoRR*, 2019. 85

Alessandro Raganato and Jörg Tiedemann. An analysis of encoder representations in transformer-based machine translation. In *Proc. of the EMNLP Workshop BlackboxNLP: Analyzing and Interpreting Neural Networks for NLP*, pages 287–297, Association for Computational Linguistics, Brussels, Belgium, November 2018. https://www.aclweb.org/anthology/W18-5431 DOI: 10.18653/v1/w18-5431 91

Alessandro Raganato, Jose Camacho-Collados, and Roberto Navigli. Word sense disambiguation: A unified evaluation framework and empirical comparison. In *Proc. of the Conference of the European Chapter of the Association for Computational Linguistics*, pages 99–110, Valencia, Spain, 2017a. DOI: 10.18653/v1/e17-1010 62

Alessandro Raganato, Claudio Delli Bovi, and Roberto Navigli. Neural sequence learning models for word sense disambiguation. In *Proc. of the Conference on Empirical Methods in Natural Language Processing*, pages 1156–1167, 2017b. DOI: 10.18653/v1/d17-1120 62

Alessandro Raganato, Tommaso Pasini, Jose Camacho-Collados, and Mohammad Taher Pilehvar. XL-WiC: A multilingual benchmark for evaluating semantic contextualization. In *Proc. of the Conference on Empirical Methods in Natural Language Processing (EMNLP)*, 2020. 67

Inioluwa Deborah Raji and Joy Buolamwini. Actionable auditing: Investigating the impact of publicly naming biased performance results of commercial AI products. In *Proc. of the AAAI/ACM Conference on AI, Ethics, and Society, AIES'19*, pages 429–435, New York, 2019. DOI: 10.1145/3306618.3314244 103

Shauli Ravfogel, Yanai Elazar, Hila Gonen, Michael Twiton, and Yoav Goldberg. Null it out: Guarding protected attributes by iterative nullspace projection. In *Proc. of the 58th Annual Meeting of the Association for Computational Linguistics*, pages 7237–7256, July 2020. https://www.aclweb.org/anthology/2020.acl-main.647 DOI: 10.18653/v1/2020.acl-main.647 106, 107

Emily Reif, Ann Yuan, Martin Wattenberg, Fernanda B Viegas, Andy Coenen, Adam Pearce, and Been Kim. Visualizing and measuring the geometry of BERT. In H. Wallach, H. Larochelle, A. Beygelzimer, F. d'Alché-Buc, E. Fox, and R. Garnett, Eds., *Advances in Neural Information Processing Systems 32*, pages 8594–8603, Curran Associates, Inc., 2019. http://papers.nips.cc/paper/9065-visualizing-and-measuring-the-geometry-of-bert.pdf 93

Nils Reimers and Iryna Gurevych. Sentence-BERT: Sentence embeddings using Siamese BERT-networks. In *Proc. of the Conference on Empirical Methods in Natural Language Processing and the 9th International Joint Conference on Natural Language Processing (EMNLP-IJCNLP)*, pages 3973–3983, Association for Computational Linguistics, Hong Kong, China, November 2019. https://www.aclweb.org/anthology/D19-1410 DOI: 10.18653/v1/d19-1410 100

Joseph Reisinger and Raymond J. Mooney. Multi-prototype vector-space models of word meaning. In *Proc. of the Annual Meeting of the Association for Computational Linguistics*, pages 109–117, 2010. 38, 57, 66

Philip Resnik. Using information content to evaluate semantic similarity in a taxonomy. In *Proc. of the International Joint Conferences on Artificial Intelligence (IJCAI)*, pages 448–453, 1995. 66

Philip Resnik and David Yarowsky. Distinguishing systems and distinguishing senses: New evaluation methods for word sense disambiguation. *Journal of Natural Language Engineering*, 5(2):113–133, 1999. DOI: 10.1017/s1351324999002211 61

Leonardo F. R. Ribeiro, Pedro H. P. Saverese, and Daniel R. Figueiredo. Struc2Vec: Learning node representations from structural identity. In *Proc. of the 23rd ACM SIGKDD International Conference on Knowledge Discovery and Data Mining, KDD'17*, pages 385–394, New York, 2017. DOI: 10.1145/3097983.3098061 45

Sebastian Riedel, Limin Yao, Andrew McCallum, and Benjamin M. Marlin. Relation extraction with matrix factorization and universal schemas. In *Proc. of the Conference of the North American Chapter of the Association for Computational Linguistics: Human Language Technologies (HLT-NAACL)*, pages 74–84, 2013. 51

Anna Rogers, Aleksandr Drozd, and Bofang Li. The (too many) problems of analogical reasoning with word vectors. In *Proc. of the 6th Joint Conference on Lexical and Computational Semantics (*SEM)*, pages 135–148, 2017. DOI: 10.18653/v1/s17-1017 51

Sascha Rothe and Hinrich Schütze. AutoExtend: Extending word embeddings to embeddings for synsets and lexemes. In *Proc. of the Annual Meeting of the Association for Computational Linguistics*, pages 1793–1803, Beijing, China, 2015. DOI: 10.3115/v1/p15-1173 65, 68

Herbert Rubenstein and John B. Goodenough. Contextual correlates of synonymy. *Communications of the ACM*, 8(10):627–633, 1965. DOI: 10.1145/365628.365657 37

Sebastian Ruder. An overview of multi-task learning in deep neural networks. *ArXiv Preprint ArXiv:1706.05098*, 2017. 101

Sebastian Ruder. Neural transfer learning for natural language processing. Ph.D. Thesis, National University of Ireland, Galway, 2019. 80

Sebastian Ruder, Ivan Vulić, and Anders Søgaard. A survey of cross-lingual word embedding models. *ArXiv Preprint ArXiv:1706.04902*, 2017. DOI: 10.1613/jair.1.11640 33

Rachel Rudinger, Jason Naradowsky, Brian Leonard, and Benjamin Van Durme. Gender bias in coreference resolution. In *Proc. of the Conference of the North American Chapter of the Association for Computational Linguistics: Human Language Technologies, Volume 2 (Short Papers)*, pages 8–14, New Orleans, LA, June 2018. https://www.aclweb.org/anthology/N18-2002 DOI: 10.18653/v1/n18-2002 104

M. Sahlgren. An introduction to random indexing. In *Methods and Applications of Semantic Indexing Workshop at the 7th International Conference on Terminology and Knowledge Engineering, TKE*, 2005. 29

Gerard Salton and M. McGill. *Introduction to Modern Information Retrieval*. McGraw-Hill, New York, 1983. 27

Gerard Salton, A. Wong, and C. S. Yang. A vector space model for automatic indexing. *Communications of the ACM*, 18(11):613–620, 1975. DOI: 10.1145/361219.361220 5, 7, 26, 27

Victor Sanh, Lysandre Debut, Julien Chaumond, and Thomas Wolf. DistilBERT, a distilled version of BERT: smaller, faster, cheaper and lighter. *NeurIPS EMC² Workshop*, 2019. 87

Naomi Saphra and Adam Lopez. Understanding learning dynamics of language models with SVCCA. In *Proc. of the Conference of the North American Chapter of the Association for Computational Linguistics: Human Language Technologies, Volume 1 (Long and Short Papers)*, pages 3257–3267, Minneapolis, MN, June 2019. https://www.aclweb.org/anthology/N19-1329 DOI: 10.18653/v1/n19-1329 110

Natalie Schluter. The word analogy testing caveat. In *Proc. of the Conference of the North American Chapter of the Association for Computational Linguistics: Human Language Technologies, Volume 2 (Short Papers)*, pages 242–246, 2018. DOI: 10.18653/v1/n18-2039 38

Tobias Schnabel, Igor Labutov, David Mimno, and Thorsten Joachims. Evaluation methods for unsupervised word embeddings. In *Proc. of the Conference on Empirical Methods in Natural Language Processing*, pages 298–307, Association for Computational Linguistics, Lisbon, Portugal, September 2015. https://www.aclweb.org/anthology/D15-1036 DOI: 10.18653/v1/d15-1036 39, 40

Karin Kipper Schuler. VerbNet: A broad-coverage, comprehensive verb lexicon. Ph.D. Thesis, University of Pennsylvania, 2005. 67

Mike Schuster and Kaisuke Nakajima. Japanese and Korean voice search. In *International Conference on Acoustics, Speech and Signal Processing*, pages 5149–5152, 2012. DOI: 10.1109/icassp.2012.6289079 31, 84

Hinrich Schütze. Word space. In *Advances in Neural Information Processing Systems 5*, pages 895–902. Morgan-Kaufmann, 1993. http://papers.nips.cc/paper/603-word-space.pdf 7, 31

Hinrich Schütze. Automatic word sense discrimination. *Computational Linguistics*, 24(1):97–123, 1998. 55, 57

Roy Schwartz, Roi Reichart, and Ari Rappoport. Symmetric pattern based word embeddings for improved word similarity prediction. In *Proc. of the 19th Conference on Computational Natural Language Learning*, pages 258–267, 2015. DOI: 10.18653/v1/k15-1026 31

Rico Sennrich, Barry Haddow, and Alexandra Birch. Neural machine translation of rare words with subword units. In *Proc. of the 54th Annual Meeting of the Association for Computational Linguistics (Volume 1: Long Papers)*, pages 1715–1725, 2016. DOI: 10.18653/v1/p16-1162 31

Ehsan Sherkat and Evangelos E. Milios. Vector embedding of Wikipedia concepts and entities. In *International Conference on Applications of Natural Language to Information Systems*, pages 418–428, Springer, 2017. DOI: 10.1007/978-3-319-59569-6_50 66

Vered Shwartz, Yoav Goldberg, and Ido Dagan. Improving hypernymy detection with an integrated path-based and distributional method. In *Proc. of the 54th Annual Meeting of the Association for Computational Linguistics (Volume 1: Long Papers)*, pages 2389–2398, 2016. DOI: 10.18653/v1/p16-1226 51

Jasdeep Singh, Bryan McCann, Richard Socher, and Caiming Xiong. BERT is not an interlingua and the bias of tokenization. In *Proc. of the 2nd Workshop on Deep Learning Approaches for Low-Resource NLP (DeepLo)*, pages 47–55, Association for Computational Linguistics, Hong Kong, China, November 2019. https://www.aclweb.org/anthology/D19-6106 DOI: 10.18653/v1/d19-6106 92

Samuel L. Smith, David H. P. Turban, Steven Hamblin, and Nils Y. Hammerla. Offline bilingual word vectors, orthogonal transformations and the inverted softmax. In *Proc. of the International Conference on Learning Representations (ICLR)*, 2017. 36

Richard Socher, Brody Huval, Christopher D. Manning, and Andrew Y. Ng. Semantic compositionality through recursive matrix-vector spaces. In *Proc. of the Joint Conference on Empirical Methods in Natural Language Processing and Computational Natural Language Learning*, pages 1201–1211, Association for Computational Linguistics, 2012. 98

Richard Socher, Alex Perelygin, Jean Wu, Jason Chuang, Christopher Manning, Andrew Ng, and Christopher Potts. Parsing with compositional vector grammars. In *Proc. of the Conference on Empirical Methods in Natural Language Processing (EMNLP)*, pages 455–465, Sofia, Bulgaria, 2013a. 50

Richard Socher, Alex Perelygin, Jean Wu, Jason Chuang, Christopher D. Manning, Andrew Ng, and Christopher Potts. Recursive deep models for semantic compositionality over a sentiment treebank. In *Proc. of the Conference on Empirical Methods in Natural Language Processing*, pages 1631–1642, Association for Computational Linguistics, Seattle, WA, October 2013b. https://www.aclweb.org/anthology/D13-1170 98

Anders Søgaard, Sebastian Ruder, and Ivan Vulić. On the limitations of unsupervised bilingual dictionary induction. In *Proc. of the 56th Annual Meeting of the Association for Computational Linguistics (Volume 1: Long Papers)*, pages 778–788, 2018. http://aclweb.org/anthology/P18-1072 DOI: 10.18653/v1/p18-1072 36, 37

Anders Søgaard, Ivan Vulić, Sebastian Ruder, and Manaal Faruqui. Cross-lingual word embeddings. *Synthesis Lectures on Human Language Technologies*, 12(2):1–132, 2019. DOI: 10.2200/s00920ed2v01y201904hlt042 34

Radu Soricut and Franz Och. Unsupervised morphology induction using word embeddings. In *Proc. of the Conference of the North American Chapter of the Association for Computational Linguistics: Human Language Technologies (HLT-NAACL)*, pages 1627–1637, Denver, CO, 2015. DOI: 10.3115/v1/n15-1186 31

Pascal Soucy and Guy W. Mineau. Beyond TFIDF weighting for text categorization in the vector space model. In *Proc. of the International Joint Conferences on Artificial Intelligence (IJCAI)*, 5:1130–1135, 2005. 27

Robert Speer and Joanna Lowry-Duda. ConceptNet at SemEval-2017 task 2: Extending word embeddings with multilingual relational knowledge. In *Proc. of the 11th International Workshop on Semantic Evaluation (SemEval)*, pages 85–89, Association for Computational Linguistics, 2017. 33

Robert Speer, Joshua Chin, and Catherine Havasi. Conceptnet 5.5: An open multilingual graph of general knowledge. In *Proc. of the AAAI Conference on Artificial Intelligence*, pages 4444–4451, 2017. 24

Gabriel Stanovsky and Mark Hopkins. Spot the odd man out: Exploring the associative power of lexical resources. In *Proc. of the Conference on Empirical Methods in Natural Language Processing*, 2018. DOI: 10.18653/v1/d18-1182 38

Gabriel Stanovsky, Noah A. Smith, and Luke Zettlemoyer. Evaluating gender bias in machine translation. In *Proc. of the 57th Annual Meeting of the Association for Computational Linguistics*, pages 1679–1684, Florence, Italy, July 2019. https://www.aclweb.org/anthology/P19-1164 DOI: 10.18653/v1/p19-1164 104

Sandeep Subramanian, Adam Trischler, Yoshua Bengio, and Christopher J. Pal. Learning general purpose distributed sentence representations via large scale multi-task learning. In *International Conference on Learning Representations*, 2018. 101

Tony Sun, Andrew Gaut, Shirlyn Tang, Yuxin Huang, Mai ElSherief, Jieyu Zhao, Diba Mirza, Elizabeth Belding, Kai-Wei Chang, and William Yang Wang. Mitigating gender bias in natural language processing: Literature review. In *Proc. of the 57th Annual Meeting of the Association for Computational Linguistics*, pages 1630–1640, Florence, Italy, July 2019. https://www.aclweb.org/anthology/P19-1159 DOI: 10.18653/v1/p19-1159 105

Simon Šuster, Ivan Titov, and Gertjan van Noord. Bilingual learning of multi-sense embeddings with discrete autoencoders. In *Proc. of the Conference of the North American Chapter of the Association for Computational Linguistics: Human Language Technologies (NAACL-HLT)*, pages 1346–1356, San Diego, CA, 2016. DOI: 10.18653/v1/n16-1160 61

Ilya Sutskever, James Martens, and Geoffrey Hinton. Generating text with recurrent neural networks. In *Proc. of the 28th International Conference on Machine Learning (ICML-11)*, pages 1017–1024, New York, 2011. 32

Ilya Sutskever, Oriol Vinyals, and Quoc V. Le. Sequence to sequence learning with neural networks. In *Advances in Neural Information Processing Systems*, pages 3104–3112, 2014. 17, 18, 99

Mohamed Ali Hadj Taieb, Torsten Zesch, and Mohamed Ben Aouicha. A survey of semantic relatedness evaluation datasets and procedures. *Artificial Intelligence Review*, pages 1–42, 2019. DOI: 10.1007/s10462-019-09796-3 38

Jian Tang, Meng Qu, Mingzhe Wang, Ming Zhang, Jun Yan, and Qiaozhu Mei. Line: Large-scale information network embedding. In *Proc. of the 24th International Conference on World Wide Web, WWW'15*, pages 1067–1077, International World Wide Web Conferences Steering Committee, Republic and Canton of Geneva, Switzerland, 2015. DOI: 10.1145/2736277.2741093 45

Wilson L. Taylor. Cloze procedure: A new tool for measuring readability. *Journalism Quarterly*, 30:415–433, 1953. https://ci.nii.ac.jp/naid/10024758642/en/ DOI: 10.1177/107769905303000401 82

Ian Tenney, Dipanjan Das, and Ellie Pavlick. BERT rediscovers the classical NLP pipeline. In *Proc. of the 57th Annual Meeting of the Association for Computational Linguistics*, pages 4593–4601, Florence, Italy, July 2019a. https://www.aclweb.org/anthology/P19-1452 DOI: 10.18653/v1/p19-1452 91, 92

Ian Tenney, Patrick Xia, Berlin Chen, Alex Wang, Adam Poliak, R. Thomas McCoy, Najoung Kim, Benjamin Van Durme, Samuel R. Bowman, Dipanjan Das, and Ellie Pavlick. What do you learn from context? probing for sentence structure in contextualized word representations. In *Proceeding of the 7th International Conference on Learning Representations (ICLR)*, 2019b. 110

Fei Tian, Hanjun Dai, Jiang Bian, Bin Gao, Rui Zhang, Enhong Chen, and Tie-Yan Liu. A probabilistic model for learning multi-prototype word embeddings. In *COLING*, pages 151–160, 2014. 58

Rocco Tripodi and Marcello Pelillo. A game-theoretic approach to word sense disambiguation. *Computational Linguistics*, 43(1):31–70, 2017. DOI: 10.1162/coli_a_00274 62

Yulia Tsvetkov, Manaal Faruqui, Wang Ling, Guillaume Lample, and Chris Dyer. Evaluation of word vector representations by subspace alignment. In *Proc. of the Conference on Empirical Methods in Natural Language Processing (EMNLP)*, pages 2049–2054, Lisbon, Portugal, 2015. DOI: 10.18653/v1/d15-1243 39, 40

Ke Tu, Peng Cui, Xiao Wang, Philip S. Yu, and Wenwu Zhu. Deep recursive network embedding with regular equivalence. In *Proc. of the 24th ACM SIGKDD International Conference on Knowledge Discovery and Data Mining, KDD'18*, pages 2357–2366, New York, 2018. DOI: 10.1145/3219819.3220068 45

Joseph Turian, Lev Ratinov, and Yoshua Bengio. Word representations: A simple and general method for semi-supervised learning. In *Proc. of the 48th Annual Meeting of the Association for Computational Linguistics*, pages 384–394, Uppsala, Sweden, 2010. 29

Peter D. Turney. Mining the Web for synonyms: PMI-IR versus LSA on TOEFL. In *Proc. of the 12th European Conference on Machine Learning*, pages 491–502, 2001. DOI: 10.1007/3-540-44795-4_42 38

Peter D. Turney. Measuring semantic similarity by latent relational analysis. In *Proc. of the International Joint Conferences on Artificial Intelligence (IJCAI)*, pages 1136–1141, 2005. 51

Peter D. Turney and Michael L. Littman. Measuring praise and criticism: Inference of semantic orientation from association. *ACM Transactions on Information Systems (TOIS)*, 21(4):315–346, 2003. DOI: 10.1145/944012.944013 27

Peter D. Turney and Patrick Pantel. From frequency to meaning: Vector space models of semantics. *Journal of Artificial Intelligence Research*, 37:141–188, 2010. DOI: 10.1613/jair.2934 7, 26, 27

Amos Tversky and Itamar Gati. Similarity, separability, and the triangle inequality. *Psychological Review*, 89(2):123, 1982. DOI: 10.1037/0033-295x.89.2.123 55

Shyam Upadhyay, Manaal Faruqui, Chris Dyer, and Dan Roth. Cross-lingual models of word embeddings: An empirical comparison. In *Proc. of the 54th Annual Meeting of the Association for Computational Linguistics (Volume 1: Long Papers)*, 1:1661–1670, 2016. DOI: 10.18653/v1/p16-1157 33

Shyam Upadhyay, Kai-Wei Chang, James Zou, Matt Taddy, and Adam Kalai. Beyond bilingual: Multi-sense word embeddings using multilingual context. In *Proc. of the 2nd Workshop on Representation Learning for NLP*, Vancouver, Canada, 2017. DOI: 10.18653/v1/w17-2613 61

Dmitry Ustalov, Alexander Panchenko, and Chris Biemann. Watset: Automatic induction of synsets from a graph of synonyms. In *Proc. of the 55th Annual Meeting of the Association for Computational Linguistics (Volume 1: Long Papers)*, 1:1579–1590, 2017. 22

Tim Van de Cruys, Thierry Poibeau, and Anna Korhonen. Latent vector weighting for word meaning in context. In *Proc. of the Conference on Empirical Methods in Natural Language Processing*, pages 1012–1022, Edinburgh, Scotland, UK, 2011. 56

Florentina Vasilescu, Philippe Langlais, and Guy Lapalme. Evaluating variants of the Lesk approach for disambiguating words. In *Proc. of LREC*, 2004. 63

Ashish Vaswani, Noam Shazeer, Niki Parmar, Jakob Uszkoreit, Llion Jones, Aidan N. Gomez, Lukasz Kaiser, and Illia Polosukhin. Attention is all you need. In *Advances in Neural Information Processing Systems 30*, pages 5998–6008, 2017. 21, 73, 74, 81

Loïc Vial, Benjamin Lecouteux, and Didier Schwab. Sense vocabulary compression through the semantic knowledge of wordnet for neural word sense disambiguation. In *Global WordNet Conference*, 2019. 62, 93

Jesse Vig and Yonatan Belinkov. Analyzing the structure of attention in a transformer language model. In *Proc. of the ACL Workshop BlackboxNLP: Analyzing and Interpreting Neural Networks for NLP*, pages 63–76, Association for Computational Linguistics, Florence, Italy, August 2019. https://www.aclweb.org/anthology/W19-4808 DOI: 10.18653/v1/w19-4808 91

Luke Vilnis and Andrew McCallum. Word representations via Gaussian embedding. In *Proc. of the International Conference on Learning Representations (ICLR)*, 2015. 31

S. V. N. Vishwanathan, Nicol N. Schraudolph, Risi Kondor, and Karsten M. Borgwardt. Graph kernels. *Journal of Machine Learning Research*, 11:1201–1242, August 2010. http://dl.acm.org/citation.cfm?id=1756006.1859891 42

Elena Voita, David Talbot, Fedor Moiseev, Rico Sennrich, and Ivan Titov. Analyzing multi-head self-attention: Specialized heads do the heavy lifting, the rest can be pruned. In *Proc. of the 57th Annual Meeting of the Association for Computational Linguistics*, pages 5797–5808, Florence, Italy, July 2019. https://www.aclweb.org/anthology/P19-1580 DOI: 10.18653/v1/p19-1580 90

Denny Vrandečić. Wikidata: A new platform for collaborative data collection. In *Proc. of the International Conference on World Wide Web*, pages 1063–1064, 2012. DOI: 10.1145/2187980.2188242 23

Thuy Vu and D. Stott Parker. K-Embeddings: Learning conceptual embeddings for words using context. In *Proc. of the Conference of the North American Chapter of the Association for Computational Linguistics: Human Language Technologies (HLT-NAACL)*, pages 1262–1267, 2016. DOI: 10.18653/v1/n16-1151 58

Ivan Vulić and Marie-Francine Moens. Bilingual word embeddings from non-parallel document-aligned data applied to bilingual lexicon induction. In *Proc. of the 53rd Annual Meeting of the Association for Computational Linguistics and the 7th International Joint*

Conference on Natural Language Processing (Volume 2: Short Papers), 2:719–725, 2015. DOI: 10.3115/v1/p15-2118 33

Ivan Vulić and Marie-Francine Moens. Bilingual distributed word representations from document-aligned comparable data. *Journal of Artificial Intelligence Research*, 55:953–994, 2016. DOI: 10.1613/jair.4986 34

Ivan Vulić, Simon Baker, Edoardo Maria Ponti, Ulla Petti, Ira Leviant, Kelly Wing, Olga Majewska, Eden Bar, Matt Malone, Thierry Poibeau, et al. Multi-simlex: A large-scale evaluation of multilingual and cross-lingual lexical semantic similarity. *ArXiv Preprint ArXiv:2003.04866*, 2020. 38

Eric Wallace, Shi Feng, Nikhil Kandpal, Matt Gardner, and Sameer Singh. Universal adversarial triggers for attacking and analyzing NLP. In *Proc. of the Conference on Empirical Methods in Natural Language Processing and the 9th International Joint Conference on Natural Language Processing (EMNLP-IJCNLP)*, pages 2153–2162, Association for Computational Linguistics, Hong Kong, China, November 2019. https://www.aclweb.org/anthology/D19-1221 DOI: 10.18653/v1/d19-1221 90

Alex Wang, Yada Pruksachatkun, Nikita Nangia, Amanpreet Singh, Julian Michael, Felix Hill, Omer Levy, and Samuel R. Bowman. SuperGLUE: A stickier benchmark for general-purpose language understanding systems. *ArXiv Preprint 1905.00537*, 2019a. 89, 95, 102, 109

Alex Wang, Amanpreet Singh, Julian Michael, Felix Hill, Omer Levy, and Samuel R. Bowman. GLUE: A multi-task benchmark and analysis platform for natural language understanding. In *Proc. of International Conference on Learning Representations (ICLR)*, 2019b. DOI: 10.18653/v1/w18-5446 89, 95, 102

Daixin Wang, Peng Cui, and Wenwu Zhu. Structural deep network embedding. In *Proc. of the 22nd ACM SIGKDD International Conference on Knowledge Discovery and Data Mining, KDD'16*, pages 1225–1234, New York, 2016. DOI: 10.1145/2939672.2939753 48, 54

Tianlu Wang, Jieyu Zhao, Mark Yatskar, Kai-Wei Chang, and Vicente Ordonez. Balanced datasets are not enough: Estimating and mitigating gender bias in deep image representations. In *Proc. of the IEEE/CVF International Conference on Computer Vision (ICCV)*, October 2019c. DOI: 10.1109/iccv.2019.00541 106

Zhen Wang, Jianwen Zhang, Jianlin Feng, and Zheng Chen. Knowledge graph and text jointly embedding. In *Proc. of the Conference on Empirical Methods in Natural Language Processing (EMNLP)*, pages 1591–1601, 2014a. DOI: 10.3115/v1/d14-1167 66

Zhen Wang, Jianwen Zhang, Jianlin Feng, and Zheng Chen. Knowledge graph embedding by translating on hyperplanes. In *Proc. of the AAAI Conference on Artificial Intelligence*, pages 1112–1119, 2014b. 50

Koki Washio and Tsuneaki Kato. Neural latent relational analysis to capture lexical semantic relations in a vector space. In *Proc. of the Conference on Empirical Methods in Natural Language Processing*, 2018a. DOI: 10.18653/v1/d18-1058 52, 53

Koki Washio and Tsuneaki Kato. Filling missing paths: Modeling co-occurrences of word pairs and dependency paths for recognizing lexical semantic relations. In *Proc. of NAACL*, pages 1123–1133, 2018b. DOI: 10.18653/v1/n18-1102 52, 53

Warren Weaver. Translation. *Machine Translation of Languages*, 14:15–23, 1955. 62

Jason Weston and Antoine Bordes. Embedding methods for NLP. In *EMNLP Tutorial*, 2014. 50

John Wieting, Mohit Bansal, Kevin Gimpel, and Karen Livescu. Charagram: Embedding words and sentences via character n-grams. In *Proc. of the Conference on Empirical Methods in Natural Language Processing*, pages 1504–1515, 2016. DOI: 10.18653/v1/d16-1157 31

Adina Williams, Nikita Nangia, and Samuel Bowman. A broad-coverage challenge corpus for sentence understanding through inference. In *Proc. of the Conference of the North American Chapter of the Association for Computational Linguistics: Human Language Technologies, Volume 1 (Long Papers)*, pages 1112–1122, 2018. DOI: 10.18653/v1/n18-1101 100

Ian H. Witten, Timothy C. Bell, and Alistair Moffat. *Managing Gigabytes: Compressing and Indexing Documents and Images*, 1st ed., John Wiley & Sons, Inc., 1994. DOI: 10.1109/tit.1995.476344 31, 84

Shijie Wu and Mark Dredze. Beto, bentz, becas: The surprising cross-lingual effectiveness of BERT. In *Proc. of the Conference on Empirical Methods in Natural Language Processing and the 9th International Joint Conference on Natural Language Processing (EMNLP-IJCNLP)*, pages 833–844, Association for Computational Linguistics, Hong Kong, China, November 2019. https://www.aclweb.org/anthology/D19-1077 DOI: 10.18653/v1/d19-1077 92

Yonghui Wu, Mike Schuster, Zhifeng Chen, Quoc V. Le, Mohammad Norouzi, Wolfgang Macherey, Maxim Krikun, Yuan Cao, Qin Gao, Klaus Macherey, Jeff Klingner, Apurva Shah, Melvin Johnson, Xiaobing Liu, Lukasz Kaiser, Stephan Gouws, Yoshikiyo Kato, Taku Kudo, Hideto Kazawa, Keith Stevens, George Kurian, Nishant Patil, Wei Wang, Cliff Young, Jason Smith, Jason Riesa, Alex Rudnick, Oriol Vinyals, Gregory S. Corrado, Macduff Hughes, and Jeffrey Dean. Google's neural machine translation system: Bridging the gap between human and machine translation. *ArXiv*, 2016. 14, 73

Zhaohui Wu and C. Lee Giles. Sense-aware semantic analysis: A multi-prototype word representation model using Wikipedia. In *Proc. of the AAAI Conference on Artificial Intelligence*, pages 2188–2194, Citeseer, 2015. 58, 68

Zhibiao Wu and Martha Palmer. Verbs semantics and lexical selection. In *Proc. of the 32nd Annual Meeting on Association for Computational Linguistics, ACL'94*, pages 133–138, Las Cruces, New Mexico, 1994. DOI: 10.3115/981732.981751 44

Qizhe Xie, Zihang Dai, Yulun Du, Eduard Hovy, and Graham Neubig. Controllable invariance through adversarial feature learning. In I. Guyon, U. V. Luxburg, S. Bengio, H. Wallach, R. Fergus, S. Vishwanathan, and R. Garnett, Eds., *Advances in Neural Information Processing Systems 30*, pages 585–596, Curran Associates, Inc., 2017. http://papers.nips.cc/paper/6661-controllable-invariance-through-adversarial-feature-learning.pdf 106

Chao Xing, Dong Wang, Chao Liu, and Yiye Lin. Normalized word embedding and orthogonal transform for bilingual word translation. In *Proc. of the Conference of the North American Chapter of the Association for Computational Linguistics: Human Language Technologies*, pages 1006–1011, 2015. DOI: 10.3115/v1/n15-1104 35

Chang Xu, Yalong Bai, Jiang Bian, Bin Gao, Gang Wang, Xiaoguang Liu, and Tie-Yan Liu. RC-NET: A general framework for incorporating knowledge into word representations. In *Proc. of the 23rd ACM International Conference on Conference on Information and Knowledge Management*, pages 1219–1228, 2014. DOI: 10.1145/2661829.2662038 32

Ruochen Xu, Yiming Yang, Naoki Otani, and Yuexin Wu. Unsupervised cross-lingual transfer of word embedding spaces. In *Proc. of the Conference on Empirical Methods in Natural Language Processing*, pages 2465–2474, Association for Computational Linguistics, 2018. http://aclweb.org/anthology/D18-1268 DOI: 10.18653/v1/d18-1268 37

Yadollah Yaghoobzadeh and Hinrich Schütze. Intrinsic subspace evaluation of word embedding representations. In *Proc. of the Annual Meeting of the Association for Computational Linguistics*, pages 236–246, 2016. DOI: 10.18653/v1/p16-1023 55

Yadollah Yaghoobzadeh, Katharina Kann, T. J. Hazen, Eneko Agirre, and Hinrich Schütze. Probing for semantic classes: Diagnosing the meaning content of word embeddings. In *Proc. of the 57th Annual Meeting of the Association for Computational Linguistics*, pages 5740–5753, Florence, Italy, July 2019. https://www.aclweb.org/anthology/P19-1574 DOI: 10.18653/v1/p19-1574 8

Bishan Yang, Wen-tau Yih, Xiaodong He, Jianfeng Gao, and Li Deng. Embedding entities and relations for learning and inference in knowledge bases. In *Proc. of the International Conference on Learning Representations (ICLR)*, 2015. 50

Xuefeng Yang and Kezhi Mao.   Learning multi-prototype word embedding from single-prototype word embedding with integrated knowledge. *Expert Systems with Applications*, 56:291–299, 2016. DOI: 10.1016/j.eswa.2016.03.013 63

Zhilin Yang, Zihang Dai, Yiming Yang, Jaime G. Carbonell, Ruslan Salakhutdinov, and Quoc V. Le. XLNet: Generalized autoregressive pretraining for language understanding. *CoRR*, 2019. http://arxiv.org/abs/1906.08237 87

Mo Yu and Mark Dredze. Improving lexical embeddings with semantic knowledge. In *Proc. of the Annual Meeting of the Association for Computational Linguistics*, pages 545–550, 2014. DOI: 10.3115/v1/p14-2089 32

Dayu Yuan, Julian Richardson, Ryan Doherty, Colin Evans, and Eric Altendorf.   Semi-supervised word sense disambiguation with neural models. In *Proc. of the International Conference on Computational Linguistics (COLING)*, pages 1374–1385, 2016. 62

W. W. Zachary. An information flow model for conflict and fission in small groups. *Journal of Anthropological Research*, 33:452–473, 1977. DOI: 10.1086/jar.33.4.3629752 41

Brian Hu Zhang, Blake Lemoine, and Margaret Mitchell.   Mitigating unwanted biases with adversarial learning. In *Proc. of the AAAI/ACM Conference on AI, Ethics, and Society, AIES'18*, pages 335–340, Association for Computing Machinery, New York, 2018. DOI: 10.1145/3278721.3278779 105

Meng Zhang, Yang Liu, Huanbo Luan, and Maosong Sun. Earth mover's distance minimization for unsupervised bilingual lexicon induction. In *Proc. of the Conference on Empirical Methods in Natural Language Processing*, pages 1934–1945, Association for Computational Linguistics, Copenhagen, Denmark, September 2017a. https://www.aclweb.org/anthology/D17-1207 DOI: 10.18653/v1/d17-1207 37

Meng Zhang, Yang Liu, Huanbo Luan, and Maosong Sun. Adversarial training for unsupervised bilingual lexicon induction. In *Proc. of the 55th Annual Meeting of the Association for Computational Linguistics*, pages 1959–1970, 2017b. DOI: 10.18653/v1/p17-1179 36

Jieyu Zhao, Tianlu Wang, Mark Yatskar, Vicente Ordonez, and Kai-Wei Chang. Men also like shopping: Reducing gender bias amplification using corpus-level constraints. In *Proc. of the Conference on Empirical Methods in Natural Language Processing*, pages 2979–2989, Association for Computational Linguistics, Copenhagen, Denmark, September 2017. https://www.aclweb.org/anthology/D17-1323 DOI: 10.18653/v1/d17-1323 103

Jieyu Zhao, Yichao Zhou, Zeyu Li, Wei Wang, and Kai-Wei Chang. Learning gender-neutral word embeddings. In *Proc. of the Conference on Empirical Methods in Natural Language Processing*, pages 4847–4853, Association for Computational Linguistics, Brussels,

Belgium, October–November 2018.   https://www.aclweb.org/anthology/D18-1521 DOI: 10.18653/v1/d18-1521 105, 106

Zhi Zhong and Hwee Tou Ng. It makes sense: A wide-coverage word sense disambiguation system for free text. In *Proc. of the ACL System Demonstrations*, pages 78–83, Uppsala, Sweden, 2010. 62

Authors' Biographies

MOHAMMAD TAHER PILEHVAR

Mohammad Taher Pilehvar is an Assistant Professor at the Tehran Institute for Advanced Studies (TeIAS) and an Affiliated Lecturer at the University of Cambridge. Taher's research is primarily in Lexical Semantics with a special focus on representation learning for word senses. Taher has co-instructed multiple tutorials at *ACL conferences and co-organized four SemEval tasks and an EACL workshop on semantic representation. Taher has contributed to the field of lexical semantics with several publications in the recent years, including two best paper nominees at ACL (2013 and 2017) and a survey on vector representations of meaning.

JOSE CAMACHO-COLLADOS

Jose Camacho-Collados is a UKRI Future Leaders Fellow and a Lecturer at the School of Computer Science and Informatics at Cardiff University (United Kingdom). Previously, he was a Google Doctoral Fellow, completed his Ph.D. at Sapienza University of Rome (Italy), and had pre-doctoral experience as a statistical research engineer in France. His background education includes an Erasmus Mundus Masters in Human Language Technology and a 5-year B.Sc. degree in Mathematics (Spain). Jose's main area of expertise is Natural Language Processing (NLP), particularly computational semantics or, in other words, how to make computers understand language. In this topic, together with Taher Pilehvar, he has written a well-received survey on vector representations of meaning, which was published in the *Journal of Artificial Intelligence Research* and established the basis of this book. His research has pivoted around both scientific contributions through regular publications in top AI and NLP venues such as ACL, EMNLP, AAAI, and IJCAI, and applications with direct impact in society, with a special focus on social media and multilinguality. He has also organized several international workshops, tutorials, and open challenges with hundreds of participants across the world.

Printed in the United States
by Baker & Taylor Publisher Services